Andrew Preshous   Rachael Roberts
Joanna Preshous   Joanne Gakonga

IELTS Foundation

Student's Book Second edition

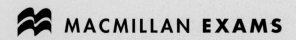

MACMILLAN **EXAMS**

Contents

IELTS Foundation is designed to help you improve your IELTS score and progress towards your goal of studying at an English speaking university. There are 12 topic-based units which cover each of the four IELTS academic modules and all task types, as well as giving guided support and exam-focused practice. Units are carefully graded in order to develop your language skills, increase your knowledge of grammar and vocabulary, and familiarize yourself with the IELTS exam format. Improving these areas will help build your confidence and give you a solid foundation, not only for IELTS, but also for further academic study.

What do you need to do to improve your IELTS score?

1 You need to learn about the exam format

For any exam, learning about the structure and about the task types will help you to succeed, and IELTS is no exception. *IELTS Foundation* takes you though all parts of the exam, giving techniques and advice to help you approach the different task types. *Exam Information*, *Tip* and *Strategy* boxes provide useful guidance throughout the book.

2 You need to improve your productive language skills

IELTS Foundation gives you step-by-step guidance with each task type in the *Writing* module. At the back of the book there are model answers for each of the *Writing* questions with comments to help you improve your own writing techniques.

There are also activities to prepare you for the *Speaking* module, including opportunities to practise each of the three parts and sample audio answers. For both *Writing* and *Speaking* there are useful language boxes containing vocabulary and phrases to use in these IELTS modules.

3 You need to improve your receptive language skills

For the *Reading* module there are not only a variety of texts and IELTS tasks, but also exercises to help you deal with unknown vocabulary and improve your active reading skills.

IELTS Foundation gives you numerous chances to develop your active listening skills whilst completing different task types for the *Listening* module. Complete audioscripts are available at the back of the book.

4 You need to improve your language accuracy

Throughout the book, essential grammar exercises have been built into each unit. These have been selected as areas where students at your level most often make mistakes in writing and speaking. The language work is put into context, to show you how grammar really works in English, particularly in academic situations. There are also further practice activities in the *Grammar and vocabulary bank* at the back of the book.

5 You need to increase your vocabulary

Vocabulary is very important, particularly in the *Reading* and *Writing* modules. There are vocabulary-building exercises throughout the book and extra practice exercises in the *Grammar and vocabulary bank* at the back of the book. In addition, there is a particular focus on developing your knowledge of collocations and on building your academic vocabulary.

6 You need to improve your academic study skills

In order to achieve your academic goals it is important to not only improve your English, but also to develop your study skills. *IELTS Foundation* includes strategies to help you learn more effectively and develop your ability to work independently when studying IELTS and in other academic contexts.

1 Studying overseas

Reading

1 Discuss these questions with another student.
- Why do students go overseas to study?
- What are the benefits of living and studying in another country? What are the difficulties that students experience?

2 Check the meaning of the following words and phrases. Which ones are benefits of living abroad, which ones are difficulties, which ones could be both?

> experiencing a different lifestyle   a different climate   being independent
> experiencing a new culture   missing friends and family   meeting new people
> feeling lonely   the language barrier   feeling homesick   a change in diet

3 When people first arrive in a new country they often suffer from *culture shock*. What do you think this means?

4 Read the first paragraph of the text and see if you were right. Which of the difficulties from exercise 2 are mentioned?

What is culture shock?

'Culture shock' describes the impact of moving from a familiar culture to one which is unfamiliar. It is an experience described by people who have travelled abroad to work, live or study; it can be felt to a certain extent even when abroad on holiday. It includes the shock of a new environment, meeting lots of new people and learning the ways of a different country. It also includes the shock of being separated from the important people in your life. These may include family, friends, colleagues or teachers: people you would normally talk to at times of uncertainty, people who give you support and guidance. When familiar sights, sounds, smells or tastes are no longer there you can miss them very much. If you are tired and jet-lagged when you arrive, small things can be upsetting and out of all proportion to their real significance.

5 According to the author there are many different causes of culture shock. Underline any you can find in the text.

6 What do you know about the climate, food, language, dress and rules of behaviour in Britain?

7 Now read the rest of the article and compare your ideas with the author's.

Climate

Many students find that the British climate affects them a lot. You may be used to a much warmer climate, or you may just find the greyness and dampness, especially during the winter months, difficult to get used to.

Food

You may find British food strange. It may taste different, or be cooked differently, or it may seem lighter or heavier than what you are used to.

Language

Constantly listening and speaking in a foreign language is tiring. Although you may have learned English very thoroughly, it is possible that the regional accents you discover when you arrive in the UK make the language harder to understand than you thought. People may also speak quickly and you may feel too embarrassed to ask them to repeat what they have said.

Dress

If you come from a warm climate, you may find it uncomfortable to wear heavy winter clothing. Not all students will find the style of dress different, but for others people's dress may seem immodest, unattractive, comical or simply drab.

'Rules' of behaviour

Every culture has unspoken rules which affect the way people treat each other. For example, the British generally have a reputation for punctuality. In business and academic life keeping to time is important. You should always be on time for lectures, classes and meetings with academic and administrative staff. Social life is a little more complicated. Arranging to meet and see a film at 8pm means arriving at 8pm. But if you are invited to visit someone's home for dinner at 8pm you should probably aim to arrive at about 8.10, but not later than 8.20. When going to a student party an invitation for 8pm probably means any time from 9.30pm onwards!

Glossary	
dampness	slight wetness in the air
immodest	clothing or behaviour that shocks or embarrasses some people
comical	funny
drab	dull or boring, colourless
reputation	the opinion that other people have about someone
punctuality	not being late

8 Are these aspects of culture similar or different in your country? Discuss with other students.

9 The adjectives (1–7) appear in the next part of the text. Match them to the definitions (a–g) and then check your answers in a dictionary.

1 relaxed
2 confused
3 confident
4 excited
5 frustrated
6 curious
7 hostile

a calm and not worried
b behaving in a very unfriendly or threatening way
c wanting to find out about something
d certain about your abilities and not nervous or frightened
e unable to understand something or think clearly about it
f very happy and enthusiastic because something good is going to happen
g feeling annoyed and impatient because you are prevented from achieving something

10 Look at the diagram showing the stages of culture shock marked 1–5.
Now match the stages 1–5 with paragraphs A–E.

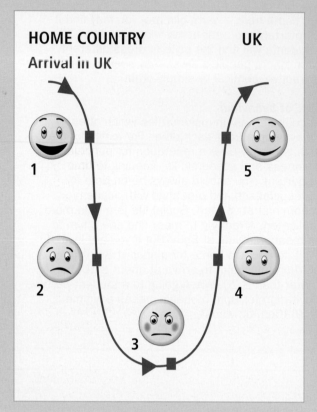

A Differences and similarities are accepted. You may feel relaxed and confident and you become more familiar with situations and feel well able to cope with new situations based on your growing experience.

B When you first arrive in a new culture, differences are intriguing and you may feel excited, stimulated and curious. At this stage you are still protected by the close memory of your home culture.

C Differences and similarities are valued and important. You may feel full of potential and able to trust yourself in all kinds of situations. Most situations become enjoyable and you are able to make choices according to your preferences and values.

D A little later, differences create an impact and you may feel confused, isolated or inadequate as you start to notice more and more cultural differences and family and friends are not immediately available for support.

E Next you may reject the differences you encounter. You may feel angry or frustrated, or hostile to the new culture. At this stage you may be conscious mainly of how much you dislike it compared to home. Don't worry as this is quite a healthy reaction. You are reconnecting with what you value about yourself and your own culture.

Strategy
Read all the choices carefully and underline key words in the question (see first example). Eliminate answers which are clearly wrong.
Make sure you can find the answer in the text and underline it, making a note of which question it answers.

Multiple choice
11 Choose the correct letter, A, B, C or D.

1 According to the writer, you may feel positive when you first arrive in a new culture because
  A you have no experience of this culture yet.
  B you are still thinking about your own country.
  C your family and friends are not with you.
  D you do not notice any differences to your own culture.

2 According to the writer, in stage 3 it is normal to feel
  A negative about the new culture.
  B frightened of asking for help.
  C worried about your health.
  D negative about your own culture.

3 This text was written
  A to advise international students returning home.
  B to advertise international study to students from around the world.
  C to warn international students of the dangers of living abroad.
  D to help international students who have just arrived in a new country.

12 Work in pairs. Discuss which country you would like to live or study in. What do you think you might enjoy about living there?

Adjectives ending in *-ing/-ed*

Adjectives can have two forms.

To describe how we feel:

I am bor<u>ed</u> because I have nothing to do.

To describe the effect something has on us:

This film is bor<u>ing</u> – there's no action in it.

1 Underline the correct alternative.

  0 Have you ever had an <u>*embarrassing*</u>/*embarrassed* experience?

  1 What is the most *exciting*/*excited* thing about living abroad?

  2 What do you find *frustrating*/*frustrated* about learning English?

  3 Do you think trying new foods is an *interesting*/*interested* experience? Why/Why not?

  4 What makes you feel *relaxing*/*relaxed*?

  5 Which makes you most *confusing*/*confused* – English grammar or spelling?

  6 Do you find visiting new places *fascinating*/*fascinated*? Why/Why not?

2 Ask your partner the questions. Give reasons and examples.

I had a very embarrassing experience on my first day in England. I got lost and was late for my first class. I was so embarrassed!

3 Respond to the situations using *-ed* and *-ing* adjectives. Choose from the adjectives in the box, using a dictionary to check meaning. There may be more than one possible answer.

> annoyed/annoying   disappointed/disappointing   exhausted/exhausting
> frightened/frightening   satisfied/satisfying   shocked/shocking
> surprised/surprising

  0 Your team lost the cup final.

    It was very disappointing when my team lost the cup final./I was very disappointed when my team lost the cup final.

  1 You watched a horror film. _____

  2 You finished painting your bedroom. _____

  3 You did a 15 kilometre walk. _____

  4 You passed an exam that you had expected to fail. _____

  5 Your bus was very late. _____

  6 You saw a young child smoking. _____

4 Tell your partner about the following. Try to use both *-ed* and *-ing* adjectives.

  – a disappointing experience

  – something you are frightened of

  – something that you find very annoying

  – a time when you were exhausted

  – something that you find shocking

IELTS Listening Section 1: Predicting answers

You are going to hear a conversation between a student, Li Cha, and a university admissions officer. Look at the form and answer these questions.

1 What are the speakers talking about?
2 What type of answers do you expect for questions 1–3, 5 and 6?
3 What type of answers do you expect for questions 4 and 7–10?

Questions 1–10

🔊 1.1 Listen and complete the form. Write no more than three words or a number for each answer.

**Exam information
Listening: Section 1**
Number of people: two (a dialogue)
Context: everyday social situation
Example situation: a student asking about accommodation, or someone telephoning to hire a car

Name: Li Cha

Tutor: Stephen Ennis

Age: **1** .... Class: **2** ....

Start: 14th February Finish: **3** ....

Lives in: **4** .... Mobile number: **5** ....

Years of study of English: **6** ....

Hobbies: **7** .... , emailing friends, **8** ....

University choice: **9** ....

Future plans: work with **10** ....

Forming questions

See *Grammar and vocabulary bank* on page 150.

1 Look at the form and write questions.

1. What's your name?

Name: 1 .... Age: 2 ....
Nationality: 3 ....
Years of study of English: 4 ....
Hobbies: 5 ....
Reason for taking IELTS: 6 ....
Future plans: 7 ....

2 In pairs ask each other the questions and complete the form.

IELTS Speaking Part 1

1 Correct the mistakes in these questions.

**Exam information:
Speaking: Part 1**
In Part 1 of the Speaking module the examiner will ask you general questions about yourself.

0 Are you work or study? *Do you work or study* ?
1 Where you live? .... ?
2 How often speak you English? .... ?
3 What do you in your free time? .... ?
4 Do you can speak any other languages? .... ?
5 How are you travelling to work/school? .... ?
6 When did you came to this country? .... ?
7 Do you have got any brothers or sisters? .... ?
8 Can you say me about your home town? .... ?

2 Interview your partner by asking the questions. Then report back to your class with information you found out in the last two activities.

Ahmed is from Saudi Arabia. He is 21 years old and has three brothers and a sister. He likes ...

Expanding answers

3 Look at these extracts from a Speaking Part 1 question. Which student gives the best answer? Why?

Examiner: *Do you work or study?*
Student A: *I'm a student.*

Examiner: *Do you work or study?*
Student B: *I'm doing a Business Foundation course in the UK because I want to go to university in October.*

TIP

In the exam it is better to give longer answers and extra information about the topic.

4 Look at the short answers (a–d) and match them to the questions in exercise 1.
  a In Birmingham. ....
  b Yes, three. ....
  c Yes, a brother and a sister. ....
  d In September. ....

5 Choose the most suitable extra information (1–4) for the short answers (a–d).
  1 I have a younger brother who's still at school and my sister is studying law in the USA. ....
  2 When I first arrived I was very nervous and I didn't understand anything but I soon made friends and settled down. ....
  3 I share a flat with some friends. It's great because it's near the city centre. ....
  4 I speak Arabic with my family but I had to learn French at school and I also speak a little Spanish. ....

Giving reasons and examples

6 Ask your partner the following question:

Why are you learning English?

Look at the following sample answers and the words used to give reasons.

  1 *Because* .... it will give me the chance speak more to people from other countries.
  2 *As* .... it will help me to get a better job in the future.
  3 *So that* .... I can go to university in the UK.
  4 *The reason* .... I am studying English *is that* .... I really enjoy learning other languages.

7 How could you expand your answers to give more information? Match the sentences (a–d) below to the answers (1–4) above.
  a I really want to work in business. ....
  b I also speak Arabic and Urdu. ....
  c It will help me communicate wherever I go. ....
  d At the moment I'm doing a 1-year Foundation course. ....

Practice

Ask and answer the questions with a partner, giving reasons for your answers.
  – Do you prefer arts or science subjects?
  – Do you think your country is expensive to live in?
  – Do you like the climate in this country?
  – Which country would you most like to live in: Australia or USA?
  – Which sports do you like playing most?
  – What other activities do you enjoy doing in your free time?

**Exam information
Writing: Task 1**
You may be asked to
describe, summarize
or explain a chart,
diagram, table or
graph.
Number of words:
at least 150
Time allowed:
20 minutes

IELTS Writing Task 1

1 Discuss these questions in small groups. Give reasons and examples.

1 Which are the most popular countries for students to study overseas?
2 Which countries do most overseas students to the UK come from?
3 Which subjects do you think are most popular with international students in the UK?
4 Have numbers of applications to UK universities gone up or down in recent years?

Understanding visual information

2 Look at diagrams 1–4 to see if you were right. Which diagram provides information that answers each question?

3 Look at diagrams 1–4 and identify which one is:

a a pie chart **b** a line graph **c** a bar chart **d** a table

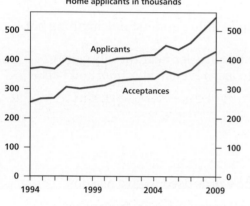

Figure 1 Applicants to UK Universities 1994–2009

Home applicants in thousands

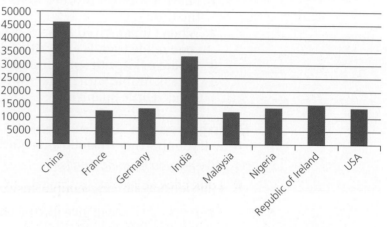

Figure 3 Country of Origin for Higher Education Students in the UK 2008–9

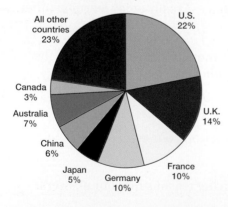

Figure 2 Global Destinations for International Students at Tertiary Level 2006.

Figure 4 International Student Numbers by Subject Area 2009/10

International students in HE 2009/10 by subject of study	No of international students	% in subject who are international
Business & administrative studies	116,190	33%
Engineering & technology	50,880	32%
Social studies	33,620	16%
Computer science	24,655	24%
Languages	24,145	17%
Subjects allied to medicine	22,795	7%
Creative arts & design	21,410	12%
Law	19,045	20%
Biological sciences	17,545	10%

TIP
Make sure you understand
what the diagram shows.

4 Choose the best alternative from the words in *italics*.

Figure 1
1 The number of student applications *increased/decreased* in the period 1994–2009.
2 Between 2005 and 2006 the number of applications *rose/fell*.

Figure 2
3 Around a *half/quarter* of all students go to the USA to study.
4 China is *more/less* popular than Australia for international students.

Figure 3

  5 The number of students from China is much *greater/smaller* than those from other countries.

  6 Just *under/over* 35,000 students came from India to study in the UK.

Figure 4

  7 The number of international students studying Social Studies was *higher/lower* than the number studying Languages.

  8 The *most/least* popular subject is Business and Administrative Studies.

5 Now complete these sentences using words or phrases from the box. Refer to Figures 1–4.

a quarter	decreased	just over	higher	least popular	more popular	rose	lower

  1 The UK is _____ than France for overseas students.

  2 The number of Irish students in the UK is _____ than the number from the United States.

  3 The _____ subject for international students was Biological Sciences.

  4 Between 2008 and 2009 the number of applicants to UK universities _____ .

  5 Just under _____ of students go to other unnamed countries.

  6 The number of applicants to UK universities _____ in the period 1997–8.

  7 There were _____ 45,000 Chinese students studying at university in the UK.

  8 The number of students studying Computer Science was _____ than the number studying Engineering and Technology.

The opening paragraph

6 Look back at the line graph in exercise 3 and read the exam instruction below.

The graph below shows the number of students who applied and were accepted at UK universities between 1994 and 2009.
Summarize the information by selecting and reporting the main features, and make comparisons where relevant.

Read the opening paragraph and choose the correct alternatives from the words in *italics*. One or two correct answers may be possible.

> The graph (1) *shows/is showing/showed* the number of applications and acceptances at universities in the UK in the (2) *time/period/years* 1994–2009. (3) *During/At/From* this period student applications (4) *went up/increased/rose up* and the number of acceptances had a similar (5) *line/pattern/trend*.

TIP
The opening paragraph should contain general information, but don't copy the words in the diagram. Try to describe what the diagram shows in your own words.

7 Discuss these questions with a partner.

  1 Which tense is used in the first sentence?

  2 Is the information and words used in the first sentence the same as in the exam instruction?

  3 Which tense is used in the second sentence? Why?

  4 Does the second sentence contain general information about the graph or specific details?

  5 What kind of information will the next paragraph contain?

Practice

8 Write a similar opening paragraph for one of the other diagrams in exercise 3. When you have finished, look at the model answers on page 160.

Exam information
Speaking: Part 2
In Speaking Part 2
the examiner will
give you a topic on
a card. You have one
minute to prepare a
talk and make notes
on this subject. You
have to speak for
1–2 minutes.
The examiner will
then ask you one or
two questions on
the topic.

IELTS Speaking Part 2

1 Discuss with a partner:
  – Which subjects did you study at school?
  – Which subjects did you enjoy? Which did you dislike? Why?

2 Now look at the exam information and the following task.

> **Part 2**
>
> Describe a subject that you enjoyed at school.
>
> You should say:
> – what the subject is
> – how long you studied it
> – why this subject is useful
>
> and explain why you found this subject enjoyable.

3 Further questions:
  – What do you like most about this subject?
  – Do you think you will use this subject in your future work or studies?

Exam information
Listening: Section 2
Number of people:
one (monologue)
Context: everyday
social situation
Example: a tour
guide talking about
a museum visit, a
talk about facilities
in a university.

IELTS Listening Section 2

1 You are going to hear Professor Gooding, a New Zealander, talking about her experiences of living in Indonesia, Egypt, Finland, Japan and China.
  – What do you think she liked about living in these countries?
  – What do you think she found difficult?

Summary completion

Questions 1–4

⊙ **1.2** Listen to the first part of the talk and complete the sentences below. Write NO MORE THAN TWO WORDS OR A NUMBER for each answer.

> The talk was organized by the (1) .... Students' Society.
>
> The subject of Professor Gooding's talk is her experiences of (2) ....
>
> Her age was (3) .... when she first left New Zealand.
>
> She was especially (4) .... by Indonesian architecture.

Table completion

Questions 5–10

⊙ **1.3** Listen to the second part of the talk and complete the table.

Complete the table below as you listen. Write NO MORE THAN THREE WORDS for each answer.

Country	Positive point	Difficulty
Indonesia	5	looking different/being tall
6		extreme heat
Finland	cross-country skiing	7 ....
8	could speak the language	9 couldn't ....
China	satisfying job	10 couldn't ....

Dependent prepositions

2 After many adjectives, verbs and nouns we use a preposition. Complete the following sentences from exercise 1 with the correct preposition. Then listen to Professor Gooding again and check your answers.

    0 I was interested ___*in*___ learning all about the country.
    1 I was particularly fascinated _____ the architecture.
    2 Life in Indonesia is very different _____ life in New Zealand.
    3 I'm very keen _____ spicy food.
    4 I was pretty good _____ cross-country skiing.
    5 I was a bit nervous _____ going to a country where I couldn't read anything.
    6 He was really enthusiastic _____ his work.

3 Look at sentences 0 and 5 in exercise 2. What happens to the form of the verb after a preposition?

4 Fill in the missing dependent prepositions in the table below.

Three countries you are interested _____ visiting.	1
A culture you are fascinated _____	2
A country where life is very different _____ your own.	3
A country you wouldn't be keen _____ visiting.	4
A language you'd be enthusiastic _____ learning.	5
A city you'd be nervous _____ visiting.	6

5 Work in small groups. Roll a dice and look at the sentence with this number. Then talk about it for 30 seconds.

Language focus

Countable/uncountable nouns

See *Grammar and vocabulary bank* on page 150.

1 Look at the nouns in the box below and answer the questions.
    1 Which nouns are countable and which are uncountable?
    2 Which of the countable nouns are singular and which are plural? Add them to the table below.

> accommodation advice children country homework information language
> luggage people sports students subjects university weather

Countable		Uncountable
Singular	Plural	

2 Correct the mistakes in the sentences below (one of the sentences is correct).
    1 Ahmed speaks four language. _____
    2 Accommodation are very expensive in London. _____
    3 The tutor gave me a very good advice. _____
    4 The bar chart shows the population of four different country. _____
    5 The weather in July is usually better than this. _____
    6 I went to the library to get some more informations about the topic.

    _____

    7 Team sports such as football and rugby is very popular in this country.

    _____

    8 When I came to the UK I had a lot of luggages. _____

Quantifiers

3 A class of students conducted a survey into which sports they enjoyed playing and watching. The bar charts show the results.

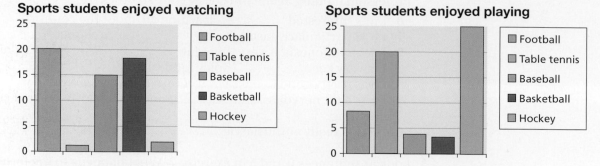

Sports students enjoyed watching — Football, Table tennis, Baseball, Basketball, Hockey

Sports students enjoyed playing — Football, Table tennis, Baseball, Basketball, Hockey

Look at the sentences describing the bar charts and correct the mistakes with quantifiers in each one. Check your answers by looking at the *Grammar and vocabulary bank* on page 150.

0 A lot of student likes playing table tennis. *A lot of students like playing table tennis.*
1 The students spend much time watching football. ....
2 Majority of the students prefer watching football to playing it. ....
3 Some of students like playing basketball. ....
4 The students don't spend many time playing basketball. ....
5 A number of students who play table tennis is larger than a number who play football. ....
6 The large number of students enjoy watching football. ....
7 Several of the student don't play any sports. ....
8 Most of students prefer playing table tennis to watching it. ....

4 Use the charts to write three more sentences about hockey and baseball using these quantifiers.

a/the number of	a lot of	many	most (of)
much several (of)	the majority of		some (of)

Note: *Lots* (*of*) is rather informal, and not suitable for academic writing.

Practice

5 In groups, carry out a class survey to find out information about your classmates: for example, what subjects they would like to study in the future, sports they enjoy, countries they would like to visit, or your own ideas.

6 Collate your results in a table like this:

Subject	Number of students
Business	9
Law	2
Medical related	3
Engineering	5

7 Use the information from your table to draw a bar chart. Write an opening statement, eg:
The bar chart shows ...
Write sentences about the data, for example
The most/least popular ...
Use percentages (*60%*) or fractions (*half, a quarter*)
Use quantifiers (*most, a number of*)

8 Present your findings to the rest of the class.

Identifying parts of speech

See *Grammar and vocabulary bank* on page 150.

1 Read this paragraph from the text on culture shock and find an example of each of these parts of speech from the underlined words in the text. Can you add another example to each group?

a verb	a noun	an adjective	an adverb	a preposition
an article		a conjunction		a pronoun

Constantly listening and speaking <u>in</u> a foreign language is tiring. <u>Although</u> you may have learned English very thoroughly, it is possible that the regional accents you discover when you <u>arrive</u> in the UK make <u>the</u> <u>language</u> harder to understand than you thought. People may also speak <u>quickly</u> and you may feel too <u>embarrassed</u> to ask <u>them</u> to repeat what they have said.

2 An understanding of the parts of speech is useful in building your knowledge of word families. eg *meet* (verb), *a meeting* (noun).

Complete the table with the missing verbs or nouns. Either the noun or verb form appears in Unit 1.

Noun	Verb		Noun	Verb
advice				invite
	inform		experience	
	arrive			choose
education				apply

3 Use one of the words in the box to complete the sentences.

1. Living overseas can be an exciting ....
2. We would like to .... you to attend an interview next week.
3. I'm not sure whether to study at home or overseas; it's a difficult ....
4. When you first .... in a new country it is common to suffer from culture shock.
5. To .... for the job you need to complete this form.
6. Most parents want to give their children a good ....
7. Your tutor will .... you on how to write this assignment.
8. We are pleased to .... you that you have passed the course.

Collocations

Collocations are words that are commonly used together, eg:
verb + noun *take an exam*, adjective + noun *a final exam*.

Adjective–noun collocations

4 Match each of the nouns with two of the adjectives in the box to make collocations.

first	full-time	higher	home	host	official	secondary	undergraduate

0. *full-time* .... student
1. .... education
2. .... language
3. .... country

5 Complete the sentences with one of the collocations from exercise 4.

1. My .... is Hindi but I also speak English and Urdu.
2. When living overseas you should respect the customs of your ....
3. Most .... gain a degree after three year's study.
4. IELTS is an exam taken by students who want to enter ....

Check your answers in the *Macmillan Collocations Dictionary*. Use the dictionary to find one more collocation for each of the nouns.

Reading

1 Work in groups. Look at the pictures. What are some of the problems and benefits of different modes of transport?

2 Check the meaning of the following words and phrases and then divide them into 'traffic problems' and 'possible solutions'.

bus lane	car pooling	congestion	congestion charging
gridlock	higher parking charges	park and ride	road pricing
	rush hour	traffic jam	

3 Which of these problems do you have where you live? Which of the possible solutions have been tried in your city? How successful were they?

4 Read the title of the article first. What do you think the answer to this question might be? Now skim the text quickly and answer the following questions.

1 How does the writer answer the question in the title?
2 Which of the problems and solutions in exercise 2 are mentioned in the text? Underline those you find.

TIP
Making predictions about what you are going to read can help you to understand the text more quickly when you read it. Look at the title and any pictures with the text first.

Does charging motorists more actually lead to less congestion?

A When London first introduced the congestion charge in 2003, almost everyone was in favour. It seemed a tough but necessary decision. Something had to be done to deal with the increasingly heavy traffic. Only the Federation for Small Businesses opposed the charge, fearing that it would damage trade for small shop-keepers. Within the first two years, however, traffic in the capital had fallen by about 30%, a dramatic improvement. The success of the scheme seemed obvious, and other cities rushed to copy it.

B Since then, however, traffic has slowly risen and congestion levels are now very similar to those in 2002. In fact, a recent survey showed that London is now the fourth most congested city in Europe. The only difference is that now motorists are paying for the privilege of sitting in gridlock. Supporters of the charge argue that without the congestion charge, the traffic jams would be even worse but, clearly, this is hard to prove either way.

C Attempts to introduce more general road pricing have stalled. The proposal was for every vehicle to be fitted with a satellite receiver to calculate exactly where and when the driver was travelling, charging from 2p per mile on uncongested roads to £1.34 on the busiest roads at peak times. An online petition against the proposal, signed by over 1.8 million people, made it very clear how the public felt about this latest tax and, for now at least, nothing further has been done to introduce it.

D Another strategy which has been implemented with the aim of reducing the number of cars on the road is that of introducing higher parking charges throughout town and city centres. However, the evidence suggests that, again, this is not reducing the amount of traffic but simply encouraging people to drive to out of town shopping centres, where parking is free. In this case, the victims are the small independent shops on our high streets.

E Ultimately all these attempts to force motorists out of their cars have failed and we need to ask ourselves why. The most obvious reason would seem to be a lack of any real alternative. Public transport in the UK is expensive, unreliable and slow. No wonder we usually choose to go by car. Milton Keynes, recently named as the most car-dependent city in Britain, has a public transport system where a ten-minute car journey during rush hour can often take up to two hours by bus. In contrast, Nottingham, the least car-dependent city according to the survey, has invested in 30 miles of cycle tracks, an efficient bus service and a nine-mile network of trams, used by 10 million passengers a year.

F Clearly we need to support any measure which will reduce congestion, both for our own convenience and, more importantly, to curb global warming. However, more thought needs to be given to the solutions. Perhaps the government needs to consider spending more money on transport infrastructure before making motorists pay more for using their cars.

Locating information

5 Work in pairs. Match the adjectives (1–6) with the nouns (a–f) to make collocations from the article.

1	tough	a	improvement
2	dramatic	b	bus service
3	uncongested	c	decision
4	efficient	d	times
5	heavy	e	roads
6	peak	f	traffic

6 Choose three of the collocations and write true sentences about your town or city.

See *Grammar and vocabulary bank* on page 151 for more on collocations.

7 Read the text again. Which paragraph (A–F) has the following information?

1 The current traffic situation in the capital. ....
2 One reason why people are reluctant to stop driving. ....
3 How the British public felt about paying per mile driven. ....
4 The short term effects of a congestion charge. ....

Yes, No, Not given

8 Do the following statements reflect the opinion of the writer of the text?

Write
YES (Y) If the statement agrees with the views of the writer.
NO (N) If the statement contradicts the views of the writer.
NOT GIVEN (NG) if it is impossible to say what the writer thinks about this.

0 A congestion charge seemed essential to reduce traffic in the capital. ...Y...
1 The government probably brought in a congestion charge in order to raise money for other projects. ....
2 It is clear that the congestion charge has prevented London from being even more congested. ....
3 Higher parking charges tend to encourage people to walk rather than drive.
....
4 People would probably use their cars less often if public transport was more efficient. ....
5 Public transport should be free, or very cheap, to encourage more people to use it. ....

Singular or plural

1 These phrases are taken from the reading text. Underline the subject and verb in the sentence. Is the verb singular or plural?

0	almost <u>everyone</u> <u>was</u> in favour	<u>singular</u>/plural
1	traffic has slowly risen	singular/plural
2	congestion levels are now very similar	singular/plural
3	all these attempts to force motorists out of their cars have failed	singular/plural
4	Public transport in the UK is expensive, unreliable and slow.	singular/plural
5	Perhaps the government needs to consider	singular/plural

2 Look at the *Grammar and vocabulary bank* on page 151. Now look at the subject–verb agreement in each of these sentences. Is it correct or incorrect? Rewrite the incorrect sentences.

0 Nobody seem to enjoy travelling to work by train. *Nobody seems* ....
1 One of my sisters drive a sports car. ....
2 Many of my colleagues shares the drive to work. ....
3 Much of my work involves visiting different companies. ....
4 Most people in my country owns a car. ....
5 Some of the students in my class cycle to college.
6 Neither of us travels on public transport much. ....

3 Choose the correct form of the verb and complete the sentences with your opinions about the problem of congestion. Then compare ideas with a partner.

1 Public transport in my country *is/are* ....
2 Traffic congestion *is/are* ....
3 People *is/are* starting to worry more about ....
4 The government *has/have* to ....
5 The environment *is/are* ....

IELTS Listening Section 3

1 Look at the pictures. Which of the words in the box can you use to describe them?

bottle bank	dustbin	landfill	litter	recycling bin	rubbish
	scrap metal		waste		

2 Which two categories could you divide the words in the box into? What are the differences in meaning between the words in each category?

3 ⊙ **1.4** Listen and write down the numbers you hear. Use numbers and symbols rather than words where possible.

4 You are going to hear a conversation between a student and a lecturer.

Short answer questions

Questions 1–6

Look at questions 1–6. What kind of answer are you looking for in each case?

⊙ **1.5** Now listen and answer the questions. Write NO MORE THAN THREE WORDS OR A NUMBER for each answer.

1 How much waste, on average, does one person in Britain produce each year?

....

2 What proportion of our waste is biodegradable? ....
3 What percentage is glass? ....
4 How much waste is buried? ....
5 Why is some waste burned? ....
6 By when will the amount of waste sent for landfill have to be reduced?

....

Questions 7–10

🔊 1.6 Complete the sentences below. Write NO MORE THAN THREE WORDS for each answer.

7 The two major aims of the government and environment agencies are to .... waste whenever possible.

8 Because people are sometimes too lazy to take their recycling to a special site, councils also often provide bins to keep at home for ....

9 In Switzerland the government encourages people not to throw things away by putting a tax on ....

10 Generally speaking, the situation has got better over the ....

Sentence completion

5 Use the correct form of the verbs in the box to complete these extracts from Listening Section 3. Check your answers in the audioscript on pages 166 and 167.

conserve	dispose of	minimize	produce	protect	recycle	reduce

1 On average we .... 30 million tonnes of solid household waste every year ... and obviously it's vital that waste is .... and .... in a way that .... our environment and our health.

2 New European law requires us to .... amounts of waste, and by 2020 we will only be able to send 10 million tonnes of this for landfill and the rest will have to be .... , burned or treated in a different way.

3 What we need to do is to .... raw materials, like tin and aluminium, while still protecting the environment and public health.

Present simple vs present continuous

1 Look at this extract from the audioscript for the listening task. Underline examples of the present simple and the present continuous as in the example.

J: They're responsible for household 'dustbin' collections, or taking away all the rubbish you produce in the home. In recent years, many more sites have been set up to collect waste separately for recycling. There are often containers in car parks or outside supermarkets for people to put bottles in: clear, green and brown bottles are separated. Also newspapers and magazines can be recycled as well as tins made of aluminium. One of the problems of this, though, is that most people are not bothering to take their rubbish there. To overcome this, some local councils also provide special containers, often called 'recycling bins', for residents to collect glass and paper in. They put these outside their houses at the same time as their rubbish, and they are collected and recycled.

L: I see. So are you saying that recycling is more important than actually reducing waste?

J: No. Nowadays, many products are increasingly being designed with reuse or recycling in mind and I think, in general, people are far more aware about these issues.

2 Write the examples from the text under the correct heading to describe their use. The present simple can be used to describe:

1 a regular habitual action

....

....

2 something which is generally true

....

....

Language focus

The present continuous can be used to describe:

1 something in progress at this specific moment

....

....

2 a changing, developing or temporary situation happening around now but not necessarily at this specific moment

....

....

3 Which of the following verbs are 'state' verbs and not usually used in continuous tenses?

| belong | develop | eat | grow | know | love | realize | seem | smell | want |

4 Some state verbs can be used in the continuous form with a slightly different meaning. Discuss the difference in meaning between the verbs in these pairs of sentences with a partner.

1
a What are you thinking about?
b What do you think about climate change?

2
a I feel sure that more could be done to reduce congestion.
b I'm feeling a bit sick.

3
a Most people in developed countries have a car.
b I'm having a lot of trouble with my car at the moment.

5 Complete the following text with the verbs in brackets in the correct tense (present simple or continuous).

Every year, UK households (1) .... (throw away) 8.3 million tonnes of food. Shockingly, research (2) .... (show) that most of this could actually have been eaten. The majority of the waste (3) .... (happen) as a result of buying food in bulk, which then (4) .... (go bad) before we can eat it. Most of us probably (5) .... (know) that we are wasting too much food, but we probably (6) .... (not realize) that it costs us, on average, £680 a year.
The amount of waste produced by British households (7) .... (grow) year by year and we (8) .... (currently send) most of it to be buried in landfill sites. The good news is that scientists (9) .... (develop) new ways to use food waste to create gas, which can then be used to produce energy.

6 Work in pairs. Make a list of things which can be recycled, then discuss which of these things *you* currently recycle.

– How do you do this? (collection from your house, going to a bottle bank, etc).
– If you don't recycle any of these things, what is it that prevents you?
– Is it difficult or inconvenient?
– What would make you more likely to recycle these things?

See *Grammar and vocabulary bank* on page 151.

The environment

1 What topic do the pictures relate to? Use the words in the box and any others that you know to describe the pictures and talk about what they show.

carbon dioxide	climate	consequences	efficiently	emissions
essential	greenhouse	renewable	the planet	wasting

2 Read the short text below. Don't worry about the gaps, just try to get the general idea. Which do you think would be the best title?

A Global warming – who cares?
B We can stop global warming.
C Why we can't stop global warming.
D The history of global warming.

Average global temperature has risen by 0.8 degrees Celsius since the start of the industrial revolution. That may not sound like much, but the (1) .... are enormous. The polar ice caps are shrinking year by year. Extreme weather situations are on the increase. Climate change is already damaging (2) .... and that's only the beginning. However, we can do something about it. It is not a threat coming from outer space. It is people, us, who are causing (3) .... change by polluting the atmosphere with too much (4) .... (CO_2) and other (5) .... gases. If we started it ourselves, we can stop it ourselves too. We can – and must – cut CO_2 (6) .... by 50% by the year 2050. The industrial countries will have to cut theirs by as much as 80%. If we do this, we can keep the rise in global temperature below the 2 degrees Celsius mark. Scientists agree that this is (7) .... if we are to prevent the climate from getting completely out of control. (8) .... forms of energy – solar power, wind, water can supply half the world's energy requirements by the middle of this century. But only if we stop (9) .... energy and take action to use it more (10) ....

3 Look at the text again and identify what part of speech is needed in each gap. Then choose from the words in the box in exercise 1 to complete the text.

4 What can be done to prevent or slow climate change? Work in pairs or small groups and write your ideas in the table below.

Individual actions	Government actions
Walking more and driving less	Providing cheap and efficient public transport to encourage people not to use their cars.

IELTS Writing Task 2

1 Look at the following essay question. Do you agree, disagree, or partly agree? Discuss your ideas with a partner.

Individual actions have little or no effect on climate change. For this reason, worthwhile change can only be made at governmental level.

To what extent do you agree or disagree?

Give reasons for your answer and include any relevant examples from your own knowledge or experience.

Write at least 250 words.

2 Now read the following model answer. Does the writer agree with the statement, disagree or partly agree? Which paragraph gives you the writer's opinion most clearly?

In recent years it has become more and more obvious that climate change is real and that it is starting to affect our planet badly. If we continue to pollute the atmosphere with current levels of CO_2, the consequences will be enormous. Clearly, change must happen, but whose responsibility is it?

Some people argue that the problem is so huge that only international governmental action can have any real impact. Certainly, it is essential for governments to work together on solutions, signing up to agreements and, more importantly, keeping them. On a national level, we need to remember that most pollution is caused by industry and that this can only be controlled effectively by government action. For example, industries could be made to pay a carbon tax on their emissions.

However, while the government must take a lead on dealing with climate change, we are also all individually responsible for our own carbon footprint. The average person in the UK is responsible for about 10 tonnes of carbon emissions a year, while someone in the developing world only uses around 0.3 tonnes a year. If we are to prevent temperatures rising by more than 2 degrees, we will all need to use no more than 1.3 tonnes a year by 2050. This will require a considerable lifestyle change for the average British person. We will need to stop flying regularly, driving when we could just as easily walk and so on.

In conclusion, I would maintain that to protect our planet, and all our futures, we will need a combination of effective international agreements, strong government policies and changes in individual behaviour.

Topic sentences

3 A *topic sentence* is the sentence within a paragraph which gives the reader the main idea of the paragraph. The other sentences give more information, adding details or examples. Underline the topic sentences in each paragraph of the sample essay.

4 For each topic sentence, identify the topic and the main idea about it.

In recent years it has become more and more obvious that climate change is real and that it is starting to affect our planet badly.

The topic is climate change. The main idea is that it is having a bad effect.

5 What supporting ideas or information have been added to each main idea? Which paragraph does not have any supporting information? Why?

Topic sentence:
Some people argue that the problem is so huge that only international governmental action can have any real impact.

Supporting ideas:
Certainly, it is essential for governments to work together on solutions, signing up to agreements and, more importantly, keeping them. On a national level, we need to remember that most pollution is caused by industry and that this can only be controlled effectively by government action. For example, industries could be made to pay a carbon tax on their emissions.

TIP
While the topic sentence usually starts the paragraph, it can also go at the end (or occasionally elsewhere).

6 Look at the three sentences below. Together they make a paragraph. Identify the topic sentence and then add the supporting sentences to make a coherent paragraph.
  a *By the end of the 21st century, if current trends continue, the global temperature is likely to be higher than at any other time in the last two million years.*
  b *Climate change is a reality.*
  c *Our planet is hotter today than it has been in two thousand years.*

7 Write a paragraph using the following topic sentence. The topic sentence can go at the beginning or the end of the paragraph. Make sure that the other sentences are clearly related to the topic sentence. Remember that they can be used to add detail or examples.

Many people believe that the threat of climate change has been exaggerated.

Practice

8 Look at the following question and underline the key words.

People will never be willing to make the dramatic lifestyle changes needed to control climate change. For this reason, governments must force people to do so.

To what extent do you agree or disagree?

Give reasons for your answer and include any relevant examples from your own knowledge or experience.

Write at least 250 words.

TIP
Make sure that you really understand the question. A question may have several parts; make sure that you answer all of them.

9 The first paragraph or introduction explains the background and says what you understand by the question, but in your own words. Which of the following introductions would be most suitable for the essay question above?

    1 *I think that it is very important that we should all look after our planet. After all, it is the only one we have. There are lots of small actions that we can all take such as switching off computers and televisions, rather than leaving them on standby or walking short distances rather than going in the car.*

    2 *Nowadays, most people are aware of the threat of climate change and are willing to make small changes to the way they live. However, for the majority of people this does not include such things as giving up their car or giving up flying abroad.*

    3 *Governments must force people to make changes or the problem of climate change will never be solved. If necessary, people who continue to pollute the planet should be sent to prison.*

10 Now make a list of ways in which you agree with the statements and/or disagree with the statement. Also try to think of examples to back up your opinions.

11 Divide your ideas into two or three paragraphs, with one main idea in each paragraph. Write your paragraphs. This is the main part of your essay, and you should write about 200 words in total in these paragraphs.

12 The conclusion should sum up the main points and give your final opinion (though you can also mention your opinion in the introduction if you prefer). Write your conclusion, using one of the following stems to start the paragraph.

> **Useful language**
> In conclusion, I would maintain/argue/say that ...
> To sum up, we can see that/it is clear that ...
> To conclude, I agree that ...

Editing

13 Check grammar, vocabulary and spelling. Make sure that you leave yourself a few minutes to check your work for any obvious grammar (for example articles, tenses, plurals, third person, subject–verb agreement, etc.), vocabulary or spelling mistakes. You will not have time to change the main content of your essay but you might notice some errors that can be easily corrected.

14 When you have finished your answer, compare it with the model answer on page 160.

1 Look at the topics below and make a list of vocabulary from the unit which you could use to discuss each one.

- Should cars be banned in city centres?
- Why bother recycling?
- What alternative sources of energy are there and which is our best option?

2 🔘 **1.7** Listen to three different people talking about these topics. Which of the items of vocabulary you listed do they use?

3 Listen again and complete the table.

Topic	Opinions	Reasons
Should cars be banned in city centres?		
Why bother recycling?		
What alternative sources of energy are there and which is our best option?		

4 Listen again. Which of the phrases in the box below do you hear?

Useful language

Personal
In my view/opinion …
I personally think that…
I'd rather (+ base form)/I prefer (to + base form or -ing) …
I (strongly/firmly/personally/honestly) believe/think/feel that …
I'm convinced that …
If you ask me, …

More impersonal
Some people say/argue/think that …

Backing up opinions with examples
For example/instance, …
In my experience/country …

5 Choose one of the topics in exercise 1 and write five sentences, giving your opinions, with reasons, and using appropriate vocabulary.

6 Find a partner who has chosen the same topic as you (if possible) and without using your written sentences, talk about the topic together.

Working out meaning from context

1 Look at the headline of the article. What reasons can you think of why this might be happening?

2 Read the article and check your predictions.

Car use is dropping

A Car use is falling in Britain in a historic change of direction that will have important implications for transport, mobility and society in general, expert panellists agreed at a meeting held yesterday evening. Nobody knows why the decline is occurring, but it mirrors what is happening in other industrialized countries. Car sales have fallen by more than a fifth in Japan since 1990, while in the United States millions more cars are scrapped each year than are purchased.

B One factor in the decline may be the regeneration of cities like London and Manchester, where more and more homes have been built near to the centre making car ownership and use unnecessary. And indeed research in the US – where four in five people now live in towns and cities – suggests that this does play a part as growing numbers of cars have lessened mobility, through congestion, rather than improving it.

C There is evidence that the fall is particularly marked among the young. Socializing on the internet, rather than in person, has been found to be a factor in a drop in the number of US teenagers with driving licences, from 12 million in 1978 to under 10 million now.

3 It is often possible to work out the meaning of an unknown word by using the context.

For example, for the word *implications* in paragraph A:
- First decide what part(s) of speech the word or phrase is. In this case it is a noun.
- Then look at the sentence before and after the word for any clues. The big change in the number of cars being used will *have important implications for* different areas of society: it will have a big effect or impact on them.
- When you have an idea what it might mean, try it out in the sentence to see if it makes sense.

*Car use is falling in Britain in a historic change of direction that will have **a big effect on** transport, mobility and society in general.*

The dictionary definition of *implication* is 'a possible future effect or result of an action, event, decision, etc.'

Now find a word or phrase in the text which means the same as

1 a decrease in the quality, quantity or importance of something (para A) ....
2 is very similar to something else or copies it (para A) ....
3 the process of making something develop and grow strong again (para B) ....
4 very easy to notice (para C) ....
5 one of several things which influence or cause a situation (para C) ....

Reading

1 Look at these pictures and answer the questions.
  – Which holiday would you most/least like to go on?
  – What type of person does each holiday appeal to?

2 Read the title of the passage on page 31. What do you think 'extreme tourism' is? Read the first paragraph of the article and check your predictions.

Matching headings to paragraphs

3 Read the text quickly . Do any of these holidays appeal to you? Why/Why not? Now answer the questions.

TIP
Read through each paragraph quickly to identify the main idea. There will usually be more headings than paragraphs so you will not need to use them all.

Questions 1–6
The reading passage has seven paragraphs labelled A–G. Choose the correct heading for each paragraph from the list of headings below.

List of headings	
i Sub-zero expedition	0 Paragraph A *ii*
ii The rise in adventurous travel	1 Paragraph B ....
iii An out of this world experience	2 Paragraph C ....
iv Into the depths of the jungle	3 Paragraph D ....
v Journey through heat and dust	4 Paragraph E ....
vi High and dry on two wheels	5 Paragraph F ....
vii On top of the world	6 Paragraph G ....
viii Close underwater encounters	
ix African overland safari	

Adventure, Risk and Adrenaline Rush – the appeal of extreme tourism

A Whilst for many people the idea of the perfect holiday is escaping from the routine and stress of everyday life to a faraway deserted beach, for a growing number of travellers this type of holiday no longer holds its appeal. For these adventure seekers, the chance to participate in something much more daring or dangerous is attracting more tourists each year. This type of extreme tourism involves travelling to some of the most far-flung and inhospitable corners of the earth or taking part in risky sports or activities. The most intrepid holidaymakers combine the two; dangerous activities in a hazardous environment. Here are just a few examples of the type of holidays available.

B This must be the ultimate in extreme travel destinations but is fast becoming a reality for those for whom money is no object. So far only a handful of space tourists have taken to the skies but already a number of companies are competing for the custom of the few who have the cash. All potential space tourists must go on an intensive training course prior to departing on this unique trip. The course will prepare them for the weightless environment and cramped conditions of a £1 million-a-night space hotel where, from the windows, they will be able to view the earth and see the sun rise every 80 minutes.

C Few people can actually claim to have seen Antarctica so this is really a once-in-a-lifetime experience. This inaccessible region, whose only human residents are scientists and researchers, holds records for being the driest, windiest and coldest continent, with temperatures below freezing all year round. Travellers to this region will experience 24-hour sunlight and see magnificent icebergs as well as colonies of penguins. For the most adventurous, there are plenty of unexplored mountains to climb and skidoo riding across the desert snow is also popular.

D At over 9,400,000 square kilometres, the Sahara is the largest hot desert in the world, spanning North Africa from the Red Sea to the Atlantic Ocean. Trekking on foot is not the only travel option and camel rides and 4 x 4 vehicles are also used to venture into the wilderness, where temperatures can reach 50°C during the day but can fall rapidly at night. Accommodation is under canvas in a traditional Bedouin tent and there will be little in the way of creature comforts with common hazards including sandstorms and scorpions.

E This adventure is for climbing enthusiasts looking for the ultimate challenge. At 8,850 metres high serious training is needed to reach the top of Everest and it can be difficult to acclimatise to the high altitude, but the Himalayas are fast becoming one of the ultimate tourist destinations. For those who don't wish to try for the highest summit there are plenty of opportunities for challenging climbs around Everest base camp.

F South America's spectacular Amazon basin is one of the most humid places on earth and is home to a huge array of flora and fauna. In some places rainfall here is over 2,000 mm a year and temperatures can reach around 32°C. Adventurous tourists can trek into some of the most remote and uninhabited areas of the rainforest to spot wildlife including alligators, monkeys, parrots and anacondas. There may also be opportunities to experience the way of life of some of the indigenous communities that inhabit the Amazon basin.

G For adventurers keen to get up close to the natural world, this holiday to South Africa gives travellers the chance to observe the wonders of the ocean depths including tropical reefs, whales, turtles, dolphins and sharks. The highlight of this marine safari must be the thrill of the great white shark cage dive where divers are surrounded by these amazing creatures, only separated by the bars of a reinforced cage. Not for the faint-hearted!

Short answers

Questions 7–13

Answer the questions using NO MORE THAN THREE WORDS from the text.

7 What type of person does extreme tourism appeal to?

8 What must space tourists attend to prepare for their trip?

9 Who lives in Antarctica?

10 What dangers will visitors to the Sahara come across?

11 What do Everest climbers have difficulty getting used to?

12 Whose lifestyle can travellers to the Amazon come into contact with?

13 What protects divers from the great white shark?

Synonyms

See *Grammar and vocabulary bank* on page 152.

4 Synonyms (words with the same or similar meaning) are used in written English to make a text more interesting and to avoid repetition. Find the following synonyms in the text.

   1 Three adjectives meaning *likely to kill, damage or harm* (para A)

   2 Three adjectives meaning *a long way away or distant* (para A, para F)

   3 Three nouns/noun phrases which refer to *plants, animals and other living things* (para F, para G)

   4 Three adjectives meaning *keen to try new things, brave* (para A, para C)

   5 Two adjectives and one noun which refer to *a place with no people or where people do not live* (para A, para D, para F)

5 Use one of the synonyms from exercise 4 to complete each of the sentences. Compare with a partner. Did you use the same words?

   1 My brother is very .... and always tries to find new and exciting challenges.

   2 I have always been very interested in .... and would love to go on an African safari.

   3 A trek into the Sahara will take you to .... areas where you will not see any other people.

   4 One of the most .... trips you can undertake is climbing Mount Everest.

   5 Every summer I travel to a .... Scottish village to visit my grandparents – they live a long way from the nearest city.

Articles

See *Grammar and vocabulary bank* on page 151.

1 Look at these examples of how articles are used. Match the examples with the rules.

Indefinite articles (*a/an*)

   1 on *a* faraway deserted beach

   2 £1 million-*a*-night space hotel

   3 space tourists must go on *an* intensive training course

   a Use *a/an* with countable nouns the first time they are mentioned.

   b Use *a/an* to mean *per* or *every* with distances, times, etc.

   c Use *a/an* when the noun referred to is one of many.

Definite article (*the*)

  4 holds records for being *the driest,* windiest and coldest continent
  5 see *the sun* rise every 80 minutes
  6 *the Himalayas* are fast becoming one of the ultimate tourist destinations
  7 a space hotel ... where, from *the windows* they will be able to view the earth
  8 *The course* will prepare them

  d Use *the* with singular, countable nouns, after they are first mentioned or if it is clear which one is being talked about.
  e Use *the* with nouns which are unique.
  f Use *the* with superlatives.
  g Use *the* with rivers, seas, deserts and mountain ranges.
  h Use *the* when it is clear which one is being talked about.

No article (–)

  9 wildlife including *alligators, monkeys, parrots* and *anacondas*
  10 those for whom *money* is no object
  11 Few people can actually claim to have seen *Antarctica*

  i Use no article with most countries, regions and continents.
  j Use no article with plural countable nouns used in a general sense.
  k Use no article for uncountable nouns used in a general sense.

2 Look at these sentences taken from the text and fill in the missing articles (– = no article). Then check your answers against the text.

  1 .... most far-flung and .... inhospitable corners of .... earth.
  2 .... Sahara is .... largest hot desert in .... world, spanning .... North Africa from .... Red Sea to .... Atlantic Ocean.
  3 .... rainfall here is over 2,000 mm .... year.
  4 ... whose only human residents are .... scientists and .... researchers ...
  5 .... travellers to this region will experience .... 24-hour sunlight and see .... magnificent icebergs
  6 this holiday to .... South Africa
  7 .... wonders of .... ocean depths including .... tropical reefs, ... whales, ... turtles ...
  8 only separated by .... bars of .... reinforced cage.

Quiz

3 Work in pairs to do the general knowledge quiz. Think carefully about the use of articles in your answers.

  1 Which sea separates North Africa from Europe? ....
  2 Who lives in Buckingham Palace, London? ....
  3 What rises in the sky in the morning? ....
  4 How often is there a new moon? ....
  5 What wild cats might you see on an African safari? ....
  6 Why is Mount Everest so famous? ....
  7 In which continent are Japan and Thailand? ....
  8 What are England, Scotland, Wales and Northern Ireland known as? ....
  9 What is the Great White? ....
  10 What is the highest mountain range in South America? ....

IELTS Listening Section 1: Prediction

1 You want to travel by train to Edinburgh and you phone the train enquiry line. Think about the type of information you want and write down:

    1 three questions you might ask, eg *How much does a ticket to Edinburgh cost*?
    2 three questions the train enquiry person might ask you, eg *What time do you want to travel?*

2 You are going to hear a conversation between a student and a train enquiry assistant. Look at questions 1–6. What type of answers are needed? eg. 1. a date.

Table completion

Questions 1–6

🎧 **1.8** Now listen and fill in the information in the spaces in the boxes.

Date of travel	1
Journey type	2
Class	3

Outward journey	Depart Birmingham	08.05	5 ....
	Arrive Edinburgh	4	14.35
	Change of train?	Direct	Change at Stockport
Return journey	Depart Edinburgh	16.45	18.05
	Arrive Birmingham	20.21	21.57
	Change of train?	Direct	6 ....

TIP
Look at the parts of the table that are already complete. These will help you predict the type of answer that is needed.

Questions 7–10

🎧 **1.9** Listen to the second part of the recording and answer questions 7–10.

Type of ticket	Apex Super Saver	Apex Peak Saver	9	Off Peak Saver
Advance purchase necessary?	14 days	8	None	None
Travel on Friday possible?	Yes	Yes	Yes	10 ....
Price	7 £	£41.30	£54	£38

TIP
Check if the numbering goes across or down the table.

Labelling a diagram

Questions 11–14

🎧 **1.10** The student is at the train station information desk. Listen to the final part of the recording and answer questions 11–14.

TIP
Look at the diagram before you listen. Look for key features and their positions, eg if it is a plan, where is the speaker standing? If it is a process, where does it start and finish?

The train station

12

13

café

14

newsagent's

11

You are here → *i*

IELTS Writing Task 1

1 Name the country where you can see these attractions.
   – Can you identify them?
   – Would you like to visit this destination? Why/Why not?

2 Read this Task 1 question. Which country do most visitors come from?

The table below shows how many tourists from five countries visited Australia in different years from 2006 to 2010. Summarize the information by selecting and reporting the main features, and make comparisons where relevant.

Country of residence	2006	2007	2008	2009	2010
New Zealand	979	976	1030	1006	1011
Japan	631	582	505	396	335
Canada	99	104	113	117	118
China	267	319	346	352	360
Germany	143	144	148	153	159
France	61	65	71	83	93

Visits (thousands)

TIP
When describing data you only need to write about the most significant information, not all the figures shown in the diagram.

Selecting and reporting the main features

3 Which of these statements would be the most suitable general description for the data above?

   1 The number of visitors to Australia from most countries decreased from 2006 to 2010.
   2 The number of visitors to Australia from most countries increased from 2006 to 2010.

4 Look at the table again. Which three statements from the list below would be suitable to include as important information and which three would you not include? Give reasons.

   1 Over the whole period New Zealand had the most visitors to Australia.
   2 From 2006 to 2010 the biggest increase in tourists was from China.
   3 There were 148,000 visitors from Germany in 2008.
   4 The number of visitors from France increased between 2007 and 2008.
   5 Visitors from Japan to Australia almost halved over this period.
   6 Chinese tourists visiting Australia increased by about 6,000 from 2008 to 2009.

5 Look at this model answer to the question. Quickly read the text and underline one statement about each of the countries.

The table shows that the number of visitors to Australia from most countries increased from 2006 to 2010. There was a significant increase in tourists from New Zealand, China and France over this period while numbers from Canada and Germany rose gradually. However, visitors from Japan to Australia dropped dramatically.

The biggest increase in tourism was from China and numbers went up significantly by approximately 100,000 to reach 360,000 in 2010. Although visitors from New Zealand to Australia fell slightly from 2006 to 2007, over the whole period this country had the most visitors with a notable increase from 979,000 to over a million. There were fewer visitors from France but numbers rose considerably.

Contrary to the general trend, visitors from Japan to Australia almost halved over this period with a significant decrease.

Overall, the table indicates that Australia increased in popularity as a tourist destination for most countries in this five year period.

Describing trends and changes over time

6 Look at the sample answer again.

1 Underline the verbs that mean 'go up' or 'go down'.
2 Complete the table. Which tense is used in the answer? Why?

Up ▲		Down ▼	
Infinitive	Tense:	Infinitive	Tense: ....
go up	....	drop	....
....	rose	fall	....
increase	....	....	decreased

3 Find adverbs in the model answer and complete the table below. Why are adverbs like these useful for Task 1?

Adverbs describing a big change	Adverbs describing a slower, more regular change	Adverbs describing a small change
significantly	steadily	slightly

7 Look at the examples below.

China

2006	2007
267	319

The number of visitors from China increased significantly between 2006 and 2007.

Germany

2008	2009	2010
148	153	159

Tourist numbers from Germany rose gradually from 2008 to 2010.

1 Write a sentence describing the trend shown in the data in the boxes.

Canada

2009	2010
117	118

Japan

2008	2009
505	396

2 Write further statements about New Zealand (2006–2007) and France (2006–2008).

Adding specific details to general statements

8 It is important to use numbers or figures from the data to support your statements.

Read the following sentences. Note the extra details underlined.

The biggest increase in tourists was from China and numbers went up significantly by approximately 100,000 to reach 360,000 in 2010.
Over the whole period New Zealand had the most visitors with a notable increase from 979,000 to over a million.

Add extra details using figures from the table to these sentences from the model answer.

1 There were fewer visitors from France but numbers rose considerably by ....

2 ... visitors from Japan to Australia almost halved over this period with a significant decrease from ....

Practice

9 Read the information and choose the key points you want to include in your answer.

What general trends does the table show? What specific details will you need to include?

The table below shows UK residents' visits abroad by country of visit from 2004 to 2008. Summarize the information by selecting and reporting the main features, and make comparisons where relevant.

	2004	2005	2006	2007	2008
Egypt	345	564	694	510	664
India	657	796	958	972	956
Poland	304	637	1,236	1,552	1,578
Spain	13,883	13,837	14,428	13,869	13,819
USA	4,167	4,241	3,986	3,923	4,003

Visits (in thousands)

10 When you have finished, compare it with the model answer on page 161.

IELTS Listening Section 2: Listening for gist

1 ⊙ **1.11** You will hear someone talking to a class about a trip. Listen and answer these questions.

  1 Where is the trip to?
  2 How long will the trip last?

2 Listen again and answer the exam task questions.

Multiple choice
Questions 1–5

Circle the appropriate letter.

  1 Mary Golding is
    A a student.
    B a coordinator.
    C the Student Officer.
    D the French teacher.

  2 How many students can go on this trip?
    A 4
    B 10
    C 30
    D 20

  3 The trip begins on
    A Wednesday 4th April.
    B Saturday 31st March.
    C Saturday 4th April.
    D Friday 30th March.

  4 They will cross the Channel
    A by coach.
    B by plane.
    C by ferry.
    D by train.

  5 They will return home at around
    A 11am.
    B 10pm.
    C 11pm.
    D 9am.

Classification
Questions 6–10

⊙ **1.12** Listen to the second part of the talk. During the trip to Paris, will you have to pay for these activities?

Write
FREE (F) if it is free.
INCLUDED (I) if it is included in the cost of the trip.
PAY (P) if you have to pay for it yourself.

  6 a boat ride ....
  7 The Eiffel Tower ....
  8 a cathedral ....
  9 art galleries ....
  10 the train journey to Paris ....

Speaking

1 Look at the pictures of tourist attractions. In which country do you think they are? How could you describe each place? Which of the following features would you expect to find in each place?

> a friendly atmosphere   a peaceful environment   beautiful views
> colourful markets   historic buildings   interesting museums and galleries
> lively nightlife   spectacular scenery   street cafés
> traditional local customs   unspoilt countryside

2 Label the map with the locations and geographical features.

> **1** a castle in the north east (of the country)
> **2** a city between the mountains and the sea
> **3** a town next to a forest
> **4** a beach on the east coast
> **5** an island off the south coast
> **6** a river in the west of the country
> **7** a mountainous region in the west
> **8** a village next to a lake

IELTS Speaking Part 2

Part 2

A Describe a tourist destination you have enjoyed visiting.

You should say
– where the place is
– when you first went there
– what this place is like

and explain why you enjoyed visiting it.

B Describe a place you would like to visit in the future.

You should say
– where the place is
– what is the place like/why it is famous
– what you would do there

and explain why you would like to visit this place.

Making notes

TIP
You will have one minute so write only key words, not full sentences.

3 In Part 2 of the Speaking exam you have one minute to think about what you are going to say and make notes. Look at a student's notes for one of the two tasks above. Which of the tasks has she chosen?

- Disneyland
- Florida, USA
- favourite films, characters
- rides
- souvenirs
- love Disney
- dream since childhood
- family

4 ⊙ 1.13 Listen to the student give her talk using the notes she made. As you listen think about questions 1–5.
  1 Did she cover all the points on the card?
  2 Did she talk for long enough?
  3 What does she say to start the talk?
  4 How does she introduce the final part of the talk?
  5 How could the talk be improved?

5 You are now going to do Task A. First, spend one minute preparing ideas and making notes. Work in pairs. Speak for 1–2 minutes on the topic and get your partner to time you. Make sure you include all points on the card. When you have finished your partner will tell you what you did well and what you should do to improve.

Presentation

Think of a place anywhere in the world you would love to go to. Carry out research using the guidelines below and then present your ideas to the group.

- Location.
- How to get there.
- Why this place is famous.
- Why you are interested in visiting it. If possible use visuals to illustrate your talk.

Editing

1 Checking your work carefully and correcting your own mistakes will help you improve your accuracy in written work as well as being very useful for your future studies. Look at the following Writing Task 1 showing the purpose of overseas visits to the UK and read the sample answer.

Purpose of visit	2004	2005	2006	2007	2008
Holiday	9,275	9,713	10,566	10,758	10,923
Business	7,470	8,168	9,019	8,845	8,124
Visiting friends or relatives	7,861	8,687	9,406	9,720	9,727
Miscellaneous	3,149	3,401	3,722	3,456	3,113
All visits (total)	27,755	29,969	32,713	32,779	31,887

Visits (in thousands)

The total number of overseas visits to UK decreased from 2004 to 2008. Most people visited the UK for the purpose of hollidays and this figure went up slightly. Travel to visit friends or relatives and for business reasons increased but visits for miscellaneous purposes decrease.

A biggest increase was visiting friends or relatives which rise significantly from 7,861,000 to 8,124,000. Holidays also went up considerably from 9,275,000 to 10,923,000. Miscellaneous reasons droped dramatically from 3,149,000 to 3,113,000.

Overall, the number of overseas residents' visits to the UK increased in this period.

1 Find errors relating to the content (one for each category):
– general trends ....
– specific details ....

2 Find and correct errors relating to language:
– two spelling errors ....
– two articles errors ....
– two verb tense errors ....
– two adverbs describing trends errors ....

Collocations

2 All these words can collocate with the verb *travel* or the noun *traveller*. Use them to complete the word map.

| adventurous | air | budget | business | experienced | extensively |
| frequent | independently | keen | overseas | rail | regularly |

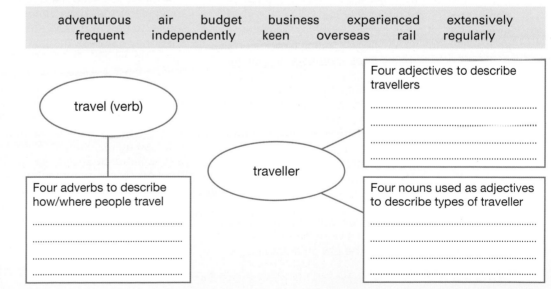

travel (verb)

traveller

Four adjectives to describe travellers
....
....
....
....

Four adverbs to describe how/where people travel
....
....
....
....

Four nouns used as adjectives to describe types of traveller
....
....
....
....

MACMILLAN
Collocations
DICTIONARY
FOR LEARNERS OF ENGLISH

See *Grammar and vocabulary bank* on page 152 for further practice.

Reading

1 Which of the following are against the law in your country? Which do you think are against the law in the UK?
- Riding a bicycle on the pavement
- Carrying a weapon
- Parking on pavements
- Using a mobile phone while driving
- Dropping litter
- Driving through red lights
- Not wearing a seatbelt in the car
- Eating or drinking while driving
- Speeding (breaking the speed limit while driving)
- Downloading music from illegal websites

2 Which of these 'crimes' do you think are commonly committed in the UK? Read the text quickly and tick the ones that are mentioned. Which of the crimes in exercise 1 are not mentioned?

Our daily dose of crime

Most people are pretty law-abiding you might think. Well, think again. According to a recent survey, the average British citizen breaks the law 500 times a year, or about eight times a week.

Some of the offences most commonly committed are downloading music illegally, riding bicycles on the pavement and dropping litter. Motorists are among the worst offenders, with common crimes including parking on the pavement, eating or drinking behind the wheel, using a non hands-free mobile phone while driving or not putting on a seatbelt.

The survey polled 2,000 adults about these crimes and found that 25% of those polled were not at all worried about the fact that they were actually breaking the law. Their arguments were either that the crimes were not very serious or that it was acceptable because 'everyone does it'.

John Sewell, who works for www.onepoll.com, which carried out the poll, said: 'It's worrying to think that so many people are breaking the law on a daily basis.

'And it's an even bigger concern that many aren't at all bothered about it.

'But these so-called minor crimes are committed so regularly, they have almost become legal, which seems to be the reason so many people aren't fazed when they do break the law.'

Speeding, which can, of course, have serious consequences, was one of the most common laws to be broken. Over 50% of people admitted to breaking the speed limit at times and 35% of people admitted to eating and drinking while driving. Texting and using a mobile phone while driving was also quite common. Peter Gray, spokesman for the National Society for the Prevention of Road Accidents, commented, 'After many years of campaigning, Britain now has one of the best road safety records in the world. However, there are still around six people dying on our roads each day. Without doubt this number could be significantly reduced if people would just follow the law.'

True, False, Not given

TIP
Be careful – even if you think the answer is True or False from your own knowledge, you must be able to find evidence in the text.

3 Do the following statements agree with the information in the text?

Write
TRUE (T) if the statement agrees with the information.
FALSE (F) if the statement contradicts the information.
NOT GIVEN (NG) if there is no information on this.

1 More than half the people questioned consider the crimes unimportant. ....
2 Some of the minor crimes have recently become legal. ....
3 More than a thousand people admitted to speeding. ....
4 35% of people admitted to using a mobile while driving. ....
5 There are fewer road accidents in Britain than there used to be. ....

4 Discuss these questions.
   – Do you think these crimes are minor?
   – Which do you consider to be the most serious?
   – How should people who commit these crimes be punished? A fine? A warning? A prison sentence? No punishment?

5 Read the text about crazy driving laws on page 44. Are any of the crimes from the previous text mentioned?

6 Read the text again and answer the questions.

Table completion

Questions 1–8
Complete the table. Choose NO MORE THAN THREE WORDS OR A NUMBER from the passage for each answer.

Name	Crime	Punishment
Michael Thompson	Signalled to other motorists about a **1**	a fine and costs
2 .... Keith Pemberton **3**	eating whilst driving	**4** .... a £60 fine a fine
Michael Mancini	**5** .... while waiting in his car	a £60 fine and **6** ....
Gary Saunders	**7** .... at the wheel	no punishment except a **8** ....

Crazy driving laws

Should a driver be punished for warning of a speed trap ahead? David Williams investigates some cases in which the police appear to have overreacted.

Michael Thompson provoked sympathy and disbelief in equal measure when he was fined £175, ordered to pay £250 costs and a £15 'victim surcharge' after being found guilty of wilfully obstructing a police officer in the course of her duties.

The crime meriting such severe punishment? The semi-retired man simply did what many motorists often do and warned oncoming drivers that there was a police speed trap around the corner, by flashing his headlamps.

Thompson insisted he was performing his 'civic duty' by warning fellow motorists and one solicitor at court criticized the prosecution as a waste of taxpayers' money.

In words that resonated with many of Britain's 34 million motorists, the solicitor said the driver should be praised for his actions.

Not everyone was as sympathetic, however. On national radio phone-ins many criticized his actions; had he not prevented speeding drivers from getting their just deserts?

It turns out that Thompson is in good company; numerous driver prosecutions and penalties have been at least as contentious.

In December 2003 Sarah McCaffery was stopped by police who thought she was using her mobile phone while making a left turn in her Ford Ka.

In fact, she was doing nothing more sinister than eating an apple. Police nevertheless issued her with a £30 ticket, saying she was not in proper control of her car. The 23-year-old from Hebburn, in the North-East, decided to fight back and appealed, but was nevertheless convicted by magistrates.

Stranger still was the case of a man fined for blowing his nose. When Michael Mancini found himself stuck in a queue of traffic with a runny nose, he instinctively reached for his handkerchief.

The simple act of pulling out a tissue and blowing his nose earned him a £60 fine because he was 'not in proper control of his vehicle'.

Policeman Stuart Gray also handed out three penalty points, even though Mancini had the handbrake on at the time.

The case echoes that of salesman Keith Pemberton, from Cheshire, who was fined £60 for eating a sandwich at the wheel in March 2007.

Company director Gary Saunders was stopped in the same city for laughing while driving in 2009, but escaped with a ticking-off.

Motoring, clearly, is not a laughing matter – but justice can prevail. Mr Mancini took his protest to court and the public prosecutor in Ayr decided not to prosecute. 'I knew it would cost me hiring a lawyer but it was worth it out of principle,' said Mr Mancini.

Kevin Story was spotted by police munching a chocolate bar on the M3 and issued with a fine for 'not being in control of his vehicle'. Police later gave him a break and said the fine would be quashed as it was 'inappropriate'.

Hampshire's Assistant Chief Constable Colin Smith said: 'We accept that the issue of a fixed penalty ticket, while intended to promote road safety, was inappropriate action by a well-meaning policeman.

'Officers usually deal sensitively and with common sense. If we are found to be over-zealous, we are more than happy to admit that officers are human and sometimes make mistakes.'

The Automobile Association (AA) advises drivers stopped by police to be courteous and not to challenge them. It says that nine times out of 10 no action will be taken.

'In the light-flashing case, the driver said the police officer did not let him off with a warning because he "challenged" him,' says Edmund King, of the AA.

'We urge drivers to keep their cool and police not to overreact to minor misdemeanours. It would save everybody an awful lot of time and money.'

TIP
To help you with this type of task, first underline the people from organizations in the text to help you find the information more easily.

Questions 9–13
Look at the following statements and the list of people or organizations in the box below. Match each statement to the correct person/organization A–E. You may use any letter more than once.

9 Errors are sometimes made by enthusiastic police officers. ....
10 Taking people to court for less serious motoring crimes is a misuse of public money. ....
11 Motorists should keep calm and be polite to police to avoid action being taken. ....
12 It is a driver's public obligation to warn other drivers of speed traps. ....
13 The police should not make too much of relatively small crimes. ....

A Michael Mancini
B The AA
C Michael Thompson
D Assistant Chief Constable Colin Smith
E A solicitor for Michael Thompson

Vocabulary

Crime and the law

1 The following words are all related to crime and the law and appear in the text. Use a dictionary to check the meanings and then complete the summary of the text.

TIP
For each space decide what part of speech the word might be – verb, noun or adjective.

appealed	convicted	court	guilty	justice	lawyer
magistrates	penalty	prosecution	solicitor		

One example of crazy driving laws was the case of Michael Thompson who was found (1) .... of warning other motorists about speed traps.
He received a heavy (2) .... from (3) .... although his (4) .... thought the case was a waste of taxpayers' money. A similar case was that of Sarah McCaffery who, even though she (5) .... , was (6) .... of eating whilst driving. However, (7) .... prevailed when another motorist, Michael Mancini successfully managed to avoid (8) .... when he hired a (9) .... and took his case to (10) ....

Discussion

2 Discuss the following questions in small groups.
  – How serious do you think the crimes mentioned in the passage are?
  – What might the consequences of these crimes be?
  – What punishments (if any) do you think are appropriate?

3 Do you agree that prosecuting people for this type of crime is a waste of police time and taxpayers' money? Why/Why not?

See *Grammar and vocabulary bank* on page 153 for collocations with *crime*.

IELTS Listening Section 2: Note completion

1 Work in pairs. Look at this note completion exercise and discuss these questions.

TIP
It can be difficult to write down answers and continue to listen at the same time. Predicting the kind of information you are listening for will help.

   1 Neighbourhood Watch is the subject of this listening. What do you think it is and how might it prevent crime?

   2 What kind of information is missing in each gap? (eg a location, a date)

   3 What kind of word or words will grammatically fit the space? (eg a noun, a verb)

2 Listen to a talk about Neighbourhood Watch.

Questions 1–6

○ 1.14 Listen to the first part of the talk and complete the notes below using NO MORE THAN THREE WORDS for each answer.

Neighbourhood Watch is a partnership between the Police and
1 ....
In the past, people didn't 2 .... If people saw something unusual they would 3 ....
Nowadays people often move to different parts of the country so we don't have as much 4 .... Two crimes mentioned by the policeman are a neighbour's house being 5 ....
and 6 ....

Multiple choice
Questions 7–10

○ 1.15 Listen to the second part of the talk and choose the correct letters, A, B or C.

   7 Becoming a 'nosy neighbour' will help if we see something
     A embarrassing.
     B suspicious.
     C worrying.

   8 One suggestion to help your neighbours is to
     A watch their house while they are not there.
     B walk along the road.
     C take photographs of strange behaviour.

   9 Which of the following suggestions is *not* mentioned as a way to help the Neighbourhood Watch scheme?
     A Take a job as part of the committee.
     B Sell newsletters.
     C Give out newsletters.

  10 Being a member of Neighbourhood Watch may also lower your
     A blood pressure.
     B security costs.
     C home insurance.

1 Complete the table below with the crimes, criminals, verbs and definitions.

Crime	Criminal	Verb	Definition
shoplifting	2	to shoplift	to steal something from a shop
1	burglar	to burgle	to enter a building illegally in order to take something
mugging	mugger	3	to attack someone in a public place and steal their money or possessions
(armed) robbery	4	to rob (at knifepoint/ gunpoint)	to take money or property from someone illegally (often using weapons)
vandalism	vandal	5	to damage or destroy things deliberately, especially public property
murder	murderer	to murder	6 ....

2 Complete the sentences with one of the words from the table. You may have to change the form of the word.

1 .... have painted graffiti on the town hall.
2 Remember to lock your doors and windows as there have been a number of .... in the neighbourhood recently.
3 He was found guilty of .... two people and was sentenced to life in prison.
4 We have store detectives in operation and .... will be prosecuted.
5 Most .... take place on the street or on public transport.
6 A gang of masked men .... the bank and got away with a large amount of money.

Defining relative clauses

See *Grammar and vocabulary bank* on page 152.

1 Look at these crime definitions and choose a suitable relative pronoun to complete the gaps.

where	which	who	whose

1 A mugger is a person .... attacks people in public places and steals their money and possessions.
2 A prison is a place .... criminals are kept as punishment for committing a crime.
3 A fine is money .... is paid as a punishment for breaking the law.
4 Victims are people .... lives have been affected by crime.

2 Underline the relative clause in each sentence.

3 Complete each of the spaces below with an appropriate relative pronoun. Choose from *that/which/who/whose/where/none needed*. Some will have more than one possibility.

1 Burglary is one of the most common crimes .... people commit.
2 Insurance premiums are often reduced in streets .... a Neighbourhood Watch Scheme has been set up.
3 If you make an insurance claim, you will need the crime reference number .... the police give you.
4 Many crimes .... the police investigate are never solved.
5 It often takes a long time for people .... houses have been burgled to fully recover.
6 Unfortunately, people .... have been burgled once are statistically more likely to be burgled again.

IELTS Writing Task 2

1 Look at the pictures of prison cells. What are the differences?

2 Decide whether the words in the box are associated with more modern or older prisons.

> classrooms   ensuite facilities   fewer inmates   gyms
> high walls with barbed wire   large living blocks   overcrowded, dirty conditions
> personal computers   smaller cells   steel bars on windows

3 Do you think we should have more modern or more traditional prisons? Why? Read the following question.

Many modern prisons have been designed for learning and communication with larger cells often containing personal computers. However, this policy has been criticized for turning prisons into 'holiday camps' and for 'wasting taxpayers' money.'

What are the advantages and disadvantages of a more modern prison system?

Give reasons for your answer and include any relevant examples from your own knowledge or experience.

Key stages

4 Understand the question. Underline key words in the questions and make sure you know what the task involves.

5 Generate main ideas. Look at the notes below and decide if you think they are advantages or disadvantages. Can you add any more ideas?

Advantages: ....

Disadvantages: ....

> • long-term benefits
> • expensive
> • prisoners have an easy life
> • the chance to study
> • make inmates into better citizens
> • improved facilities and living conditions

6 Add supporting information. In order to back up the main points you will need to include details and examples. Match these points to the notes above.

    1 *increased education opportunities, eg modern classrooms, computers*
    2 *reduce crime level, create safer society*
    3 *less likely to commit further crimes if given clear goals*
    4 *need to modernize outdated system eg bigger cells, – dirty, overcrowded*
    5 *waste of money, better to spend on crime prevention, eg more police training*
    6 *like a 'holiday camp', food, activities and accommodation – not a punishment*

7 Make a plan. It is important to have a clear structure. Which do you think is the best paragraph plan?

	A	B	C
Para 1	Introduction: Background about prisons	Introduction: Recent developments in prison system	Introduction: What is crime?
Para 2	Disadvantages	Advantages	Advantages and disadvantages
Para 3	Advantages	Advantages	Advantages and disadvantages
Para 4	Conclusion: Recommendations	Disadvantages	Your opinion
Para 5		Conclusion: Lower crime rates	Conclusion: More advantages

Read the sample answer below and check which paragraph plan has been used.

8 Write your answer. In order to complete the sample answer, do the two tasks below:
1 Put the advantages and disadvantages from exercise 5 in gaps a–f.
2 Now underline the supporting information referred to in exercise 6. The first is done for you as an example.

There have been significant developments in the prison system in recent times and 21st century prisons is very different from older, more traditional systems. Although many of the changes have been positive, there has also been a lot of negative criticism and many people consider the developments to be a waste of money. It is important to consider both the advantages and the disadvantages.

In terms of the advantages, (a) .... such as bigger cells, will have a beneficial effect on the prisoner. It was very important to modernize the older prisons which were often overcrowded and dirty. Another benifit is (b) .... which will motivate and interest inmates and give them more opportunities to increase their education using computers in modern classrooms. There are even better leisure facilities such as gyms.

The arguments in favour of modern prisons are based on the idea that these improved living conditions and opportunities to gain training will (c) .... with clear goals who are less likely to commit crimes in the future. The aim is to help prisoners leading a more normal life and prepare them for their return to society.

Many people, however, are against these developments and have highlighted disadvantages such as turning morden prisons into 'holiday camps'. (d) .... and can eat well, have the chance to work out in the gym or do other activities in better accommodation. To many this does not seem like appropriate punishing for their crimes. A further serious drawback is how (e) .... these changes have been. Some argue that this is a waste of money which could have been spent on improving crime prevention such as police training.

Overall, although there are strong views for and against modern prisons, the (f) .... are important as it is hoped that the system will reduce the level of crime and make the world a safety place.

9 Check your answer. In this answer there are six errors relating to grammar, vocabulary and spelling. Locate and correct these errors.

Practice

10 Now answer the following Writing Task 2 question. When you have finished, compare it with the model answer on page 161.

In recent years there has been an increase in bad behaviour, poor discipline and anti-social behaviour in schools. Tough measures and stricter punishments by schools, parents and others are necessary to stop this trend.

What are the advantages and disadvantages of stricter discipline for young people?

Give reasons for your answer and include any relevant examples from your own knowledge or experience.

compare it with the model answer on page 161.

TIP
Don't forget to follow the key stages: understand the question, generate ideas, make a plan, write your answer, check your answer.

IELTS Listening Section 3: Prediction

1 Work in pairs. Discuss these questions.
   – What are acceptable reasons for missing school?
   – What might children do instead of going to school?
   – Do you know what the consequences or punishments are for truancy in your country?

2 You are going to hear a discussion about truancy.

Table completion

Questions 1–7

🔊 1.16 Listen to the first part of the discussion and complete the table. Write NO MORE THAN THREE WORDS for each answer.

People present:
A government spokesperson
A person from a charity that aims to reduce **1** ....
A mother

Reasons why absence from school can be harmful:
Damages education
Can result in children leading a **2** ....

Strategies to prevent truancy:
Long term imprisonment
Sending parents to prison for **3** .... only.
4 ....

Reasons for truancy:
5 ....
Peer pressure
Bullying

People who should be involved in dealing with truancy:
Parents
Children
6 ....
The government
Social services

The number of children absent from school in spring: **7** ....

Exam information
In matching questions, you have a number of answers to match together. It is similar to classification, but you can only use each choice once. There will usually be more choices than you need.

Matching

Questions 8–10

🔊 1.17 Listen to the second part of the discussion. Read the statements A–F below. Which three points are mentioned? Choose three letters.
   A Truancy is a simple subject to understand.
   B Sending parents to prison may not be the best approach.
   C Focus on the boy or girl who misses school.
   D Charities work closely with schools to tackle truancy.
   E Counselling is a good idea.
   F The government has decided what to do about truancy.

TIP
Underline key words (usually nouns or verbs) in the statements. Then listen for these words or synonyms (or sometimes opposites) related to the topic.

**Exam information
Speaking: Part 3**
In Part 3 of the
speaking test the
examiner will ask
you questions
connected to the
topic in Part 2. The
questions will be on
more abstract ideas
and this part lasts
4–5 minutes.

Part 3

In this section you have to answer questions and 'express and justify opinions and to analyse, discuss and speculate about issues'.

1 Look at these questions from Speaking Part 3.
1 What are the best ways to deal with young people who break the law?
2 Why do people commit crime?
3 How can people help to prevent common crimes such as mobile phone theft?
4 Do you think police officers should have higher salaries?
5 Many people feel that films and TV influence crime rates. Do you agree or disagree with that view?
6 Do you think that it is important to have strict motoring laws and regulations?

2 🔊 **1.18** You are going to hear a student answering three of the questions. Which questions does he answer?

3 Look at the expressions in the boxes below. Choose a suitable heading for each box.
 – Giving opinions
 – Fillers (to give thinking time)
 – Making a suggestion
 – Agreeing or disagreeing

1 _____	**3** _____
I believe ... I'd say that ... Personally, I think ... Some people say that ...	Possibly, but ... I'm not sure that ... Yes, that's true (because) ... Yes, I think that's very important (as) ...
2 _____	**4** _____
One way is to ... We/people should/could ... It is a good idea to ... It would be better to ...	Well ... That's a good question ... That's a difficult one ... It's hard to say but ...

4 Now listen again and tick the expressions you hear.

5 Now look again at question 1 in exercise 1. What are the best ways to deal with young people who break the law?

6 Think about suitable ways to complete these sentences.
 – Personally I think that young people who break the law _____ because _____ .
 – I'm not sure that _____ .
 – It's a good idea to _____ .

TIP
Remember to give
reasons and examples
to support your
opinions.

7 Work in pairs. Ask and answer questions 2–6 in exercise 1 using some of the expressions in exercise 3.

Present perfect vs past simple
See *Grammar and vocabulary bank* on page 152.

1 Look at the phrases from Listening Section 3 on page 50 and match them to the uses (a–d) below.
1 ... this has actually happened to me and some of my friends.
2 Last year I left my mobile lying on a desk ...
3 ... we have only had the law for a few years ...
4 ... the number of accidents on the roads has decreased significantly.

a to show an event which happened in the past at a definite time
b to show the duration of a situation which started in the past and continues in the present
c to show an experience which took place at an unspecified time in the past
d to show an event in the past which has a significant result in the present

2 Complete these sentences using either the past simple or present perfect.
1 According to a survey, about 30% of British people .... (eat) while driving.
2 Thirty years ago cybercrime .... (not exist).
3 Absence from school .... (be) in the news a lot recently.
4 Burglaries in this area .... (decrease) since a neighbourhood watch scheme was introduced.
5 Last year car crime in the city centre .... (rise) significantly.
6 I heard on the news that two men .... (escape) from the local prison.
7 Yesterday thieves .... (steal) over £1 million in an armed raid on a post office.
8 My school .... (have) CCTV cameras for two years.

3 Choose the correct alternative and then discuss the questions.
1 *Did crime increase or decrease/Has crime increased or decreased* in your town recently?
2 When you were at school how *did the teachers punish/have the teachers punished* children who misbehaved?
3 *Did you hear/Have you heard* about any interesting crime stories in the news recently?

Class debate
4 You are going to debate a controversial topic.
1 As a class choose one of the following subjects:

Capital punishment (the death penalty) should not be allowed for any crime.

When a young person commits a crime, the parents are to blame.

2 Work in two groups. One group should argue in favour of the statement, and the other should be against.
3 Prepare your argument. Think of plenty of reasons and examples to support your opinions. Consider how the other group will present their case. How will you challenge their views? Use some of the phrases for expressing opinions, agreeing and disagreeing from this unit and Unit 2.
4 Present and debate the topic.

Using a dictionary

What do you use your dictionary for – looking up the meaning of words? A good dictionary has so much more useful information than just the meaning and is essential for learning a language.

In order to use a dictionary effectively, you need to understand the abbreviations that are used in it.

1 Match these abbreviations to their meaning.

1	[C]	**a**	uncountable noun – that cannot be used with *a/an* and has no plural form
2	Adj		
3	[T]	**b**	somebody
4	Sb	**c**	countable noun – that is used with *a/an* or a number and has a plural form
5	[U]		
6	Adv	**d**	adverb
7	[I]	**e**	something
8	Sth	**f**	adjective
9	Abbrev	**g**	abbreviation
		h	transitive verb – used with a direct object, eg *I ate my lunch.*
		i	intransitive verb – has no direct object, eg *I slept until noon.*

2 Now look in your dictionary to find an example of each one.

3 What other abbreviations does your dictionary have?

4 A good dictionary has a lot of information about each word. Find out how much your dictionary can tell you. Look up:

1 *rob*: is it transitive or intransitive?
2 *trial*: which preposition is often used before this word?
3 *legal*: what is the opposite?
4 *homicide*: is this British or American English?
5 *thief*: what is the plural form?
6 *ASBO*: what does this mean?
7 *behaviour*: find three adjectives which collocate with this
8 *yob*: is this formal or informal?
9 *time*: where would you be if you are *doing time*?
10 *fraud*: what part of speech is this?

5 Look up the words in *italics* in your dictionary and make any necessary corrections to the sentence. The error is not necessarily the word in italics.

1 He was fined for dropping *litters* in the street. ....
2 James was arrested for *stealing* a shop. ....
3 It is under the *law* to smoke in public buildings. ....
4 A witness has done a *statement* to police. ....
5 More *police* is needed to tackle crimes on the street. ....
6 Motorists face strong *fines* for speeding. ....

Reading

1 Work in pairs. What qualifications, skills and experience do employers look for when recruiting graduate employees? Which of the following do you think are the most important? Which are the least important? Give reasons for your answers.

> academic qualifications　　foreign language skills
> membership of clubs and societies　　musical ability　　sporting achievements
> volunteering in the local community　　work experience

2 The Confederation of British Industry (CBI) a organization which promotes British businesses, defines *employability* as a set of skills and knowledge which are essential for the workplace. These skills include:

1 Self-management ....
2 Teamworking ....
3 Business and customer awareness ....
4 Problem solving ....
5 Communication and literacy ....
6 Application of numeracy ....
7 Application of information technology ....

Match these employability skills with the definitions and examples below.

a the ability to write and speak clearly
b the ability to work with others
c the ability to assess a situation and find an appropriate solution
d an understanding of basic business concepts and how to meet customer needs
e a willingness to take responsibility, manage your time and improve performance
f a familiarity with common software and internet search engines
g the ability to use mathematics in practical situations

3 Skim the text opposite and choose the most appropriate title.
1 How universities can help prepare graduates for work
2 Employers' views on education and skills for the workplace
3 Work experience for university students

A The CBI recently conducted a survey into education and skills. Responses were received from 581 employers, collectively employing over 2.5 million people, or 8% of the total UK workforce. These firms came from a wide range of organizations, covering all sectors of the economy, including the public and private sector. The survey was completed by senior executives: in small and medium-sized companies, this tended to be the managing director, chief executive or chairman, while in larger firms it was usually the human resources director or equivalent.

B The survey comes at a time when firms are facing tough economic conditions and provides an authoritative barometer of business opinion on key education and skills issues. Findings from the survey confirmed that businesses in the UK have strong relationships with universities. The majority (84%) of larger firms, with 5,000+ employees, have links with universities – and 10% plan to develop links in the future.

C Three quarters (74%) of companies who have university links do so to provide work experience placements for graduates – this is more important for companies in certain sectors (eg construction) where the practical nature of the workplace makes work experience very important. It is encouraging to see business playing its part to help graduates develop the skills which are the focus of this report. Businesses see a number of benefits from engaging with universities, the main one being the ability to attract high quality graduates and post-graduates.

D The survey also suggests that small businesses are struggling to make links with universities. There are 4.3 million SMEs in the UK accounting for almost three fifths (59%) of employment. Findings suggest that a smaller proportion of these businesses currently have links with universities – only half of businesses with between 50 and 199 employees have university links, compared to 84% of the largest employers which responded.

E When senior executives were asked to rank the most important factors they consider when recruiting graduates, employability skills came out on top. Students and universities should be aware that employers place a huge value on these skills, which will help graduates secure jobs after graduation, where competition is now higher than ever due to the economic downturn. The survey results also confirmed the understanding that underpinning all of these skills, businesses also value a positive attitude: a 'can-do' approach, a readiness to take part and contribute, openness to new ideas and a drive to make those ideas happen. These findings are consistent with findings from the previous year – businesses rank employability skills and a positive attitude at the top of their list.

F Employers are very happy with the IT skills among graduates entering the workplace. It is also encouraging to see that businesses are generally satisfied with the degree to which graduates have acquired the majority of the other employability skills. But satisfactory should not be seen as good enough. There is no room for complacency when relatively small proportions express a high degree of approval. There is also some dissatisfaction (35%) in terms of graduates' awareness of business and customer issues (only 8% rate themselves as being highly satisfied) and also in relation to the level of self-management skills graduates possess (20% not satisfied), suggesting a need for improvement.

G It is not surprising that businesses think universities should focus on developing these employability skills within the student population as a priority. When asked what three things they thought universities should prioritize, 82% of employers thought this was far more important than increasing the number of students graduating from university each year. It is also positive to note that businesses think universities should focus on working with them to provide more work experience placements, so if universities want to improve their engagement with businesses a good place to start would be in relation to arranging work experience. The potential to improve engagement in the small and medium-sized firms may be greatest, where 45% of medium firms currently have no links with universities.

Glossary

CBI Confederation of British Industry – an organization which promotes British businesses

SME small and medium enterprises (businesses)

Matching headings to paragraphs

4 Now answer the exam questions on the text.

Questions 1–6

The passage is divided into seven paragraphs (A–G). Choose the correct heading for each paragraph from the list of headings below. The first has been done as an example.

List of headings

  i Employers consider employability skills a priority

  ii Employers request an increase in graduate numbers

  iii Recommendations to improve employability skills and links with business

  iv Firms with a smaller workforce lack strong ties with universities

  v Dissatisfaction with IT skills in the workplace

  vi Employers' mixed satisfaction with graduate employability skills

  vii How the survey was conducted

  viii Good connections between higher education and big business

  ix Providing practical work experience for graduates

0	Paragraph A	*vii*
1	Paragraph B	....
2	Paragraph C	....
3	Paragraph D	....
4	Paragraph E	....
5	Paragraph F	....
6	Paragraph G	....

Labelling a diagram

Questions 7–13

Re-read paragraphs E–G and complete the labels on diagrams 1-3 below. Choose NO MORE THAN THREE WORDS OR A NUMBER from the text for each answer.

TIP

Decide whether the missing information is words or a number. Find the part of the text which describes the diagrams. Use the correct number of words for each answer, and copy the words exactly as they appear in the text.

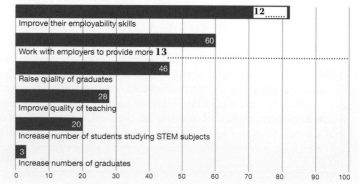

Figure 1: 7 ....
considered when recruiting graduates (%)

- 8 .... (eg teamworking, problem solving etc) — 78 / 72
- 9 .... — 54
- Relevant work experience/industrial placement — 41
- Degree subject — 28
- Degree result (1st, 2:1, 2:2 etc) — 8
- University attended — 2
- Foreign language capability

(scale 0 10 20 30 40 50 60 70 80)

Figure 2: The level to which graduates are equipped with employability skills (%)

- IT skills — 49 / 49 / 2
- Application of numeracy — 30 / 62 / 8
- Teamworking — 19 / 71 / 10
- Problem solving — 16 / 73 / 11
- Communication and literacy — 31 / 56 / 13
- Self-management — 14 / 66 / 20
- 10 .... awareness — 8 / 57 / 35

(scale 0 10 20 30 40 50 60 70 80 90 100)

■ Very satisfied ■ Satisfied ■ 11 ....

Figure 3: What should universities prioritise in terms of undergraduates (%)

- Improve their employability skills — 12 ....
- Work with employers to provide more 13 .... — 60
- Raise quality of graduates — 46
- Improve quality of teaching — 28
- Increase number of students studying STEM subjects — 20
- Increase numbers of graduates — 3

(scale 0 10 20 30 40 50 60 70 80 90 100)

Describing skills and qualities

1 Read the statements. Which of the following apply to you?

1 I believe that good things will happen. ....

2 I'm determined and willing to do things. ....

3 I'm willing to do what others ask me to do and work with others.
....

4 I want to know a lot about different things. ....

5 I'm good at finding ways to deal with problems and different situations.
....

6 I do things carefully and in an organized way. ....

7 I'm able to deal with people in a sensitive way that does not upset them.
....

8 I work hard. ....

9 I'm usually interested in and keen to do things. ....

2 The adjectives in the box are all qualities that employers look for in job applicants. Match them to the statements above.

conscientious	co-operative	diplomatic	enthusiastic	inquisitive
	methodical	motivated	positive	resourceful

3 Now match the nouns in the box with the appropriate descriptions below.

a communicator	an initiator	a planner	a quick thinker
	a relationship builder	a risk-taker	

What type of person are you if:

1 you don't mind a bit of danger? ....

2 you are good at getting activities started? ....

3 you prepare things carefully? ....

4 you speak or write clearly and effectively? ....

5 you don't need a lot of time to make up your mind? ....

6 you are good at creating and organizing teams? ....

Practice

4 Look at the extracts from the CVs of three graduates.

– Which of the words from exercises 2 and 3 could you use to describe each person?

– What type of jobs do you think would be suitable for each candidate?

Give reasons for your answers.

Name: Ben

Skills:
IT skills, plays guitar

Experience:
Set up own business and designed website
Plays in rock band
Won young businessperson award
Worked in retail
School chess champion

Name: Eve

Skills: Fluent in English and French
Good level of spoken and written Italian
First Aid skills

Experience:
Fund-raising for charity
Voluntary work overseas
Writes for student newspaper
Acted in plays
Sings in choir

Name: Raj

Skills:
Fluent in Hindi, English and Urdu
Plays violin

Experience:
Member of orchestra
Captain of university cricket team
Worked in restaurant
President of the debating society

TIP
You will often hear important information repeated in different ways. This will help you confirm your answer. Don't circle the first thing that you hear unless you are sure it's correct.

IELTS Listening Section 1

1 Sally and John are two university students who are thinking about what they will do when they graduate. Use the questions to predict the kind of information you will be listening for.

2 Now listen and answer the exam questions.

Multiple choice

Questions 1–6

🔘 1.19 Listen to the first part of the discussion and circle the correct answer, A, B, C or D.

1 Which area of business would John like to work in?
   A Sales
   B Marketing
   C Accounting
   D Human Resources

2 What job does Sally's sister have?
   A a doctor
   B a teacher
   C a singer
   D a businesswoman

3 What is Sally worried about?
   A finishing her course
   B going overseas
   C having children
   D looking for a job

4 Who is giving the talk?
   A a careers advisor
   B a professor of Business
   C a friend
   D a Human Resources representative

5 What date does the talk take place on?
   A 15th
   B 16th
   C 17th
   D 18th

6 What time do Sally and John arrange to meet?
   A 7.30pm
   B 6.30pm
   C 6.45pm
   D 7.00pm

Labelling a diagram

Questions 7–10

🔘 1.20 Listen to the second part of the discussion and label the plan below.

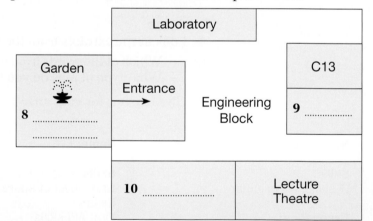

Future forms

1 Look at the following sentences from Listening Section 1. Match them to their meanings a–e below.

   1 I'm going to look for a job teaching English ...
   2 ... the talk will cover looking for work and writing applications ...
   3 What time does it start?
   4 I'll meet you there.
   5 I'm meeting Tariq in 10 minutes ...

   a a timetabled future event
   b a decision about the future made at the time of speaking
   c a future arrangement (at a specific time or place or with another person)
   d a future plan or intention made previously
   e a future fact or prediction

2 Underline the best future form to complete these extracts from the listening. Check your answers in the audioscript on page 169.

    1 I'd like to go into marketing but *I'll probably end up/I'm probably ending up/I'm probably going to end up* in Sales.

    2 There *will be/'s/is going to be* a careers talk next week which we could go to if you fancy it.

    3 Really, that'd be great! *I'm going to come/I'm coming/I'll come* and visit you!

    4 So what *will you do/are you doing/do you do* next Wednesday?

    5 Maybe – what *will he talk/'s he going to talk/does he talk* about?

3 Make questions from the following prompts, then ask your partner about the future.

    1 Where/go/after class? ....

    2 What/have to eat/this evening? ....

    3 What/do/next weekend? ....

    4 When/your course/finish? ....

    5 When/take/the IELTS test? ....

    6 What type of job/do/think/get/future? ....

See *Grammar and vocabulary bank* on page 153.

Listening

IELTS Listening Section 2

1 You are going to hear the talk mentioned in Listening Section 1. Look at the notes and flow chart below, and predict possible answers.

2 Now listen and answer the exam questions.

Table completion

Questions 1–5

◎ **1.21** Listen to the first part of the talk and complete the notes below using NO MORE THAN THREE WORDS.

Looking for a job

	Advantages	Other information
Newpapers and magazines: National Local	 – Different jobs advertised on different days – Good for jobs in **1**	Specialist industry magazines
Online sources	– Quick – Completion of applications online	Handout with **2** .... to be provided at end.
Job centre or **3**	– Efficient – service is usually **4**	Located in most towns and cities
Careers fairs	– Information about job opportunities – **5** .... with employers	Check website for future events

Labelling a flow chart
Questions 6–10

🔊 **1.22** Listen to the second part of the talk and complete the flow chart below with NO MORE THAN THREE WORDS for each answer.

Applying for a job

Contact the company for an application form and a 6 .... ← Important to mention/include 7 ....

↓

Read the job description. ← Consider your skills, qualifications and experience.

↓

Complete the application form carefully. ← Skills and experience should 8 .... the job requirements.

↓

Include a 9 .... ← Show your interest and your suitability for the job.

↓

Change needed? ← Ask someone to check it.

↓

Send off the form before 10 ....

Comparatives and superlatives
See *Grammar and vocabulary bank* on page 153.

1 Which jobs from the box below are shown? What skills and qualities would you need? What about the other jobs?

bus driver	factory worker	gym instructor	journalist
miner	police officer	Premier League footballer	teacher

2 Which would you like to do most/least? Give reasons.

3 What would be your ideal job? Give reasons.

4 Compare different jobs by using the comparative form of the adjective in brackets. The first one has been done as an example.

    0 A Premier League footballer is *richer* _____ (rich) than a teacher.
    1 A gym instructor has to be _____ (fit) than a journalist.
    2 A bus driver needs to be a _____ (good) driver than a miner.
    3 A miner has a _____ (dangerous) job than a businessperson.
    4 A journalist has a _____ (interesting) job than a bank manager.
    5 A teacher needs to be _____ (friendly) than a shop assistant.
    6 A factory worker works _____ (long) hours than a gym instructor.
    7 Being a police officer is _____ (stressful) than a factory worker.

5 Think of two other jobs and write three more sentences using comparative forms for *hard*, *boring* and *important*.

6 Use superlative forms to complete the sentences below with your own ideas. The first one has been done as an example.

    0 Of all these jobs, a miner has *the most dangerous* (dangerous) occupation.
    1 In my view, _____ (interesting) job would be a _____ .
    2 A _____ would probably be _____ (rich).
    3 A _____ gets the _____ (long) holidays.

7 Think of other jobs and write three more sentences using superlative forms for *hard*, *boring* and *important*.

Speaking

IELTS Speaking Part 2

1 Look at the task below. How long do you have to prepare? What should you do?

Part 2

Describe a job you would like to do in the future.

You should say:
– what the job is and why you would like it
– what kind of training would be useful
– what skills and qualities are needed

and also say what you would like most about this job.

---

2 Look at the example below.

I'd like to be a <u>pilot</u> because it would be <u>exciting and rewarding</u>.
<u>Flight training</u> would be useful because a pilot needs to know how to control and fly modern aircraft ...
Pilots need to be <u>brave, calm</u> and be good at <u>making quick decisions</u> ...
The thing I would like most about being a pilot would be the power and control I would have flying a plane ...

3 Now do the task using these examples as a guideline.

Part 3

TIP
Don't forget to expand your answers by adding details.

4 In pairs or small groups, ask and answer the following Part 3 questions.

    – What is the best way to prepare for a job interview?
    – Which jobs do you think are the most dangerous?
    – How can employers keep their staff happy?
    – Do you think pop and sports stars earn too much money?
    – How important is appropriate dress at work?
    – Is it better to stay in one job for a long time or have many different jobs?
    – What differences do you think will occur in the workplace in the future?

IELTS Writing Task 1

1 Unemployment is a problem in many parts of the world. Answer these questions.
  – Which age groups/sections of the population/occupations are most affected by unemployment in your country?
  – Do you know what the unemployment rate (%) is in your country?

2 Study the graph below, which shows unemployment rates in five different countries from 2005 to 2010.

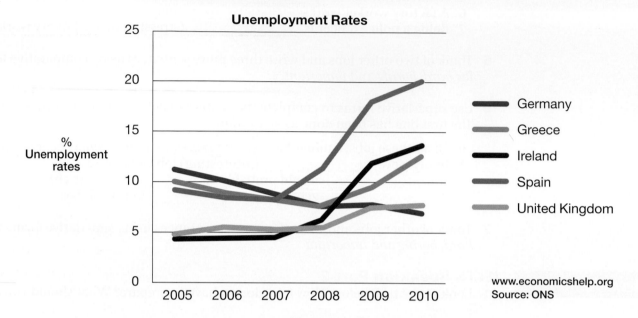

Now look at the model answer below and complete the gaps in the sentences using comparative or superlative forms of the verbs in brackets.

In most of the countries shown in the graph unemployment rates were (1) .... (high) in 2010 than in 2005. However, in Germany the rate was (2) .... (low) at the end of the period.

In Spain, unemployment rates showed (3) .... (great) differences than the other countries over the five years as it increased from 9% to over 20%. In contrast, there were (4) .... (small) changes in the UK's unemployment figures, an increase of only 2.5%.

Despite most of the countries having a small drop in unemployment rates between 2005 and 2007, the UK's unemployment figures were (5) .... (bad), with the total rising from just under 5% in 2005 to just over 5% in 2007. The situation in Ireland was (6) .... (good) with figures remaining stable.

To sum up, Spain had (7) .... (high) unemployment rates of all the countries shown in 2010, whereas Germany had (8) .... (low) figures. The (9) .... (big) change over the period was in Spain. Although the increases are not enormous, they undoubtedly have significant effects on the economy.

3 Modifiers such as *much* and *slightly/a little* can be added to comparative forms. Which shows a big difference? Which shows a small difference? Which could you add to 1 and 2 in the text above?

4 Look at the sentence below and answer the questions.

In most of the countries shown in the graph unemployment rates were higher in 2010 than in 2005. <u>However,</u> in Germany the rate was lower at the end of the period.

  1 Is the word *however* used at the start or in the middle of a sentence?
  2 Does it introduce information that is similar or different to the previous sentence?
  3 What do you notice about the punctuation?

5 *However* is a linking word used to show a contrast (difference).

Locate and underline four other words or phrases in the model answer to show contrasts.

6 Complete the rules.

1 .... is followed by a clause (subject + verb)
2 .... is followed by (subject +) *-ing* verb form (or a noun)
3 .... shows a difference between two things and comes in the middle of a sentence after a comma.
4 .... comes at the start of a sentence and is followed by a comma.

7 Use the contrast markers in brackets to link the sentences.

1 Prices rose in the first quarter. They fell slightly in the second quarter. (however).
2 Sales of laptops have increased dramatically. Sales of desktop computers have dropped. (whereas).
3 The service industry is expanding. Heavy industry is in decline. (in contrast).
4 Nurses' salaries have gone up slightly in recent years. They are still below the national average income. (although).
5 Student fees have increased in recent years. The number of undergraduates is rising steadily. (despite)

TIP

If the task shows two different charts or tables, it is a good idea to write about each one in separate paragraphs. Look for any common overall trends and comment on these in the conclusion.

8 In your country, do men generally work full-time or part-time? What about women? Who do you think earns more, men or women?

Look at the exam question and charts below. How does the situation in the UK compare to your country?

The charts below give information about workforce composition in the UK, and about average hourly earnings.

Summarize the information by selecting and reporting the main features, and make comparisons where relevant.

Total workforce composition – 24.9 million

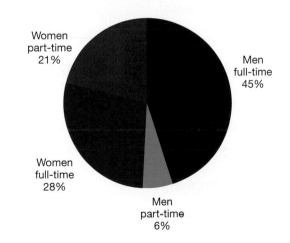

Women part-time 21%
Men full-time 45%
Women full-time 28%
Men part-time 6%

Source: Labour Force Survey, Office for National Statistics

Median hourly earnings, excluding overtime[1]

£ per hour
■ April 2010

	14
	12
	10
	8
	6
	4
	2
	0

Full-time men | Full-time women | Part-time men | Part-time women

1 Employees on adult rates, pay unaffected by absence
Source: Annual Survey of Hours and Earnings, Office for National Statistics

9 Now write your answer. When you have finished the task, compare it with the model answer on page 161.

Suffixes

1 A *suffix* is a letter or a group of letters added to the end of a word. Recognizing suffixes can help you to guess the meaning of words you don't know.

Look at these words from the reading text on page 55. What part of speech is each word? Complete the table. Use a dictionary to check your answers.

1 organiz**ation**		5 practi**cal**	
2 employab**ility**		6 place**ment**	
3 econom**ic**		7 relation**ship**	
4 priorit**ize**		8 satis**fied**	

Nouns	Verbs	Adjectives
organization		

2 Can you think of any other words with the same suffixes? Add them to the table.

3 What other words do you know in the same 'family' as the words you have found? Are there any suffixes which tell you what part of speech they are?

eg *organize* (verb), *organized* (adjective), *organization* (noun)

4 Suffixes can also carry general meanings. You can make new words within a word family by adding an appropriate suffix. Match two words in the box with each of the suffixes and their general meanings.

drive	employ	home	industrial	instruct	job
short	skill	special	success	visit	wide

1 *-less*: without (adjective) ....
2 *-ful*: full of or characterized by (adjective) ....
3 *-er*: a person doing a particular job or activity (noun) ....
4 *-or*: a person doing a particular job or activity (noun) ....
5 *-ize*: to make, cause or become (verb) ....
6 *-en*: to make, cause or become (verb) ....

5 Now choose an appropriate word from exercise 4 to complete the sentences below.
1 My brother is a .... doctor who .... in children's health.
2 The number of .... has increased in recent months due to many factories closing.
3 Unfortunately the .... had to .... their stay by two days.
4 The range of job opportunities for women has .... considerably over the last fifty years.
5 Learner .... should take lessons from a qualified ....

Word families

1 Look at this word family tree. Note how we change the part of speech by adding a suffix to the root word (the verb *employ*). We can also change the meaning of the word by adding a prefix, eg we can make the opposite of *employed* by adding the negative prefix *un-*.

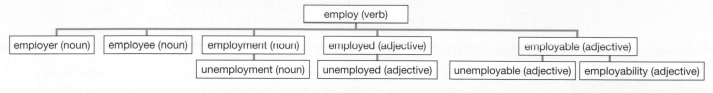

Now complete the word family tree for *manage*.

1 .... (noun)	**2** .... (noun)	**4** .... *ed* (adj)	**6** .... *able* (adj)
managerial (adj)	**3** mis .... *ment* (noun)	**5** mis .... (adj)	**7** un .... (adj)

2 How do the prefixes *mis-* and *un-* change the meaning?

3 Choose the correct alternative.
1 Graduates with work experience are more *employable/unemployed* than those without.
2 The hotel has been taken over and is now under new *managers/management*.
3 His *employers/employees* were very understanding and allowed him to work flexible hours.
4 The business has been closed down due to financial *mismanagement/unmanageable*.
5 The number of *unemployment/unemployed* has fallen steadily in recent months.

Confusing words: *job, work, career*

4 Use a dictionary to answer the following questions about *job*, *work* and *career*.
1 Which are nouns?
2 Which can also be a verb?
3 Which is/are countable?
4 Which is/are uncountable?

5 Complete the collocations with *job*, *work* or *career*. There may be more than one possible answer. Check your answers in the *Macmillan Collocations Dictionary*.
1 a distinguished ....
2 excellent ....
3 a successful ....
4 a part-time ....
5 hard ....
6 to .... effectively
7 .... security
8 a skilled ....
9 a political ....
10 to .... closely together
11 a well-paid ....
12 .... satisfaction

6 Choose the correct alternative in each sentence (some sentences may have more than one answer) Pay particular note of any collocations.
1 What's your *work/job/career*?
2 It's not easy for young people to find *work/a job/career* these days.
3 He had a long and distinguished *work/job/career* in the army.
4 He has a part-time *work/job/career* in telesales.
5 I'd like to find a temporary *work/job/career* for the summer.
6 Thank you for all your hard *work/job/career*.

See *Grammar and vocabulary bank* on page 154 for more on work vocabulary.

6 Globalization

'The idea that the world is developing a single economy and culture as a result of improved communications and the influence of very large companies.' *Macmillan Essential Dictionary*

Reading

1 Work in pairs. Below are eight possible effects of globalization. Use a dictionary to check any unknown vocabulary. Which are positive and which are negative? Which could be both?

1 growth in global trade and the world economy
2 inequalities between rich and poor nations
3 greater understanding between cultures
4 damage to the natural environmental
5 easier and cheaper travel and communication
6 more access to information
7 loss of national identity and culture
8 poverty and debt in the developing world

Locating information

2 Read the passage. Put the paragraphs in the text under the following headings. There is one positive statement and one negative statement for each heading.

Global Communications .... Global Media ....
Global Travel and Tourism .... Global Business ....

---

http://www.globalissues.com — Live Search

Favourites | Suggested Sites

Page ▾ Safety ▾ Tools ▾

A Four billion people, which is about 60% of the world's population, have no access to modern telecommunications. More than a billion people have neither a fixed line nor a mobile phone.

B The big tour operators, who own airlines, retail chains, cruise ships, hotels, self catering accommodation and car rentals, take most of the profits of holidays in developing countries – for every US dollar spent in a Third World resort, as little as 5 cents stay in the country.

C The value of world exports is over 19 trillion dollars a year, which is 36 million a minute! This is more than six times the value of exported goods 30 years ago.

D It's estimated that workers in Honduras who produce clothes for multinational companies get about 0.5% of the retail cost of the product they make.

E A phone call from UK to New York in 1990 cost about £1 a minute. In 1930, it would have cost more than £10. Today it costs as little as 2.5 pence.

F Internet, television, films, radio, newspapers, magazines are widely available. Through them we can learn about people, events and places in Africa, Asia, Latin America, Eastern Europe, Australia, Canada, Japan and North America.

G A garment worker in Bangladesh, which is one of the world's poorest countries, would have to save eight years' wages to buy a computer. In some sub-Saharan African countries, fewer than 1% of the population have access to the internet, whereas in more developed regions like North America, this figure is well over 75%, more than 100 times as many.

H Travel is cheaper, faster and more convenient today than ever before and each year there are approximately 1,000 million international tourists. People make friends in foreign countries, discover many interesting things about other people's lifestyles, cultures and customs as they visit different places. The local people, who would otherwise have few employment opportunities, benefit from jobs using their skills and sale of their crafts.

Done | Internet | Protected Mode: On | 100%

3 Which of the effects from exercise 1 are referred to? Which do you think are greater: the positive or the negative effects of globalization?

4 How has your country been affected by globalization?

Language focus

Non-defining relative clauses
See *Grammar and vocabulary bank* on page 154.

1 Both of these sentences use relative clauses. Answer the questions.

   a *It's estimated that workers in Honduras who produce clothes for multinational companies get about 0.5% of the retail cost of the product they make.*

   b *Four billion people, which is about 60% of the world's population, have no access to modern telecommunications.*

   1 Which sentence has a relative clause that identifies which person or thing is being talked about?

   2 Which sentence has a relative clause that adds extra information, or a second idea to the main idea?

2 Look at these sentences with non-defining relative clauses and identify the main idea and the extra information given.

   0 Four billion people, which is about 60% of the world's population, have no access to modern telecommunications.

   Main idea:
   Four billion people have no access to modern telecommunications.

   Extra information:
   Four billion people is about 60% of the world's population.

   1 The big tour operators, who own airlines, retail chains, cruise ships, hotels, self-catering accommodation and car rentals, take most of the profits of holidays in developing countries.

   Main idea:

   ....

   Extra information:

   ....

   2 The value of world exports is over 19 trillion dollars a year, which is 36 million dollars a minute!

   Main idea:

   ....

   Extra information:

   ....

   3 A garment worker in Bangladesh, which is one of the world's poorest countries, would have to save eight years' wages to buy a computer.

   Main idea:

   ....

   Extra information:

   ....

   4 The local people, who would otherwise have few employment opportunities, benefit from jobs using their skills and sale of their crafts.

   Main idea:

   ....

   Extra information:

   ....

3 Underline the correct alternative in these rules for non-defining relative clauses.
   1 The relative clause provides extra information and *can/cannot* be left out.
   2 *Who* or *which can/cannot* be replaced by *that*.
   3 The relative pronoun *can/cannot* be left out.
   4 Commas *are/are not* used.

4 Link the ideas in the two sentences, using commas to form one sentence.
   0 Main idea: In 2010 South Korea had more internet users than Sub-Saharan Africa.
   Extra information: South Korea is a relatively small country.

   In 2010 South Korea, which is a relatively small country, had more internet users than Sub-Saharan Africa .

   1 Main idea: Greater cultural contact has been encouraged by tourism.
   Extra information: Tourism has more than doubled over the last 20 years.

   ....

   ....

   2 Main idea: The banana is worth more than $10 billion in world trade.
   Extra information: The banana is Britain's most popular fruit.

   ....

   ....

   3 Main idea: Shima earns £28 for a month's work.
   Extra information: Shima lives in Bangladesh.

   ....

   ....

Listening

IELTS Listening Section 4

1 Which of these organizations do you know about? Match them to the descriptions below.

1 The United Nations	**a**	the international organization that controls trade between countries
2 Trade unions	**b**	campaigns on environmental issues such as the greenhouse effect
3 International Monetary Fund	**c**	an international organization that works to balance and manage the world's economy and to help countries with weak economies to develop
4 World Trade Organization		
5 Friends of the Earth	**d**	an international organization that encourages countries to work together in order to solve world problems such as war, disease and poverty
6 International Aid Organizations (such as Oxfam)	**e**	charities that raise money for famine and disaster relief
	f	organizations of workers that aim to improve pay and conditions of work

2 Predict which of these organizations are pro-globalization or anti-globalization.

3 You are going to listen to a lecture in two sections. Before each section spend half a minute reading the questions and underlining key words.

Multiple choice

Questions 1–2

🔊 1.23 Which of the following areas does the lecturer say she will cover?
Choose TWO letters A–F.

   A global inequalities
   B poverty in the developing world
   C the history of globalization
   D the key arguments for and against globalization
   E trade and economics
   F the World Trade Organization

Questions 3–5

Circle the correct letter, A, B or C.

3 Which example of an exchange of culture and technology is given?
A fast food in America
B Japan's car industry in Britain
C call centres in India

4 Globalization was put back by which of the following events?
A the Second World War
B the Great Depression
C capital expansion in 1930

5 What type of business started to increase after the Second World War?
A telecommunications businesses
B marketing companies
C multinational companies

Questions 6–7

(◎ 1.24) Listen to the second section. Which TWO arguments against globalization are mentioned? Choose two letters A–E.

A Globalization damages the environment.
B Natural resources will only be used by developed countries.
C Some organizations will help poorer nations too much.
D Cheaper imports will affect competition in richer countries.
E Salaries will increase in the developing world.

Table completion

Questions 8–10

Complete this table using ONE OR TWO WORDS OR A NUMBER.

Organization	Established	Number of member states	Role
WTO	(8)	153	Prevents members favouring home industries
IMF	1946	(9)	Provides temporary financial help
UN	1946	193	Promotes shared values between UN and the (10) ....

4 Look at these 'signposts' used by the speaker and divide them into these categories. Some signposts fit into more than one category.

1 Turning now to ...
2 Now let us look a little at ...
3 Lastly, ...
4 In the first part of today's lecture ...
5 Having looked at ... let's now consider ...
6 I will start by considering ...
7 So, we've seen that ...
8 I'd now like to move on to ...
9 Secondly, I will explain ...
10 So, let's begin with ...
11 Finally, I intend to ...

Introduction
Sequencing
Changing topic
Concluding/Summarizing

5 Listen to the lecture again and check to see if you were right. Number the signposts in the order in which you hear them.

1 Do you recognize this Mark? Where might you see it? What do you understand by Fairtrade? Have you ever bought any Fairtrade products?

Scanning

2 You are going to read an article about coffee growers in Colombia. Before you read, write the numbers in the box next to the sentence you think it refers to. Then check your predictions by quickly reading the text.

5	50	150	8.7 billion	20 million	100 million

	The value of worldwide coffee exports in dollars.
	The total number of people who earn their living from coffee.
	The number of countries which produce coffee.
	The amount of money in pence received by the farmer for each coffee sold in the West.
	The number of farmers that earn their living from coffee.
	The number of times that coffee beans can be sold between leaving the farmer and arriving in the supermarket.

3 Read the text produced by the Fairtrade Foundation about one family of coffee growers in Colombia.

True, False, Not given

Questions 1–7

Do the statements agree with the information in the reading passage?

Write

TRUE (T) if the statement is true according to the passage.

FALSE (F) if the statement is false according to the passage.

NOT GIVEN (NG) if the information is not given in the passage.

1 The Menzas have tried growing coca leaf instead of coffee. ....

2 In trade, only oil is more important than coffee. ....

3 The Menzas receive 50% of the supermarket price for their coffee. ....

4 An increase in transportation costs has had a serious effect on the price of coffee. ....

5 In the late 1990s both world and supermarket prices dropped. ....

6 Setting up a co-operative is always an effective solution for these farmers. ....

7 The farmers have less and less money to spend on their families. ....

> **TIP**
> Read the questions or T/F/NG statements through first, and guess the meaning of any words you do not understand.

A Vitelio Menza has been dependent on the coffee he grows in Colombia all his life. At 48, he still struggles to provide for his family. Like millions of other smallholders, his fortunes and those of his wife, Maria Enith, and their four children have fluctuated dramatically along with the price he receives for his crop.

B Over the years the family has suffered illness brought on by malnutrition. In other parts of the same area, some have turned to growing drugs in order to survive; higher prices are paid for coca leaf (the raw material for cocaine). The Menzas have stayed loyal to the coffee crop but not without great personal sacrifices.

C Coffee is grown in more than 50 countries in a band around the equator and provides a living for more than 20 million farmers. Altogether, up to 100 million people worldwide are involved in the growing, processing, trading and retailing of the product.

D Coffee is the second most valuable commodity after crude oil. It is the most valuable agricultural commodity in world trade – in 2000, exports worldwide totalled $8.7bn. But the journey from the Menzas' farm in Colombia to the supermarket shelf is a long and tortuous one with a succession of people taking their cut along the way.

E From tree to supermarket shelf it has been estimated the Menzas' coffee beans can change hands as many as 150 times. Paper transactions on international commodities markets account for much of this. The final price of a cup of coffee in the West will have absorbed the costs of insurance, taxes, transportation, processing, packaging, marketing, storage and much more. Of the £1.75 charged for a cappuccino in a London coffee shop, the grower will be lucky to receive the equivalent of 5p.

F Between 1994 and the end of 2001 the price of robusta beans (used chiefly in instant coffee) plummeted from around 180 cents to just 17 cents per pound, a 30-year low. The value of high-quality arabica beans has suffered similarly. While it is estimated that the world coffee trade generates $60bn in revenues, double the amount in the 1980s, producing countries retain just over 10 per cent of this, compared with 30 per cent in the 1980s.

G For the big roasters, this can be only good news: it is estimated that a company processing one million 60kg bags of coffee was $80m better off in 2001 than the previous year because of the lower prices. For small farmers, however, the drop in prices is disastrous.

H When world prices fall, growers suffer an immediate reduction in income; yet there is no noticeable reduction in supermarket prices of coffee. In contrast, when the market price of coffee gains, as it did by 50 per cent in 1994, for example, retail prices rise promptly.

I For many farmers, the collapse in prices means that they have failed to recover their production costs for several years running. This has had a devastating impact on an already precarious existence. Some have abandoned their land and gone in search of work in cities. Others have neglected or uprooted their coffee bushes. Frequently, an equally uncertain and poverty-stricken life awaits in urban shanty towns, but without the support of community and land. For those who opt to stay at home, the lack of labour for crop maintenance reduces the quality and value of the coffee, further depressing returns. The vicious circle is complete.

J But for small farmers the price of beans on the markets in New York and London is only one of the factors undermining their ability to make a reasonable living. Without the means to process or transport their crop to market, limited knowledge of the frequently changing world price and a debt driven necessity to sell their coffee the moment it is ripe (when prices are lowest), small independent farmers find themselves in a weak negotiating position. They are prey to local dealers who buy the coffee and sell it on to international markets. With only one major harvest a year, farmers are desperate for cash by the time their crop is ripe and are keen to sell at whatever price they can get. Not surprisingly, local dealers exploit this.

K The farmers' need for a quick sale is a symptom of their inability to get loans at a fair rate from banks, pushing them into the arms of loan sharks to pay for fertilizers, harvest labour and basic living costs prior to harvest. Many growers have joined with their neighbours to set up co-operative marketing ventures, which enable them to by-pass the middlemen. All too often, however, even the co-op cannot get finance to buy the crop, and members still sell to local traders (commonly called *coyotes* in Latin America) for cash, rather than wait for a better price. Evidence of low and declining living standards is clear. Producers have reported to the Fairtrade Foundation reduced spending on housing, children's education (especially where structural adjustment has led to higher school fees), health and food.

TIP
Read the instructions. This question asks for ONE OR TWO words.

Sentence completion

Questions 8–13

Choose ONE OR TWO WORDS from the reading passage for each answer.

8 The Menzas have made .... to continue growing coffee.
9 Any fall in the world price of coffee is not .... in the supermarket price.
10 A shortage of workers for .... results in a fall in quality and value.
11 Due to lack of money, transportation and knowledge, farmers do not have a strong ....
12 As there is only one coffee crop each year, farmers have very little .... by the time it is ready to harvest.
13 It is impossible for farmers to borrow money at a ....

Identifying the writer's purpose

TIP
Think about the target audience. Students? Members of the public? Is the style formal or informal?

Question 14

What is the purpose of the passage on Fairtrade? Choose A, B, C or D.

A to advise readers against buying non-Fairtrade coffee
B to explain how coffee farmers are exploited by international markets
C to advise coffee farmers like the Menzas how to make a good living
D to encourage readers to protest about the current situation

Guessing meaning from context

4 Read the text again and try to find words which mean the same as:

1 changed frequently (para A) ....
2 selling to the public (para C) ....
3 not safe or secure (para I) ....
4 a process in which one problem causes another problem, which makes the first problem worse (para I) ....
5 weakening, making less likely to succeed (para J) ....
6 getting worse (para K) ....

Money, buying and selling

Vocabulary

1 There are many words in the text connected with money and buying and selling. Match the words and definitions. When you have finished, check your answers in a dictionary.

1 revenue   **a** how much something costs to buy in a shop
2 commodity   **b** income from business activities or taxes
3 retail price   **c** how much something costs to buy in large quantities
4 market price   **d** money that someone gets from working
5 income   **e** something that can be bought and sold
6 middleman   **f** someone who lends money to people at a very high rate
7 loan shark   of interest
8 trader/dealer   **g** a person or company that buys from producers and sells
9 return(s)   to customers at a profit
10 finance   **h** profit on money invested
                    i money used to pay for something such as a large project
                    j someone who buys and sells things

2 Divide these phrases from the text into two categories: expressions which describe prices going up (U) and which describe prices going down (D).

1 the price of robusta beans plummeted ....
2 the drop in prices ....
3 world prices fall ....
4 reduction in supermarket prices of coffee ....
5 market price of coffee gains ....
6 retail prices rise ....

See *Grammar and vocabulary bank* on page 155 for verb + noun collocations connected with buying and selling.

The passive
See *Grammar and vocabulary bank* on page 154.

1 Talk to another student. How much coffee do you drink every day? What do you know about coffee, its history and production?

2 Read these facts about coffee and underline all the passive verbs.

Did you know ...?

- Coffee was first brought to Europe by traders from the Middle East in the 15th century and started to be cultivated in the Americas in the 18th century. Today coffee is drunk all over the world.
- At various times in history, coffee has been given as a medicine to cure a variety of ailments. Nowadays it is believed that coffee has both positive and negative effects on health.
- Coffee is grown between the Tropic of Cancer and the Tropic of Capricorn.
- One quarter to one third of the world's coffee is produced by Brazil.
- Coffee beans must be roasted, then ground into a powder, before being mixed with hot water to extract the flavour ready for drinking.

3 Find an example from the text of each passive form and complete the table.

Present simple	... *is (are) grown*
Past simple	
Present perfect	
Modal verbs	
Infinitive form	
Gerund (-*ing*) form	

4 Read the text again. Which sentences include an 'agent' (which tells us who performs the action)?

5 Find an example in the text for each of the reasons (1–3) we use the passive below. The passive is used:
   1 when the action/event/process is more important than the agent mentioned.
   2 when it is obvious who the agent is – it does not need to be stated because everyone knows who it is.
   3 when the agent is unknown, unimportant or refers to people in general.

6 Change the facts about tea from the active to the passive. Remove the agent if appropriate.
   1 People think that tea originated in China thousands of years ago.

   ....

   2 People drink more tea than any other beverage except water.

   ....

   3 Farmers must usually grow tea in tropical and sub-tropical climates, although some growers have also produced it in Britain and northern states of the US.

   ....

   4 Portuguese traders first imported tea to Europe in the 16th century.

   ....

   5 People began to use teabags widely in the middle of the 20th century.

   ....

   6 Nowadays China produces almost a quarter of the world's tea.

   ....

IELTS Writing Task 1: Describing a process

1 In IELTS Writing Task 1 you may be asked to describe a process using information taken from pictures or a diagram.

Describe the process to your partner using the words and pictures.

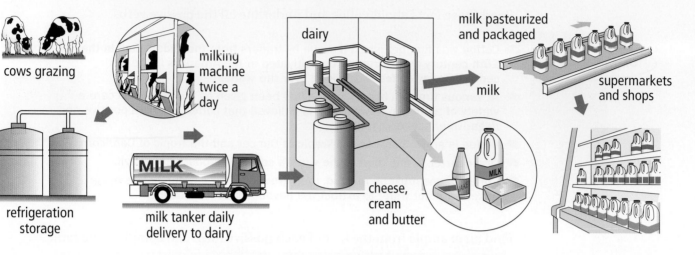

2 Choose the best opening sentence for the diagram.

    1 The diagram shows how we get milk from cows.
    2 The diagram shows how farmers produce milk.
    3 The diagram shows how milk is produced on farms.

3 Read the sentences below and put them in the correct order to describe the process in the diagram.

    a .... The milk is packaged in plastic containers, which could be of various sizes from 0.5 litres to 2 litres.
    b .... The milk is cooled and stored in large, refrigerated containers.
    c .... These are delivered to supermarkets and shops.
    d .... At the dairy, milk is made into various products including cheese, cream, butter and milk for drinking. The milk is usually pasteurized in order to kill any bacteria. This is done by heating it to 72 degrees for a very short time, usually about 16 seconds.
    e .... The cows, which are fed on grass, are milked. This usually happens twice a day, using a milking machine.
    f .... The milk is collected on a daily basis by tankers and is delivered to the dairy.

4 Underline the passive forms in a–f in exercise 3. Which tense is used? Why?

Sequencers

5 Rewrite the sentences in exercise 3 by adding an appropriate linking word from the box below to the sentences to show the stages or sequence of the process. Note that some sequencers are interchangeable.

After that	At the following stage	Finally	First	Next	Then

6 Look at the sentences in exercise 3 again. Why is the milk pasteurized? Underline the phrase which gives you the answer.

TIP
Use the information shown in the diagram but you may have to change or add more words to make complete sentences.

TIP
When describing a process it is important to explain why something happens.

7 Underline the connecting words/phrases in these sentences. Then add them to the text in exercise 3 in the appropriate places to explain the different stages in the process.

    1 as this produces more milk overall than once a day
    2 because it stays fresher longer at around 4 degrees C
    3 and therefore ensure that it is safe for consumption
    4 so that they can be sold

Practice

8 Work in pairs. The diagram below shows how sugar is produced from sugar beets.

Add the missing verbs to the diagram then describe the process to your partner. Use passive forms when necessary.

add	cut up	evaporate	extract	filter	heat
remove	shake	spin	unload	wash	

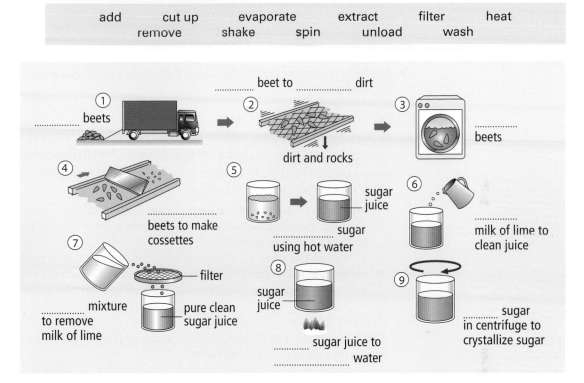

.... beet to .... dirt

① beets
.... beets

② dirt and rocks

③ .... beets

④ .... beets to make cossettes

⑤ sugar juice — .... sugar using hot water

⑥ .... milk of lime to clean juice

⑦ .... mixture to remove milk of lime — filter — pure clean sugar juice

⑧ sugar juice — .... sugar juice to .... water

⑨ .... sugar in centrifuge to crystallize sugar

9 Summarize the information by selecting and reporting the main features and make comparisons where relevant. When you have finished, compare your answer with the model answer on page 162.

> **Strategy**
> – Decide if the process has a beginning and end point or whether it is a cycle.
> – Write a clear introductory statement about the process.
> – Describe the process in a logical order using the pictures, vocabulary and sequencing words.
> – Give explanations where necessary.
> – Use verbs in the correct tense and decide if the active or passive voice is appropriate.
> – Organize your answer into paragraphs.
> – Check your answer carefully.

IELTS Speaking Part 2

1 ⊙ **2.1** Listen to this example of a Part 2 answer. Complete the missing details by identifying the topic question and the key points the speaker had to include.

> **Part 2**
>
> Talk about a successful (1) .... you know.
>
> You should say;
> what kind of (2) ....
> why you think (3) ....
> how (4) ....
>
> and also say whether your country has (5) ....

2 Comment on the candidate's performance.

3 Make brief notes, then talk about the points on this card to your partner for 1–2 minutes.

IELTS Speaking Part 3

4 In Part 3 of the IELTS Speaking module the examiner will ask you some questions related to the topic you were talking about in Part 2. Read the sample questions below.

Nowadays there is more contact between countries on a global level so the world is often described as a 'global village'.

1 How can richer countries help poorer countries?
2 Do you think it is better to buy well-known international products or locally produced goods?
3 What are the main roles of international organizations such as the United Nations?
4 How has global communication changed in the last 50 years?
5 Are cheap holidays and increased global tourism necessarily a good thing?

Balancing the argument

TIP
Do not give short answers in Part 3. Give your opinions and supporting reasons.

5 ⊙ **2.2** Listen to a possible answer to one of the Part 3 questions above and decide which question is being answered.

6 Listen again and answer these questions.
  1 What two reasons in favour of this point does the student give?
  2 What two reasons against this point does the student give?

7 Look at the audioscript on page 171 and answer these questions.
  1 What phrase does the speaker use to indicate that there are arguments on both sides?
  2 What phrase does she use to give her opinion?
  3 What other phrases do you know to give opinions?

In Part 3 you do not have any preparation time and need to respond to questions quickly. Here are some phrases that may help you.

> **Useful language**
>
> **If you think you understand the question, but you're not sure**
> I'm not exactly sure what you mean, but ...
> That's a rather difficult question, but perhaps ...
>
> **If you need a second to think about it**
> That's a good/an interesting question.
> Let me see ...

Academic writing style

1 Read these two short texts about English as a global language and answer these questions.

   1 Is the content of the two texts the same or different?

   2 Which text is more academic in style?

A One of the consequences of globalization is the spread of English as a world language. Although it is not the most widely spoken first language, English is the most used second language and it is thought that it is spoken by approximately one billion people worldwide. It is extensively used in many fields, including business and education and is also a requirement for a number of professions including medicine.

B More and more people all over the world speak English now. Why is that? I think one of the reasons is that international travel and communication have got a lot quicker and easier. English isn't the biggest first language in the world but It's the most popular second language and I think there are about a billion people who speak it all over the world – don't you think that's incredible? People use it all the time for loads of different things like business and education etc and it's important for some peoples' jobs too, eg doctors.

2 Complete these features of academic English by choosing the correct alternative.

   1 It uses more *formal/informal* language than everyday English.

   2 It *uses/doesn't* use subjective language (*I think, that's incredible*).

   3 It uses the *active/passive* more than everyday English.

   4 It generally uses *more/fewer* words than everyday English.

   5 It *does/doesn't* use contractions (*don't, it's*).

   6 It *does/doesn't* address the reader or ask questions.

3 Look at the next paragraph of the text in exercise 1. Replace the underlined words and phrases with the words in brackets to make them more academic.

   1 People <u>all over the place</u> hear or speak English <u>every day</u>. (*on a daily basis, worldwide*)

   2 It <u>crops up</u> <u>all the time</u> in <u>books, magazines, newspapers, in films, on TV and the radio and in songs</u>. (*appears, the media, constantly*)

   3 <u>So</u> even <u>people</u> who <u>say</u> they <u>don't</u> speak English <u>are probably familiar with a couple of</u> <u>words</u>. (*vocabulary, do not, claim, those, some, may recognize, therefore*)

   4 <u>In a similar way</u>, people recognize names <u>like</u> McDonald's and Starbucks <u>all over the world</u> <u>because of</u> the spread of <u>big</u> multinational companies. (*globally, large, similarly, such as, due to*)

4 Sentences 1 and 4 would be better in the passive. Why? Rewrite them.

English ....

....

Similarly, names such as McDonald's and Starbucks ....

....

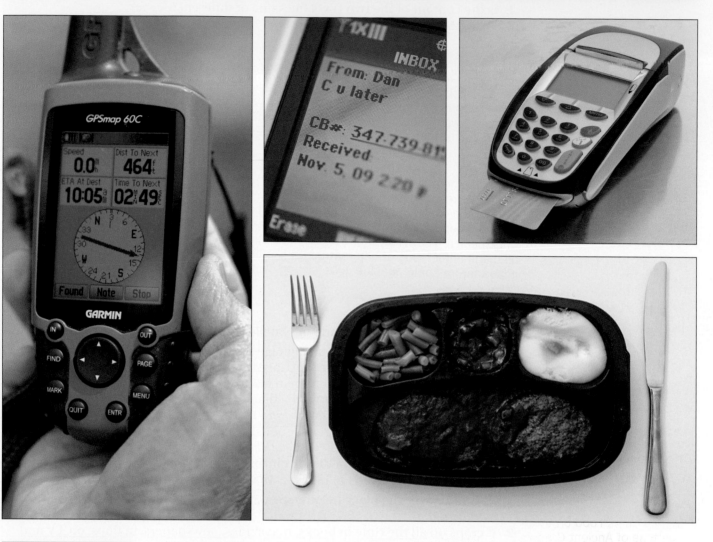

1 Look at the pictures. How many of the inventions pictured do you own or use? Can you imagine what life would be like without these things?

2 Match the date of invention with the product. Then scan the text to check your answers.

1892	PlayStation™
1949	Sony Walkman®
1970s	trainers
1978	bar codes
1979	GPS technology
1994	TV dinners

3 Discuss the following questions.
- Which of the items in the text has changed the world most?
- Which invention is the most important to you?
- What did people use before these items were invented?

Top 10 'inventions' that changed the world

A GPS technology Originally developed as a navigation system by the United States military, the Global Positioning System uses a network of satellites around the Earth to pinpoint the exact position of a receiver anywhere on the planet. Since its development in 1978, it is now used in cars, aircraft and boats. Geologists use it to track the movements of continental plate tectonics and glaciers while conservation scientists have tagged turtles with GPS receivers to follow their epic migrations.

B The Sony Walkman® In 1979 Sony spawned the era of wearable technology with its iconic personal stereo. It enabled music fans to listen to their music while on the move without inflicting their choices on those around them. It provided the soundtrack to millions of morning commutes. The Walkman quickly changed listening habits and became hugely popular as jogging culture took the 1980s by storm – here was something that allowed you to listen to your music while you worked out. This wearable technology has now evolved, thanks to Apple, into the iPod and has changed music for ever.

C The bar code These boring sets of black and white lines can now be found on almost every single item bought from a shop. At first glance, it seems hard to see how they possibly made any impact on the world, but they have fundamentally changed the way we shop. Norman Woodland first developed an early form of the bar code in 1949 by combining ideas from movie soundtracks and Morse code to help him speed up store checkouts. They now allow stores to instantly access product details, prices and stock levels with a sweep of a laser.

D TV dinners Food on the go has been around since the time of Ancient Greece, but convenience food really took off in the 1970s and transformed the way families ate meals, the high street, the countryside and national health. Traditional family dinners around the table disappeared and pre-packaged 'ready meals' eaten on the sofa became the norm. Due to hectic lifestyles, the products, which were often frozen, were designed to make life easier for time-pressed consumers.

The popularity of processed food, however, is also blamed for driving the obesity crisis. With high fat, salt and sugar content to make the meals last longer on the shelves, the diet of the Western world has deteriorated.

E PlayStation™ Although games consoles had been around for some time, Sony's PlayStation took gaming out of spotty teenagers' bedrooms and into adult living rooms when it was released in 1994. Here was a computer with more power than the average family PC. As of July 2008 more than 102 million PlayStation units had been sold, while the next generations, PlayStation 2 and PlayStation 3, have also been turned into best sellers. The gaming industry is now worth almost as much as the film industry, taking in more than £15 billion in 2008.

F Social networking Around the world, every day, more than three billion minutes are spent by computer users on Facebook. Along with other social networking sites such as MySpace™ and Twitter, it has completely changed the way we interact and who we interact with. Millions of people now communicate tiny details of their professional and personal lives by poking, twittering and posting. Online social networking has allowed people to rekindle friendships with friends they lost touch with years ago. Others chat online with complete strangers on the other side of the world. In 1967 American psychologist Stanley Milgram conducted the 'small world' experiment to prove the strength of old fashioned social networks. In the digital age, his 'six degrees of separation' have almost become redundant.

G Text messages Text messaging has created a new vocabulary and new grammar that is almost incomprehensible to those who do not use it. LOL and FYI have now passed into everyday English. It has also changed the way people use their thumbs – the old QWERTY keyboard layout suddenly became redundant. Among 13–17 year olds, text messaging now outweighs old fashioned phone calls by seven to one.

H Electronic money In the UK there were 7.4 billion purchases made during 2008 with plastic cards. Combined with internet banking, cards have made the cheque almost redundant. Credit cards gave us greater convenience for spending, greater security and the ability to spend money anywhere in the world. They also brought us internet fraud and record levels of debt that have contributed to the global credit crunch.

I Microwaves Not the ovens, but the electromagnetic waves. Microwaves – electromagnetic radiation with wavelengths ranging between 1 millimetre and one metre – are used by mobile phones, wireless broadband internet and satellite television. They also gave us a new way of cooking food while the US military has developed a 'less-than-lethal' weapon that can blast victims with a heatwave.

J Trainers Nightclub bouncers might not like them, but trainers changed fashion and the feet of generations. The Goodyear® Metallic Rubber Shoe Company was the first to use a new manufacturing process that melded rubber to cloth in 1892, but it was not until the 1970s they took off. With the help of celebrity endorsements by sporting superstars such as basketball legend Michael Jordan, trainers turned from being purely practical clothing for sport into a fashion item. The Army now reports that young people are increasingly growing up without ever wearing leather shoes and their feet are now too soft to wear traditional military boots.

4 Read the text again and answer the questions.

Locating information

Questions 1–7

The passage has ten paragraphs labelled A–J. Which paragraph contains the following information?

1 how the invention has developed into a different brand and product ....
2 a reference to the time spent using the invention ....
3 a comparison between two different sectors of the entertainment business ....
4 a reference to product promotion by famous names ....
5 the name of the person who invented the product ....
6 an example of how the armed forces are using the invention ....
7 a reference to how the device is used to study wildlife ....

Multiple choice

Question 8

Which ONE of the following is NOT mentioned as a benefit of the personal stereo?

A It allowed users to listen to music and exercise simultaneously.
B It allowed users to listen to music whilst working.
C It allowed users to listen to music without disturbing other people.
D It allowed users to listen to music on their way to work.

Questions 9–10

Which TWO of the following are mentioned as positive effects of the inventions?

A giving users more choices in their leisure time
B creating global consumers
C allowing families to spend more time together
D giving shoppers more choice of products
E allowing people to renew old contacts

Questions 11–13

Which THREE of the following are mentioned as negative effects of the inventions?

A difficulties for non-users
B a decline in language skills
C a decrease in the amount of time families spend together
D widespread unemployment
E a deterioration in young people's ability to think for themselves
F a rise in the amount of money owed
G a decline in healthy eating habits
H an increase in addiction to technology

Language focus

Dependent prepositions

1 Complete the expressions with the correct preposition. Then look back at the text to check your answers.

1 Technology has had a huge impact .... the way we communicate and interact .... each other. (paras C & F)
2 Increased use of the internet has been blamed .... a decrease in traditional forms of communication. (para D)
3 Most new gadgets are designed .... make life more convenient. (para D)
4 Social networking sites have let me find old friends I had lost touch .... (para F)
5 Text message language may have contributed .... a decline in language skills amongst young people. (para H)
6 Credit cards combined .... internet banking, have made spending money much easier than in the past. (para H)

See *Grammar and vocabulary bank* on page 155.

Expressing purpose

2 Match the sentence beginnings (1–6) with their endings (a–f) to make sentences expressing purpose.

1 The bar code was created
2 Sports stars are used
3 People use social networking sites
4 Motorists use GPS
5 TV dinners were created
6 People use abbreviated language

a *for* advertising trainers.
b *to* make life more convenient for busy people.
c *in order to* speed up the shopping process.
d *so that* they can keep in touch with friends.
e *so as to* make texting easier.
f *so as not to* get lost.

3 The *italic* phrases in exercise 2 tell us how/why something is used.
Now choose the correct alternative to complete the grammar rules.

1	*for*		infinitive/-*ing* form/subject + verb
2	*so that*		infinitive/-*ing* form/subject + verb
3	*so as (not) to*	is followed by	infinitive/-*ing* form/subject + verb
4	*in order to*		infinitive/-*ing* form/subject + verb
5	*to*		infinitive/-*ing* form/subject + verb

4 Rewrite these sentences using the expressions in brackets from exercise 3.

1 People use credit and debit cards. They can shop online safely. (so that)

....

2 People use personal stereos when travelling. They don't disturb other people. (so as not to)

....

3 TV dinners are often frozen. They are easy to prepare quickly. (so as to)

....

4 People like wearing trainers. They are comfortable and fashionable. (to)

....

5 Personal stereos are small and light. They are portable. (in order to)

....

6 Microwave ovens use microwave radiation. It cooks food. (for)

....

5 Think of a gadget that you use regularly. Tell your partner what you use it for but don't mention what the gadget is. Your partner should guess what you are talking about, eg:

A: *I use this to save time.*
B: *Is it a washing machine?*
A: *No. I use it for heating things?*
B: *Is it an oven?*
A: *No. I use it in order to cook food quickly.*
B: *A microvave?*
A: *Correct.*

IELTS Writing Task 1: Describing how something works

1 Work in pairs. Discuss these questions.
   – Would you like to go up in a hot air balloon? Why/Why not?
   – How do you think they work?

2 The diagrams below show how a hot air balloon flies. Put the words in the box below in the correct place in the pictures. Use a dictionary for any unknown vocabulary.

basket	gas burner	jets of flame	nylon
safety harness	steel ropes	valve	vehicle

How a hot air balloon works

1
Hot air balloon used for sport

Rip-proof **(c)** .... – light and strong

(b) ....

(a) ....

2
Quick release rope attached to **(d)** ....

Balloon inflated by fans (cold air)

Crown rope attached to balloon

3
Propane
(e) ....
....

Powerful **(f)** .... heat air

4
Wind slightly different at different altitudes

Height maintained/ changed using the blast valve

Direction/ speed determined by wind – not much control

(g) ....

5
Blast **(h)** .... – controls flow of gas to the burner

3 The first sentence should state the purpose of the object. Reorder the prompts below to make an introductory sentence.

is used for/up to four people/a hot air balloon/and usually carries/sport and leisure

....

....

TIP
To answer this question you need to use relevant vocabulary and verbs that describe the diagram. Many of these will be shown in the pictures but you may need to change the verb form.

4 The verb forms in the box are in the correct form. Use them to complete the text below. Which tense is used? Why?

consists of	controls	heats	is attached	is inflated
made of	rises	stand	to launch	to wear

A sports hot air balloon (1) .... a large bag, known as the envelope, attached by steel ropes to a basket in which the passengers and pilot (2) .... The balloon itself is (3) .... rip-proof nylon, so as to be light and very strong. A quick release rope (4) .... to a vehicle and the balloon (5) .... by fans blowing cold air. A crown rope is also attached so as not (6) .... the balloon before the pilot is ready.

A propane gas heater is used to send powerful jets of flame upwards into the balloon. This (7) .... the air inside the balloon in order to lift it. When the air is hot, the balloon (8) ....

When the balloon is flying, its speed and direction are determined by the wind which varies at different altitudes. However, the pilot, who needs (9) .... a safety harness, can maintain or change the height by using the blast valve. This (10) .... the flow of gas to the burner so that the balloon can go up or down.

Organizing your answer

5 Match each paragraph to the statements below.
  1 How the balloon is controlled in the air ....
  2 A general description of the balloon ....
  3 How the balloon takes off ....

Expressing purpose

6 Read the text in exercise 4 again and find and underline five different ways to express purpose.

7 Use the expressions to improve these sentences.
  0 Pilots wear safety harnesses because they don't want to fall out of the basket.
  Pilots wear safety harnesses so as not to fall out of the basket.

  1 Balloons are usually bright colours because they should be easily visible.

  ....

  2 Mobile phones are small and light because people want to carry them in pockets or handbags.

  ....

  3 Modern computers have large memories because people want to store many files.

  ....

Practice

8 The diagram shows how a fire extinguisher works.

Summarize the information by selecting and reporting the main features, and make comparisons where relevant.

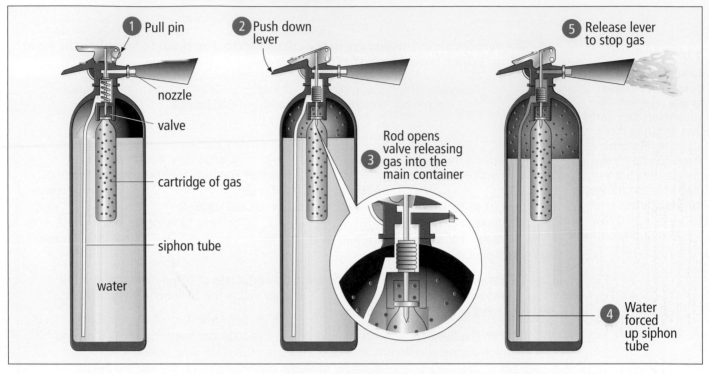

9 Consider the questions below to help you organize your answer.
- What is the general purpose of a fire extinguisher? *What is it used for?*
- What components does it consist of? *Identify the key parts.*
- How does it work? *Use the numbers to describe the process.*
- How will you conclude the description? *How do you turn it off?*

10 Write your answer in at least 150 words. When you have finished, compare it with the model answer on page 162.

Describing objects

Vocabulary

1 Complete the table with the adjectives and adjective phrases in the box.

> 1 metre in diameter   10 cm high/long/wide/deep   a shade of pink
> bigger/smaller than a ...   cylindrical   flat   leather   light/dark brown
> metal   metallic grey   plastic   the size of a ...   two parts
> round   three sections   tiny   wooden

Shape	Size	Structure	Material	Colour
It is ... *flat*	It is ...	It contains ... It consists of ...	It's made of ... It is	It is ...

2 Add two more examples to each column.

3 Use the vocabulary to describe some objects in your classroom or your bag to your partner, eg a pencil, a table. Ask your partner to guess what object you are describing.

1 Work in pairs to answer these questions.
 – What type of music do you listen to?
 – How do you listen to music?
 – Have your listening habits changed at all in the last 10 years?

2 Match the key vocabulary in A–D with the pictures of different types of music format. Use the key vocabulary and add any other other expressions from *Vocabulary* exercise 1 to describe and compare them.

Long-playing record (LP)

Cassette tape

Compact disc (CD)

MP3 player

A ....

late 1990s	lightweight	pocket-sized

B ....

1940s	30cm diameter	black vinyl	card sleeve

C ....

1980s	circular	12cm diameter	1.2mm thick	polycarbonate plastic

D ....

1960s	10cm x 6.5cm	magnetic coated tape	rectangular case

See *Study skills* section for a Writing Task 1 describing the development of these objects.

Exam information
In IELTS you will only hear the recording once. In Sections 2 and 4 it is important that you follow the 'flow' and structure of the talk or lecture. Use the questions and layout to help you follow the monologue.

1 Look at the visuals of robots and discuss these questions with a partner.
– What do you think these robots are used for?
– What other tasks can robots perform?
– Would you like a robot in your home? Why/Why not?

2 You are going to hear a lecture about the history of robotics.

Table completion
Questions 1–5

◎ 2.3 Listen to the first part of the lecture. Complete the table USING NO MORE THAN THREE WORDS OR A NUMBER.

History of robotics			
Ancient civilizations			
Greek mythology	Talos: made of bronze and guarded island of Crete		
Roman mythology	Vulcan: two female robots made of gold to **1**		
Later developments			
Date	**Inventor**	**Robot/machine**	**Has the ability to ...**
1774	Pierre and Henri Louis Jacquet-Droz	Robot boy Robot woman	draw and **2** .... play a piano
about 1774	**3**	Mechanical duck	flap wings, quack, pretend to eat and drink
4	Joseph Jacquard	Textile machine	punch cards
1834	Charles Babbage	Analytic engine	to carry out **5** ....

Multiple choice

Questions 6–7

(•) 2.4 Now listen to the second part of the lecture.

Choose TWO letters A–F.

Which two facts are mentioned about the robots Unimaton or Shakey in the 20th century?

A It was first developed in the mid-1960s.
B It provided the name for the earliest robot company.
C It was used in the steel industry.
D It was controlled by a human operator.
E It was controlled by a computer to move a box.
F It was used to switch a lamp on and off.

Question 8

Choose the correct letter, A, B or C.

Since the 1970s hundreds of robots have been designed for many uses including

A driving small cars.
B building doors for houses.
C conducting operations.

Note completion

Questions 9–10

Complete the notes below. Write NO MORE THAN THREE WORDS for each answer.

> 1967: Japan behind US in robot technology
> Currently: Japan (9) .... in robotics.
> Famous products:
> Aibo (Sony): robot dog – sold well
> Asimo (Honda): looks human, works in home.
> Future: Asimo operated using (10) .... for power.

Vocabulary

Word building

1 Look at the sentences below with missing words. For each sentence decide what type of word is missing – a verb, noun, adjective or adverb.

2 Use the words in brackets to form new words to complete the sentences. Use a dictionary to check your answers.

1 There have been many .... in the way we communicate over the past fifty years. (develop)
2 Designing new products requires you to think .... (create)
3 Alexander Graham Bell .... the telephone in 1876. (invent)
4 The screen on my digital camera has a .... of 8cm. (wide)
5 The factory has increased .... due to high demand from customers. (produce)
6 The .... of this MP3 player is modern and fashionable. (design)
7 Sony are one of the leading .... of personal stereos. (manufacture)
8 My workplace has been .... with the latest computer system. (equip)
9 The first mobile phone was the size of a large brick and was 2kg in .... (weigh)
10 The fire extinguisher contains a .... cartridge of gas. (cylinder)

See *Grammar and vocabulary bank* on page 155 for synonyms of *make* and collocations with *make* and *do*.

IELTS Speaking Part 2

1 Read the task below.

> **Part 2**
>
> Describe an item of technology that has had a big impact on your life.
>
> You should say:
> – what type of item it is and when you got it
> – what you use the item for
> – how often you use it
>
> and also say what difference it has made to your life.

Use the word map to help you write notes.

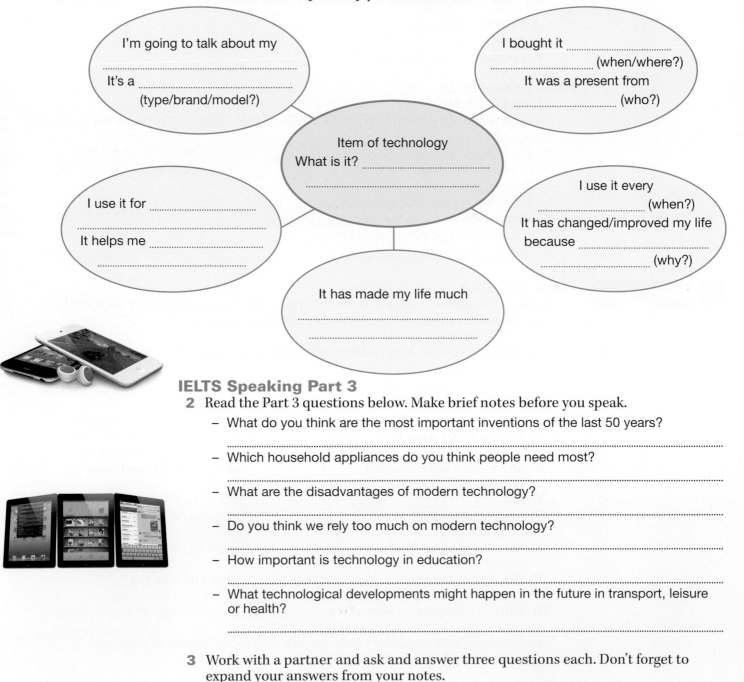

I'm going to talk about my
....
It's a ....
(type/brand/model?)

I bought it ....
.... (when/where?)
It was a present from
.... (who?)

Item of technology
What is it? ....
....

I use it for ....
....
It helps me ....
....

I use it every
.... (when?)
It has changed/improved my life
because ....
.... (why?)

It has made my life much
....
....

IELTS Speaking Part 3

2 Read the Part 3 questions below. Make brief notes before you speak.

– What do you think are the most important inventions of the last 50 years?

....

– Which household appliances do you think people need most?

....

– What are the disadvantages of modern technology?

....

– Do you think we rely too much on modern technology?

....

– How important is technology in education?

....

– What technological developments might happen in the future in transport, leisure or health?

....

3 Work with a partner and ask and answer three questions each. Don't forget to expand your answers from your notes.

Editing

1 Read the Writing Task 1 question below.

The diagrams on page 85 show the stages in the development of different music formats from records to MP3 players.

Summarize the information by selecting and reporting the main features, and make comparisons where relevant.

Read the sample answer below for the writing task and answer these questions.

1 Look at the first three paragraphs. There are six mistakes underlined. Correct them and say why they are wrong.

2 Look at the rest of the text. There are six more mistakes. Find them and correct them.

3 Compare answers with your partner.

There <u>has</u> been many developments in music formats since the creation of vinyl records in the late 19th century to digital music in the 21st century.

Long-playing records (LPs) <u>invented</u> in the 1940s and were flat, <u>circle</u> objects with a 30cm <u>daimeter</u>, made of black vinyl with a hole in the middle. Records were kept in a paper or card sleeve.

In the 1960s cassette tapes were introduced. These <u>are consisted of</u> magnetic-coated tape wound around two spools and covered with a plastic shell. These were <u>considerable</u> smaller than vinyl records, at 10cm long and 6.5cm wide. Cassettes were kept in a rectangular plastic case.

Compact discs (CDs) have appeared in the 1980s. These were circular and more smaller than records with a diameter of 12cm. They were made of 1.2mm thick polycarbonate plastic and came in a square plastic case.

In the late 1990s significant changes took place in the way people listened music. Nowadays people download digital music onto MP3 players, that are small items of technology designed fitting into a pocket and carry thousands of song.

Phrasal verbs with different meanings

2 A phrasal verb is a verb + a preposition or adverb which may have a meaning that is very different from the individual words. Many phrasal verbs have a number of different meanings. The following phrasal verbs appear in the text on page 79.

Find the phrasal verb in the passage and decide which meaning is correct in this context.

1 work out (para B)
a to find a satisfactory way of doing something
b to do physical exercise as a way of keeping fit
c to solve a problem by doing a calculation

2 take off (para D)
a to remove a piece of clothing
b to become successful or popular
c to leave the ground and start flying (for aircraft)

3 Use your dictionary to find the correct meaning of the phrasal verbs in context.

1 It was a long lecture and I didn't manage to *take in* everything.

....

2 I've had a few problems in the last year but things are finally *looking up*.

....

See *Grammar and vocabulary bank* on page 155 for more on phrasal verbs.

> **alternative medicine** /ɔːlˈtɜːnətɪv medɪsɪn/ noun [uncount]
> medical treatment using methods that are different from the usual
> Western scientific methods.   *Macmillan Essential Dictionary*

Reading

1 How is alternative medicine different from conventional medicine?

2 Look at the statements below.

Put (C) next to those which you think are conventional medicine and (A) next to those which you think are alternative therapies. Then compare answers with your partner.

1 having an injection ....
2 having a head massage ....
3 having an operation in a hospital ....
4 taking aspirin/paracetamol for a headache ....
5 smelling aromatherapy oils ....
6 taking a herbal drink ....

3 If you have an illness, which of the following people would you consult? Why?/Why not?
– a family member
– a doctor
– a chemist
– an expert on alternative therapies

4 You are going to read a text about four different types of alternative medicine.

Classification
Questions 1–5
Quickly read the text and classify the descriptions according to which of the following they refer to, according to the text. Note that you may use the letters more than once.

– Acupuncture (A)   – Iridology (I)
– Reflexology (R)   – Chiropractic Manipulation (C)

1 was invented about 200 years ago ....
2 has been successfully used as a painkiller ....
3 involves applying pressure to neck, elbows, knees and so on ....
4 can tell the practitioner every illness the patient has had ....
5 can be performed by the patient without a qualified practitioner ....

True, False, Not given
Questions 6–9
Do the following statements agree with the information in the text?
Write
TRUE (T) if the statement agrees with the information.
FALSE (F) if the statement contradicts the information.
NOT GIVEN (NG) if there is no information on this.

6 According to Professor Ernst, acupuncture is not effective for those suffering from toothache. ....
7 Practitioners claim that reflexology can relieve the symptoms of asthma. ....
8 Dr Barrett claims that reflexology cannot be proved to work. ....
9 According to Professor Ernst patients should definitely avoid iridology. ....

What's the alternative?

Are complementary and alternative therapies worth the billions of pounds that we spend on them? And do they have the same effects as conventional medicine? The scientific community is split over whether they work.

Acupuncture

What is it? Acupuncture is one of the oldest and most commonly used alternative therapies, originating in China more than 2,000 years ago.

What is involved? Therapists stimulate pressure points throughout the body, using needles. There are 2,000 pressure points which connect to 12 main and eight secondary pathways, which are called meridians.

What is the theory? Acupuncture is believed to regulate our spiritual, emotional, mental and physical balance, which is influenced by the opposing forces of yin and yang. When yin and yang are unbalanced, our qi (pronounced 'chee'), a form of energy, becomes blocked. Western scientists have been unable to explain acupuncture, since meridians do not correspond to either blood circulation or nerve pathways. No one understands fully how acupuncture works, but there is some evidence that stimulation of pressure points increases the flow of electromagnetic signals, which may trigger the release of the body's natural painkillers such as endorphins, or immune cells.

What is the evidence? Researchers at the University of Maryland, Baltimore, discovered that patients treated with acupuncture after dental surgery had less intense pain than patients who received a placebo. The same team has also shown that acupuncture can reduce the pain of osteoarthritis when used with conventional drugs to a greater degree than when these drugs are used on their own. Professor Ernst says: 'There is good clinical evidence that acupuncture works for osteoarthritis, migraine, dental and back pain. But there is good evidence that it does not work for some treatments, such as weight loss and smoking.'

Reflexology

What is it? Reflexology is the therapeutic manipulation of the hands or feet, which, according to practitioners, have areas that correspond to parts of the body.

What is involved? As well as manual manipulation by a qualified practitioner, it is now possible to buy reflexology guides and foot massagers for do-it-yourself reflexology.

What is the theory? The practitioner can diagnose the abnormalities by feeling the hands or feet; by massaging or pressing these areas, he stimulates the flow of energy, blood, nutrients and nerve impulses to the corresponding body zone and thereby relieves ailments in that area.

What is the evidence? A study published in *Respiratory Medicine* last year described 40 asthma patients who were given ten weeks of simulated reflexology and ten weeks of real reflexology. The researchers, using both subjective tests and objective lung-function tests, could find no evidence that the reflexology helped the patients' asthma.

Practitioners claim that reflexology can cleanse the body of toxins, increase circulation, assist in weight loss and improve the health of organs. Dr Barrett, vice-president of the National Council against Health Fraud in the US says: 'There is no scientific support for these assertions.'

Professor Ernst says: 'Practitioners use reflexology as a diagnostic tool and it does not work. It can be relaxing though.'

Iridology

What is it? According to iridologists, the eye contains a complete map of every body part. This therapy was invented in the early nineteenth century by a Hungarian physician, Ignatz von Peczely, who, during his childhood, accidentally broke the leg of an owl and noticed a black stripe appear in the lower part of the owl's eye.

What is involved? The practitioner looks into the patient's eye and checks the pupil's pigmentation against iridology diagrams. Several dozen configurations exist. Herbs are then prescribed to help the patient with their diagnosed illness.

What is the theory? Iridologists believe that a person's health can be diagnosed from the colour, texture and location of pigment flecks in the eye. Some claim that the eye markings can reveal a complete history of past illnesses.

What is the evidence? According to Dr Barrett, 'there is no known mechanism by which body organs can be represented or transmit their health status to specific locations in the iris'.

Professor Ernst recently published a review of the scientific literature on iridology, but he could find only four studies that had been carried out according to correct scientific procedure. These studies suggest that iridology is not a valid diagnostic tool.

Professor Ernst says firmly: 'Patients and therapists should be discouraged from using this method.'

Chiropractic manipulation

What is it? Chiropractors diagnose and treat conditions that are due to mechanical faults in the joints, especially the spine.

What does it involve? A chiropractor manipulates joints using the hands to improve mobility and relieve pain.

What is the theory? If the spine is not functioning properly, it can cause irritation of the nerves that control posture and movement. This irritation can lead to 'referred' pain, which is felt in another part of the body. By manipulating joints, chiropractors stimulate the joint's movement receptors, which are sensors that provide feedback to the brain on where the joint is.

What is the evidence? Going to a chiropractor is now mainstream. The British Chiropractic Association reports 90,000 patient visits a week. It is one of the most regulated of the alternative therapies and yet, of those discussed here, it is potentially the most dangerous. Manipulation of the neck can tear the fragile tissue of the vertebral artery and, in the worse cases, result in a stroke.

In January this year the UCLA Medical School published a report on 681 patients who were given chiropractic help when they had lower back pain. After 6 months, 96 per cent of them still had lower back pain, leading the researchers to conclude that chiropractic manipulation had been ineffective. Professor Ernst says: 'The bottom line is that it works for a very limited number of spinal conditions, and mainly in the short term.'

Glossary

placebo a substance that is not medicine, but the person taking it believes it is medicine, and so they get better

ailment an illness, usually not a serious one

Summary completion

Questions 10–13

Complete the summary about chiropractic manipulation below. Choose NO MORE THAN TWO WORDS from the passage for each answer.

> Chiropractic manipulation is now a popular and accepted alternative therapy that uses joint manipulation to relieve pain and increase (10) ....
> Although it is one of the most controlled alternative therapies, it could also be the
> (11) .... Research concluded that the treatment was
> (12) .... for the vast majority of patients receiving it for lower back pain and overall, its success was (13) .... and largely temporary.

Multiple choice

Question 14

Choose the correct letter, A, B, C or D.
Which of the following statements best sums up the overall content of this article?

    A Alternative therapies will be more common in the future.
    B There is scientific proof that all alternative therapies are effective.
    C There is no scientific proof that alternative therapies are effective.
    D Some alternative therapies can be effective but there are limitations.

5 In groups, discuss which of these alternative methods you would be most willing to try (or have tried already). Give reasons for your choice.

6 Do you know or have you experienced any other alternative medical techniques, eg aromatherapy?

Vocabulary

Parts of the body and illnesses/conditions

1 Many parts of the body appear in the text. How many can you find? Compare your list with another student.

2 The following illnesses/conditions are mentioned in the text. Use a dictionary to check your understanding and then match them to the body parts affected.

1	migraine	**a**	bones
2	osteoarthritis	**b**	teeth
3	stroke	**c**	lungs
4	asthma	**d**	head
5	dental pain	**e**	blood/brain

3 The verbs in column A all appear in the text. Which of the nouns in column B do each of the verbs collocate with? Check your ideas in the *Macmillan Collocations Dictionary*.

A	B
to relieve	antibiotics
to prescribe	an illness
to diagnose	pain
to treat	a condition
	symptoms
	medicine

See *Grammar and vocabulary bank* on page 156 for collocations practice.

Real conditionals

See *Grammar and vocabulary bank* on page 156.

1 Discuss in pairs. On average how often do you have a cold? At what time of year do you usually catch one? What are the symptoms of the common cold? When you have a cold how do you treat it? Read this short text and compare your ideas.

A cold is a contagious viral disease which infects the soft lining of the nose. <u>If you have a cold, symptoms include a runny nose, sore throat, cough and fever.</u> It is most common during the cold winter months and affects children and adults of all ages. Most people will catch a cold two to four times a year. <u>When you catch a cold, you are contagious from the day before the illness breaks out until one to three days after you feel better. When you cough or</u> <u>sneeze, the infection can spread to other people in the air.</u> However, the most common way of catching a cold is by hand contact. <u>If you don't wash your hands carefully, you will increase your chances of catching a cold.</u>

A cold is usually a mild condition and recovery takes place within a week. <u>However, you should see a doctor if you still have symptoms after a week.</u>

2 A 'real' conditional is used to talk about a possible situation and its outcome. Look at the underlined sentences in the text above, which are all examples of real conditionals, and complete the table below.

	Possible situation	Result
Zero conditional	If you have a cold,	1 ....
	2	you are contagious from the day before the illness breaks out.
First conditional	If you don't wash your hands carefully,	3 ....
	4	the infection can spread to other people in the air.
	if you still have symptoms after a week.	5 ....

3 In which conditional is the result:
   – likely but not definite?
   – definite and always true?

4 Complete the table and answer the questions.

Zero Conditional	*If/* .... + ... ,	present simple
First conditional	*If/* .... + present simple,	*will/* .... / .... + infinitive

1 Is it possible to change the order of the clauses?
2 What happens to the comma?

5 Look at these possible situations or results and make conditional sentences. Write two for each situation.

0 When you have flu ...
   When you have flu, your symptoms include a high temperature and aches and pains.
   When you have flu, you should stay in bed and drink plenty of liquids.

1 If you break your leg ...
   ....

2 ... you might need an injection.
   ....

3 When someone has a bad back ...
   ....

4 ... you get tired easily.
   ....

Health and medical breakthroughs

Check the meaning of the phrases below. Categorize them into one of four groups.

TIP
Using a wide range of vocabulary on different topics is likely to improve your IELTS grade.

a balanced diet	a poor diet	a sedentary lifestyle	cancer
having leisure and relaxation time		HIV/AIDS	immunization
infertility treatment	keeping your mind active		lack of health education
organ transplantation	poor hygiene and sanitation		regular exercise
stem cell research	stress-related illness		viral epidemics

Types of illness and disease	Causes of ill health and disease	Ways of keeping healthy	Medical breakthroughs

Speaking

IELTS Speaking Part 3

Discuss the following questions from Part 3 of the Speaking exam. Make brief notes.

– What are the best ways to keep healthy?

....

– What are the greatest health risks in the 21st century?

....

– What are the most significant medical developments of the past 50 years?

....

– Do you agree with the saying 'Prevention is better than cure'?

....

– Do you think healthcare facilities such as hospitals need to be improved?

....

– What advances do you think will take place in medicine in the future?

....

IELTS Listening Section 3

You are going to hear part of a seminar in which students are discussing cloning. Listen and answer the questions.

Multiple choice

Questions 1–4

🔘 2.5 Choose the correct letter A, B or C.

1 What is the main topic the group are going to discuss?

    A natural cloning

    B artificial cloning

    C animal cloning

2 What do many people think of reproductive cloning, according to Barry?

    A They are excited by it.

    B They are not interested in it.

    C They are afraid of it.

3 Alice believes that having the same genes will mean that

    A Clones may be similar to identical twins.

    B Clones are likely to act like robots.

    C Clones may attack and kill people.

4 Who does Barry say will benefit most from reproductive cloning?

    A medical researchers studying personality

    B people who can't have children

    C identical twins

Questions 5–6

Choose TWO letters A–E.

Which uses and benefits of therapeutic cloning are mentioned?

    A creating a whole new human being

    B the possibility of growing a new kidney

    C producing more blood for donations

    D transplanting a new liver to a different body

    E tackling certain illnesses

Note completion

Questions 7–10

🔘 2.6 Listen to the second part of the discussion and complete the notes below. Write NO MORE THAN THREE WORDS for each answer.

Progress in Human Cloning

Barriers

Opposition from (7) .... groups
Moral/ethical grounds: 'playing God', against nature

Safety

eg Dolly the sheep: over 250 attempts to create first (8) ....
Possibility of miscarriages, deformities and other (9) ....

Ongoing/future developments

• Cloning of human leg cells
• Embryos created from (10) .... cells

Unreal conditionals

See *Grammar and vocabulary bank* on page 156.

1 An unreal conditional is used to talk about an unlikely or imaginary situation and its result.

The following sentences come from Listening Section 3 on page 95. Match the *If* clauses 1–3 with the main clauses a–c. Check your answers by looking at the audioscript on page 171.

Unlikely or imaginary situation	Result
If clause	Main clause
1 If reproductive cloning were legalized, 2 If you could grow a new heart, kidney or lung for someone, 3 If you cloned humans,	a you would address the problem of organ shortages. b we wouldn't be unique. c those with fertility problems could have children.

2 Now answer these questions.
   1 What tense or verb form is used in the *If* clause?
   2 Is the speaker talking about the past?
   3 What verb forms can be used in the second clause?
   4 Is it possible to change the order of the clauses?

Note that in the *If* clause it is considered more correct to use *were* than *was*, although native speakers will often use *was*, especially in less formal situations.

3 Make unreal conditionals from these prompts. Use *would*, *might* or *could* depending on how sure you are about the result of these situations. Remember that the *If* clause can be first or second.

   0 Human cloning isn't legal. People don't live forever.
      If human cloning were legal, people could live forever.

   1 There aren't many organ donors. There is a shortage of organs for transplantation.

      ....

   2 Hygiene and sanitation in developing countries aren't good. There is a lot of disease.

      ....

   3 We have global air travel. Disease spreads quickly around the world.

      ....

   4 People don't lead healthy lifestyles. There are many cases of heart disease.

      ....

   5 We have fertility treatments. There are fewer childless couples.

      ....

4 Write your own sentences using unreal conditionals about:
   – Immunization against common diseases
   – A cure for HIV/AIDS
   – Smoking and lung cancer

   ....
   ....
   ....
   ....
   ....
   ....

IELTS Writing Task 2: Key phrases to express impersonal views

Exam information
Task 2 examines your ability to express an opinion logically and clearly. It is usual in academic writing to express your opinions in a more impersonal way than when speaking.

Useful language
It is often said/thought that …
It could be argued that …
It is difficult to understand why …
Many people refuse to accept this …
It is (im)possible that …
It is (un)likely that …

1 Read the extracts below and decide which of the categories each of the opinions belongs to. Write *A*, *B* or *C* next to sentences 1–7.

  A Formal: appropriate for academic writing or more formal speaking.
  B Semi-formal: acceptable in some academic writing including IELTS and some academic speaking situations.
  C Informal: acceptable in everyday speech but not appropriate in academic writing.

  0 Private healthcare is growing in popularity, but it is important to consider those who are unable to afford it. [A]

  1 It's really terrible that people have to wait so long to get a hospital bed – don't you think so? ☐

  2 The majority of people accept that modern drugs are the most effective way to cure an illness. ☐

  3 I firmly believe that nurses should earn more money. ☐

  4 It could be argued that people should be offered more choice in the type of medical treatment they receive. ☐

  5 I totally disagree with the view that people should pay for their healthcare. ☐

  6 Modern drugs – the best way to cure an illness? What a load of rubbish! ☐

  7 It is widely accepted that health facilities and services need to be improved in many poorer countries. ☐

2 Choose an appropriate style (formal, semi-formal or informal) for each of the following situations.

  1 Writing an email to a tutor. ....
  2 Speaking to your host family. ....
  3 Writing an assignment at university. ....
  4 Giving a presentation at college. ....
  5 Writing a practice IELTS essay. ....
  6 Speaking to a new classmate. ....

3 Match the sentences below with the situations from exercise 2.
  a Firstly, I will talk about the history of alternative medicine and then I will look at … ....
  b Would it be possible for me to get an extension for my assignment please? ....
  c Would it be all right if I invite a friend round for dinner on Friday? ....
  d Furthermore, a balanced diet can considerably improve health and well-being. ....
  e Shall we go for a coffee after class? ....
  f This report analyses the effects of acupuncture on relieving back pain in elderly patients ....

TIP
When writing, aim to use more impersonal phrases. However, it is usually acceptable to use *I* or *my* occasionally in an IELTS essay.

Preparing to write

4 Read this Task 2 question.

Currently there is a trend towards the use of alternative forms of medicine. However, at best these methods are ineffective, and at worst they may be dangerous.

To what extent do you agree with this opinion?

Give reasons for your answer and include any relevant examples from your own knowledge.

From the reading and discussion activities earlier in the unit consider the questions below.

- What is alternative medicine? Define it. Give examples and note down any relevant vocabulary.
- Do you agree with this opinion? How effective and safe is this method of treatment in your view?
- What are its positive and negative points? Make two lists.
- How would you organize the structure of your essay? Outline the content of each paragraph.

Compare your ideas with those in the sample answer below. Do not attempt to fill in the gaps; you will do this in the next exercise.

Alternative medicine, a form of medical treatment different from Western methods, is not a new concept. (1) _____ it pre-dates conventional medicine and is still used by many people all over the world. (2) _____ it is dangerous, and feel that both alternative and conventional medicine can both be useful in the modern world. The conventional medical community is often dismissive of alternatives, as there is little scientific evidence to support the claims of their supporters.

However, (3) _____ this type of treatment can be effective. Furthermore, people often (4) _____ alternative methods such as acupuncture because of the recommendations of (5) _____ , and therefore come to the therapist with a very positive attitude, which may be part of the reason for the cure.

(6) _____ , these therapies are usually only useful for long-term chronic conditions. Acute medical problems, (7) _____ accidental injury, often require more conventional treatment.

On the other hand, despite lack of scientific proof, there is a great deal of anecdotal evidence to suggest that these therapies work. Apparently, around 60% of people worldwide rely on non-conventional treatment. In addition, far from being dangerous, they often have few or no side effects, so the worst outcome would be no change. (8) _____ the effectiveness of alternative therapies in the West is that, whilst conventional medicine is available without charge, many people are prepared to pay (9) _____ for alternatives. If they were totally unhelpful, it would be rather strange if this continued. Unsurprisingly, large drug companies take a significant interest in herbal medicine. Finally, looking at a problem from a different perspective must be beneficial.

(10) _____ conventional and alternative therapies can and should co-exist. They have different strengths, and can both be used effectively to target particular medical problems. The best solution is for alternative therapies to be used to support and complement conventional medicine.

Using an appropriate writing style

5 Choose the most suitable word or phrase from the three options to complete the gaps 1–10.

1 A It is accepted that ...
B I think that ...
C People believe that ...

2 A Everyone knows that ...
B You would think that ...
C I am unconvinced that ...

3 A It's largely possible that ...
B It is widely believed that ...
C Many people have told me that ...

4 A try
B check out
C taste

5 A mates
B companions
C friends

6 A And
B Moreover
C Also

7 A such as
B eg
C like

8 A The best argument against ...
B I'd argue for ...
C One of the strongest arguments for ...

9 A loads of money
B big prices
C considerable sums

10 A I firmly believe that ...
B It is my absolute view that ...
C I guess that ...

Practice

6 Give your opinion about each of the following statements. Use an appropriate style to give an impersonal or more personal opinion. Remember to give reasons, eg:

0 Modern drugs are the most effective way to cure an illness.

The majority of people accept that modern drugs are the most effective way to cure an illness. In many cases they provide the quickest cures.

I totally disagree that modern drugs are the most effective way to cure an illness because in many cases the side effects are worse than the illness itself.

1 Nurses should earn more money.

....

....

2 Everyone should pay for their own healthcare.

....

....

3 A hospital is the best place to recover from an illness.

....

....

Using adverbs

7 Look at the underlined adverbs from these two extracts from the model answer on page 98. Are the adverbs used to show the reader what the writer thinks or to show the reader how something is done?

<u>Apparently</u>, around 60% of people worldwide rely on non-conventional treatment.
<u>Unsurprisingly</u>, large drug companies take a significant interest in herbal medicine.

apparently	clearly	fortunately	naturally
obviously	surprisingly	unfortunately	

Now answer these questions about the adverbs in the box.

1 Which one is used to say what seems to be true, when all the facts are not known? ....
2 Which one expresses a negative opinion? ....
3 Which one expresses a positive opinion? ....
4 Which one refers to something that is different from what you might expect?

....
5 Which three refer to an opinion that is what you might expect?

....

8 Put appropriate adverbs in these sentences. More than one may be possible as the answer will depend on your opinion.

1 .... , if you have a broken leg, the hospital is the best place to go.
2 .... , many people are suspicious of alternative medicine.
3 .... , some alternative therapies can be dangerous to your health.
4 .... , when doctors make mistakes, there are often serious consequences.
5 .... , more than 30% of people claim they never visit their doctor.
6 .... , there are more than 8,000 qualified reflexology practitioners in the UK.

9 Answer this Task 2 question. When you have finished, compare your answer with the model answer on page 162.

Funding medical research into curing diseases should take priority over developing existing healthcare services and facilities.

To what extent do you agree or disagree with this opinion?

Give reasons for your answer and include any relevant examples from your own knowledge or experience.

Strategy
- Check that you understand the key words in the question.
- Decide whether you agree or disagree with the opinion.
- Note down ideas and key vocabulary related to the question and think of reasons to support your opinions.
- Outline the structure of each paragraph.
- Write your answer using an appropriate style.
- Check and edit your answer for language errors.

Avoiding repetition

1 Read this short text about acupuncture. How could the underlined parts of the text be improved?

> Acupuncture is one of the oldest alternative therapies. <u>Acupuncture</u> originated in China more than 2,000 years ago. Early practitioners <u>in China</u> aimed to balance the opposing forces of yin and yang. <u>The practitioners</u> believed that when <u>the forces of yin and yang</u> are unbalanced our qi becomes blocked.

2 Read the passage below. Look at the underlined words. Pronouns (*they, them*, etc.) and other reference links such as *then, there, this, that, these, those* and *one* are used to help avoid repeating the same words and improve the cohesion of the text.

In the first sentence of the paragraph, *there* refers to 'the lining of the respiratory passages' earlier in the sentence. What do the other underlined words refer to? (This could be a single word or a whole phrase.)

> A cough is a reflex action which happens when nerves are stimulated in the lining of the respiratory passages by something which should not be <u>there</u>. <u>This</u> may be dust, a piece of food, or phlegm caused by an infection. The lungs are normally a sterile environment, so if dirt or dust get into <u>them</u> <u>this</u> could cause <u>them</u> to become a breeding ground for bacteria and infection. Coughing clears the lungs. If <u>it</u> is painful you may try not to cough and <u>this</u> can be dangerous because <u>it</u> can lead to a chest infection and even pneumonia.

3 Use reference links to replace the underlined sections.

0 Hay fever is an allergic reaction to dust and pollen. ~~Hay fever~~ _It_ is the most common allergy in the world.

1 The nose, sinus, throat and eyes are most affected. <u>The nose, sinus, throat and eyes</u> .... become irritated and swell up.

2 People usually first start to get hay fever in childhood. <u>People</u> .... often find that the symptoms improve by the time <u>people</u> .... are thirty or forty.

3 About 5% of people worldwide have hay fever. <u>The percentage of people who have hay fever</u> .... is higher in industrialized countries, where about 15% of the population suffer from <u>hay fever</u> ....

4 If you have hay fever, don't mow the lawn if you have <u>a lawn</u> ...., and try to keep your doors and windows shut, as <u>keeping your doors and windows shut</u> .... will help to keep out the pollen.

5 People sometimes think that hay fever happens in late summer, yet <u>hay fever</u> .... does not only happen <u>in late summer</u> .... but throughout the spring and summer.

6 Some of the symptoms of hay fever are red and itchy eyes, sneezing, coughing and a runny nose. <u>The symptoms of hay fever such as red and itchy eyes, sneezing, coughing and a runny nose</u> .... can be very unpleasant and seriously affect your quality of life.

4 Look at a paragraph you have written recently. Can you improve its cohesion and avoid repetition using appropriate reference links?

Reading

1 Work in groups of three. Look at the list of intelligent animals.

chimp	crow	dolphin	elephant	octopus
orang-utan	pig	pigeon	rat	squirrel

1 Can you put them in order of intelligence?
2 Which of these signs of intelligence do you think each animal has?

follow human commands	make tools	read numbers and symbols
recognize themselves in a mirror	use sign language	use tools

2 In your groups, choose one each of the three short passages and answer the following questions.

1 What was the main aim of the research?
2 Which of the signs of intelligence in exercise 1 did the animal show?
3 Did the research prove what it had set out to find?

3 Now tell your partners about the text you read.

Betty

This experiment was carried out by the Zoology Department at Oxford University and set out to test the ability of Betty, a New Caledonian crow, to make simple tools.

A male and female crow were given a choice between a straight garden wire and a hook in order to lift a small bucket of food from the bottom of a plastic tube. After the male bird took the hook, Betty the female crow bent the tip of the straight wire to make a replacement. This was an amazing achievement as Betty had been kept in a laboratory for two years by the ecology research group and had never seen garden wire before.

In the next stage the birds were set the same challenge – to retrieve the bucket of food, but this time the researchers only provided straight wires. In nine out of ten trials, Betty bent the wire and pulled up the bucket. To bend the wire she sometimes stuck one end into sticky tape wrapped around the bottom of the tube or held it in her feet, then pulled the tip with her beak.

This species of crow is very skilful at making tools and often uses sticks and leaves in the wild. However, the fact that this bird had the ability to make the right implement for the job from unfamiliar materials, as this study proved, shows unheard of animal intelligence, say the researchers.

PROJECT DELPHIS

These studies were undertaken by Earthtrust, an international research and educational organisation, in Hawaii as part of Project Delphis. The main objective was to conduct scientific research in order to find evidence that dolphins are extremely self-aware. In addition, Earthtrust aims to raise global awareness about dolphins and to improve conservation efforts worldwide.

Although it has been well recorded that dolphins are large-brained social creatures, having the capacity for self-awareness is an even more revealing sign of intelligence. In the past only man and a few apes were thought to possess this faculty.

As with previous research carried out in this area on man and apes, self-awareness is measured by marking a subject, then observing the animal's reaction to a mirror-image – touching himself indicates self-awareness, whereas touching the mirror shows social behaviour suggesting the subject is investigating another individual.

Five bottlenose dolphins were 'marked' by putting zinc oxide on their sides and then their behaviour was videotaped through a one-way mirror. Control experiments were also conducted in order to:

A compare 'marked'/'unmarked' behaviour

B compare mirror behaviour to behaviour with a real stranger through a barred gate

C compare dolphins watching themselves on TV and in the mirror.

In the project the dolphins looked in the mirror then twisted and turned a lot revealing that they seemed to have seen the zinc oxide mark and therefore suggesting that they are self-aware. If this is the case, then such evidence provides a significant insight into animal intelligence as previously only man and apes had demonstrated the capacity for self-awareness.

Orang-utan Language Project

This research was undertaken as part of the Orang-utan Language Project at the Smithsonian National Zoological Park in New York which has been ongoing since 1995. The main purpose was to test the ability of orang-utans to communicate and the study was carried out by testing whether these creatures could remember abstract symbols and then use this system to accurately label objects. Unusually, the public could actually watch these observations take place at the zoo.

Computers with touch-sensitive screens were placed in the cages of Azy and his little sister Indah. Female orang-utans in particular are known to have good manual skills but the males tend to use their lips more. Objects were passed through the bars and when the creatures touched the screen, a particular symbol based on Arabic numerals would appear. Once a number of objects and their corresponding symbols had been introduced, more symbols were put up on the screen to increase the number of choices. Tests were then conducted on the animals to find out if they could make the correct selection and what their accuracy rate was. If they did choose the right symbol for an object, a bell rang and then rewards were given in the form of food or praise.

The results of the research show that orang-utans achieved 90% accuracy and therefore have the

ability to communicate by quickly relating abstract symbols to objects. In fact the animals have now progressed to using symbols to identify actions and they are now also using Arabic numerals to identify quantities.

Note completion

4 Now read all three passages and complete these notes about each passage. Choose NO MORE THAN THREE WORDS from the passages for each answer.

Text 1

Method used to conduct tests

The crows chose a hook or straight wire in order to **1** .... the container. After the male crow took the hook, the female bird (Betty) **2** .... the wire to make another one. Researchers gave Betty more straight wire.

She made a hook **3** .... times in ten tests.

She held the wire in her feet or put it in some **4** ....

Research findings

Crows are able to make appropriate tools from **5** .... not seen or used much, providing new evidence of animal intelligence.

Text 2

Method used to conduct tests

Zinc oxide was put on the sides of bottlenose dolphins and their behaviour was filmed through a **6** .... After looking in the mirror, the dolphins **7** .... ,suggesting they had noticed the **8** ....

Research findings

Dolphins, like **9** .... may be self-aware.

Text 3

Method used to conduct tests

Objects were passed into the orang-utans' cages and as they touched a computer screen a corresponding **10** .... would appear. They then learned which one matched which object. If they made the correct choice a **11** .... and they received **12** .... , which could be food or praise.

Research findings

Orang-utans showed the **13** .... by making connections between abstract symbols and objects.

---

5 Discuss the following questions in your groups.

– Did any of the research findings surprise you? Why/Why not?

– Do you think that how intelligent an animal is should affect how well we treat it? Why/Why not?

– How do you feel about experiments on animals to develop new products for humans? Does it make a difference if these are for new medicines or new cosmetics? Why?

Lexical links

1 Look back at the texts on pages 102 and 103. Replace each word below with another word in the text which has a similar meaning.

Text 1	Text 2	Text 3
tool (n)	*animal* (n)	*undertaken* (research) (v)
....	....	....
crow (n)	*capacity* (n)	*choice* (n)
....	....	....

2 Now look at this text. The first sentence of each paragraph is missing. Match the paragraphs and the sentences in the boxes. Then underline what lexical links helped you to do this task.

1 .... They can, and do, communicate with humans. There is a linguist chimp called Nim Chimpsky with a vocabulary of 125 signs, all used correctly. Chimps can solve problems, use tools and when they lose their teeth, even improvise a makeshift food blender. Two observers have now claimed to see chimps in the wild leaving each other 'notes'. Separate groups of chimpanzees have different ways of doing things, and pass these ways on through the generations: that is, chimpanzees have culture, just as humans have culture. In a word, they might be human. Morris Goodman, a geneticist at Wayne State University School of Medicine in Detroit, argues that chimpanzees should be included with humans in the same evolutionary grouping.

2 .... The evidence is in the DNA. Instead of comparing digits, or spinal structure, or the teeth, taxonomists – scientists who deal in evolutionary relationships – have now begun to consider the basic information of life, reproduction and development. Goodman and his colleagues report in their article that they compared 97 genes in six different species: humans, chimpanzees, gorillas, orang-utans, old world monkeys and mice. DNA is common to all life: the closer the DNA match, the closer the evolutionary link. Humans and chimps came out with a similarity of 99.4%. On the strength of this, Goodman says: think again, humans.

3 .... But at another level, he is raising an argument about human links with the rest of creation. Are humans a breed apart, with dominion over fish, flesh and fowl? Or are humans just gifted apes, lucky enough to have an edge over their nearest relatives? And if the latter, then what responsibilities do humans owe to their fellow creatures?

4 .... If apes were reclassified as human, would they then be entitled to human rights? And if apes were classified as human, would *Homo sapiens* be guilty of genocide?

A
At one level, he is reviving an argument about classification: what is it that makes animals alike, and different, and how do you logically group them?

B
Chimps have language.

C
So a small change in classification translates into a big one in moral attitudes.

D
The evidence is not in their capacity to stand upright or use computer touch screens.

IELTS Listening Section 4

1 Imagine you have been given a new machine to use. You have no idea how it works. How would you prefer to learn to use it?

A Read the instruction manual.

B Watch someone else using it.

C Attempt to do it without reading the instructions.

2 Compare your answer with others in your class. Do you prefer to learn in different ways? If you chose:

A You may learn best through words.

B You may learn best through visuals.

C You may learn best by doing.

Is this true for you?

Summary completion

Exam information
In Section 4 you will hear an academic type monologue, often a talk or lecture.

> **Strategy**
>
> Summary completion is similar to sentence completion, except that the gaps are within a paragraph summarizing the listening.
>
> Read the question carefully – usually you need to use no more than three words, but you might be asked to use a different number.
>
> Read the paragraph before you listen and think about the kind of information that is missing.
>
> Make sure your answers fit grammatically and are spelled correctly.

3 ⊙ 2.7 Listen to the talk and complete the summary below. Write NO MORE THAN THREE WORDS for each answer.

Linguistic intelligence

People with linguistic intelligence find it easy to communicate through (1) ....
They like writing and tend to think in words, not pictures.
They make good teachers, with the skills of explaining and (2) .... other people to agree with their viewpoint.
Jobs that these people might do include journalists, teachers, (3) .... politicians and writers.

Logical–Mathematical intelligence

These people find it easy to see patterns and are good at (4) .... between bits of information.
A (5) .... with this kind of intelligence is likely to become involved in science, computer programming, engineering, accounting or mathematics.

Interpersonal intelligence

These people understand how others feel and think and can (6) .... with other people.
They make good counsellors, salespeople, politicians and managers.

Intrapersonal intelligence

Often good researchers or philosophers, these people are able to understand their own feelings and are aware of their (7) ....

Visual–Spatial intelligence
People who like drawing and designing and have a good (8) ....
They can use charts and maps too.

Bodily–Kinaesthetic intelligence
Being good at dancing or athletics may indicate this is a strength. Gardner argues that skilful control over your body's movement is an intelligence, though others see these skills as something (9) ....

Musical intelligence
These people don't always (10) .... , but they are often good musicians or songwriters.

4 Discuss the following questions in pairs or small groups.
- Which intelligences do you think are strongest for you? Why?
- Does the job you do, or would like to do, reflect your intelligences?
- How do you think different intelligences might affect how people learn best?

Multiple choice

TIP
Read the question carefully to see how many answers are necessary.

5 ⊙ 2.8 Now listen to a later section of the same lecture. Here, the lecturer makes some suggestions about how people with strengths in each intelligence can study more effectively.
Circle the TWO activities he suggests for each intelligence.

1 Linguistic intelligence
   A writing
   B group discussions
   C reading
   D giving lectures
   E memorizing facts

2 Visual–Spatial intelligence
   A using word maps
   B looking at paintings
   C problem solving
   D watching videos
   E reading

3 Musical intelligence
   A tapping out rhythms
   B listening to background music
   C playing instruments
   D learning through song lyrics
   E writing music

6 Which of the following would you like in your ideal classroom? Discuss in pairs or small groups.
- lots of conversation and discussion
- music playing
- peace and quiet
- pictures on the walls
- the chance to move about whenever you want
- the latest technology

-ing form and infinitive

See *Grammar and vocabulary bank* on page 157.

1 Complete these statements with the correct form of the verb in brackets.

  0 I enjoy (make) things with my hands. *I enjoy making ...*

  1 I love (visit) art galleries. _____

  2 I dislike (work) alone. _____

  3 I appreciate (spend) time alone. _____

  4 Before I use it, I need (understand) how something works.

  _____

  5 I like (learn) the words of songs. _____

  6 I would like (speak) several foreign languages. _____

2 Which intelligences do you think the statements represent?

3 Some verbs are followed by an infinitive, some by an *-ing* form and some are followed by both. Put the examples from exercise 1 into the table.

Followed by *-ing*	Followed by infinitive	Followed by both *-ing* and infinitive
enjoy		

4 Complete these sentences. Which form do they take? Why?

  1 I learn by (do). _____

  2 I am actively interested in (make) the world a better place. _____

  3 I'm keen on (write). _____

5 Now put the verbs in the box into the same table. Use your dictionary if necessary.

> agree   avoid   begin   consider   decide   fail   forget
> hope   imagine   involve   mind   promise   practise
> refuse   remember   stop   try   want   wish

6 If either the *-ing* form or the infinitive may be used, there is usually a difference in meaning.
Look at these examples and answer the questions.

  a *I like watching music videos.*

  b *I like to learn more about myself.*

  1 Which sentence is about enjoying something?

  2 Which sentence suggests that something is a worthwhile thing to do?

  c *I tried to open the window.*

  d *Try opening the window.*

  3 Which sentence is a suggestion?

  4 Which sentence suggests effort or difficulty?

  e *I stopped to talk to him.*

  f *I stopped talking to him.*

  5 In which sentence am I now avoiding him?

  6 In which sentence did I stop doing something else in order to talk?

  g *I remember telling him.*

  h *I remembered to tell him.*

  7 Which sentence is about a memory?

  8 Which sentence is about remembering something before you do it?

TIP

The distinction between *like* + infinitive and *like* + *-ing* is true in British English, but not in American English where both could be used to suggest enjoyment.

7 Complete this text about learning with the correct form of the verb.

> Being a student involves (1) .... (take) responsibility for
> (2) .... (organize) your own time. Therefore you need
> (3) .... (learn) about planning your time and workload
> effectively. You can learn to do this through practice and through
> stopping (4) .... (think) about what works or doesn't work
> for you. Try (5) .... (set) yourself goals and targets, and
> give yourself small rewards. Don't try (6) .... (do) too
> much at once – have regular breaks. If you fail (7) ....
> (finish) a piece of work as quickly as you expected, don't feel bad, just
> be more realistic in your planning next time. If you find that you avoid
> even (8) .... (start) work, stop (9) .... (make)
> excuses and start today! You will feel much better once you do.

Vocabulary

Expressions to describe skills

1 Complete the words and phrases using words from the boxes.

aptitude	common	natural	practical

To have ...
1 a/an .... talent for .... skills
2 .... sense
3 a/an .... for

all rounder	good	high	highly	quick	uptake

To be ...
4 a/an .... learner
5 .... qualified
6 a/an .... achiever
7 .... with your hands
8 quick on the ....
9 a/an good ....

deep	pick	step	steep

Expressions
10 a .... learning curve
11 thrown in at the .... end
12 .... something up quickly
13 take it one .... at a time

2 ⊙ 2.9 Listen to Josie talking about when she learned to drive.
1 Was she successful? Why/Why not?
2 Listen again and tick any of the words and phrases in exercise 1 that you hear Josie use.

See *Grammar and vocabulary bank* on page 157 for practice in word formation.

IELTS Speaking Part 2

1 Look at the question below. Think about the question for one minute and make notes if you wish.

2 Work in pairs. Take turns to talk about the question for two minutes. Try to use some of the vocabulary on this page.

Part 2

Describe a time when you learned something new.

You should say:
– what you learned to do
– where you did it and/or who you did it with
– why you did it

and describe how successful you were, explaining why.

IELTS Speaking Part 3

3 In pairs or small groups, ask and answer the following questions. Try to use some of the vocabulary on pages 108–9.

What kind of environment helps you learn best? Do you like to listen to music while studying, for example?

Do you believe that academic achievement is the best way to measure someone's intelligence? Why/Why not?

What other kinds of intelligence can people have? Give examples.

What do you think has more impact on a child's education – family background or what happens at school? Why?

IELTS Writing Task 2: Organization and coherence: paragraphing

1 Read this Task 2 question and underline the key words in the statement. Which of the following should be included in this essay?

   a a discussion of some different ways in which a person might be considered intelligent

   b a discussion of academic achievement only

Present a written argument or case to an educated reader with no specialist knowledge of the following topic.

Academic achievement at school or university is the only true measure of a person's intelligence.

To what extent do you agree with this statement?

2 Look back at the question, then read the three introductions below and decide which is best. Why is it more suitable than the other two?

Introduction 1
Academic achievement at school or university means passing exams such as A levels or getting a Degree or Masters. There is no doubt that you need to be clever to do this.

Introduction 2
Many people believe that academic achievement at school or university is the only true measure of a person's intelligence. However, there are two sides to this statement and other people would disagree with this view.

Introduction 3
There is no doubt that people are often judged in terms of their educational success. People need to pass exams to go to university and study for a degree and the majority of jobs and careers require these types of qualifications. However, this is surely not the only way to assess intelligence.

3 What words does the best introduction use to paraphrase the question?

> **Strategy**
> A good introduction will include clear, relevant information about the topic but should not repeat the question word for word. It can also include the view of the writer which will be developed later in the essay.

4 Look at the two possible topic sentences for paragraphs 2 and 3. For each topic sentence think of some supporting ideas and examples and use them to write your own paragraph.

> **Paragraph 2**
> *There are many people who leave school at the age of 16 yet go on to have successful careers in more practical jobs.*
>
> **Paragraph 3**
> *It cannot be denied that creative or artistic ability is another form of intelligence.*

5 Now read a possible paragraph 4 and answer the questions.

> *A final example of another aspect of intelligence is knowledge, which people often acquire through self-study or experience. They may not have done well at school or university but have become 'educated' by learning about a subject independently or by dealing with a variety of real-life situations and problems. Indeed, there are many highly qualified, successful people who often lack 'common sense' and who would be less able to cope with such difficulties.*

TIP
Good writers show links between paragraphs in an essay and within a paragraph. This is shown by reference or lexical links.

   1 Which phrase introduces a further type of intelligence, and thus provides a link with the previous paragraphs? (sentence 1) ....

   2 Which word refers back to *people* in sentence 1? (sentence 2) ....

   3 Which words refer back to *self-study* in sentence 1? (sentence 2) ....

   4 Which words refer back to *experience* in sentence 1? (sentence 2) ....

   5 Which words refer back to *problems* in sentence 2? (sentence 3) ....

6 Do you think that this essay will conclude by agreeing with the statement in the question? Why/Why not?

7 Now write a suitable conclusion for this essay. When you have finished, compare your answer with the model answer on page 163.

TIP
A good conclusion should summarize the main points and refer back to the introduction, giving the writer's final opinion.

8 Read this question and underline the key words.
Present a written argument or case to an educated reader with no specialist knowledge of the following topic.

Parents and family background have more influence than teachers on a young person's learning and academic achievement.

To what extent do you agree with this statement?

9 Look at this list of key arguments that agree or disagree with the statement and add your own ideas.

Agree
Intelligence seems to be inherited.
Children need to be motivated by their parents.

....

....

Disagree
As children get older, they are less likely to listen to their parents.
Teachers can be role models.

....

....

Useful language	
Introductions	**Conclusions**
It is true to say that ...	In conclusion, ...
There is no doubt that ...	To conclude, ...
In recent years ...	To sum up, ...
Many people consider ...	Overall, it is clear that ...

10 Choose 2–3 main arguments for the main paragraphs of your essay and think of any supporting ideas or examples.

11 Now write your essay, with an introduction and conclusion. When you have finished, compare your answer with the model answer on page 163.

Listening: Section 3

IELTS Listening Section 3: Note completion

⊙ **2.10** Listen to part of a tutorial discussion between a student and tutor (Dr Williams). As you listen, complete the notes, using NO MORE THAN THREE WORDS AND/OR A NUMBER.

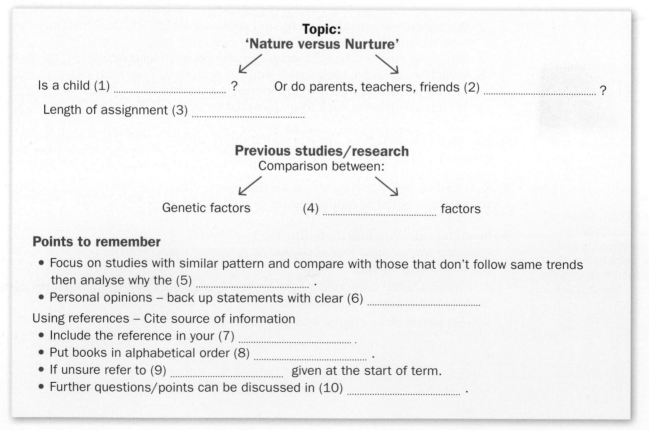

Topic:
'Nature versus Nurture'

Is a child (1) .... ?   Or do parents, teachers, friends (2) .... ?

Length of assignment (3) ....

Previous studies/research
Comparison between:

Genetic factors   (4) .... factors

Points to remember

• Focus on studies with similar pattern and compare with those that don't follow same trends then analyse why the (5) ....
• Personal opinions – back up statements with clear (6) ....

Using references – Cite source of information
• Include the reference in your (7) ....
• Put books in alphabetical order (8) ....
• If unsure refer to (9) .... given at the start of term.
• Further questions/points can be discussed in (10) ....

Hedging

1 What is the key difference between these two sentences?

    1 Many people believe that we inherit intelligence from our parents and it is often the case that children of gifted parents go on to repeat their parents' success at school.

    2 We inherit intelligence from our parents and the children of gifted parents go on to repeat their parents' success at school.

2 This feature of academic language is called 'hedging'. It is used to avoid being too direct or definite because:
- it is not always possible to be certain.
- it is more polite to be tentative.

    What other examples of hedging can you find in the sentences below?

    1 Sometimes, a teacher can have considerable influence over a child's future, inspiring them in a particular subject or possibly helping them to choose a career path.

    2 It appears that early childhood may be a key stage in a child's development.

3 Using your examples, make a list of different ways of hedging. Then compare your list with the one in the *Grammar and vocabulary bank* on page 157.

4 Rewrite the following sentences to be more tentative, using some hedging devices.

    1 Teachers have a particularly important role to play if a child lacks support from home due to emotional or financial difficulties which have a negative effect on their learning.

    ....

    ....

    2 It is possible for a child to succeed academically, even without the help of a supportive family.

    ....

    ....

Idioms

5 Complete the following idiomatic phrases with either *brain* or *mind*. Use the *Macmillan Collocations Dictionary* to check your ideas.

    1 You know a lot about this area, don't you? Can I just pick your .... ?

    2 Stop looking out of the window! Keep your .... on your work!

    3 The magician was amazing. He seemed to be able to read my ....

    4 Come on, it isn't that difficult to work out. Use your .... !

    5 Even if you think you won't enjoy it, go with an open .... rather than deciding now.

    6 No matter how hard I racked my ...., I just couldn't remember the answer.

10 Leisure time

Leisure activities

1 Look at the list of leisure activities and put them in order from those you do most often, to those you do least often. Then compare your answers in pairs or small groups.

arts and crafts	DIY	listening to music	playing computer games
reading	shopping	spending time with friends and family	
sport or exercise	using the internet	watching TV	

2 Now compare your answers with the results of a survey into leisure activities. How similar are your answers?

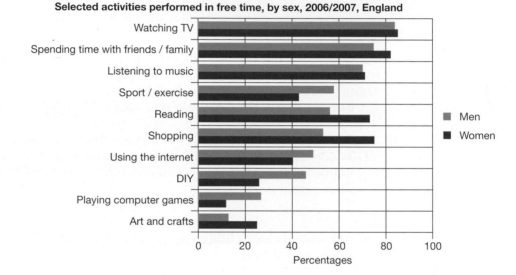

Selected activities performed in free time, by sex, 2006/2007, England

- Watching TV
- Spending time with friends / family
- Listening to music
- Sport / exercise
- Reading
- Shopping
- Using the internet
- DIY
- Playing computer games
- Art and crafts

■ Men
■ Women

Percentages

3 What differences do you notice between men and women? Do the same differences exist in your class?

4 Now look at the second bar graph. Which of these activities do you take part in? Which are popular in your country?

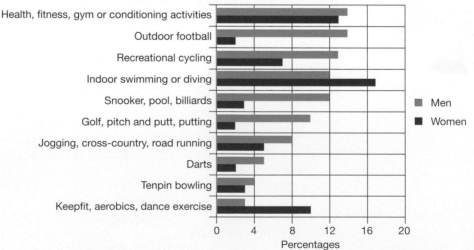

Selected sports, games and physical activities among adults, by sex 2006/2007

- Health, fitness, gym or conditioning activities
- Outdoor football
- Recreational cycling
- Indoor swimming or diving
- Snooker, pool, billiards
- Golf, pitch and putt, putting
- Jogging, cross-country, road running
- Darts
- Tenpin bowling
- Keepfit, aerobics, dance exercise

■ Men
■ Women

Percentages

5 Match the equipment in the box below to the activities in the second chart.

ball	board	club	cue	goggles	helmet	table	trainers	weights

6 What equipment do you need for the sporting or physical activities you take part in?

7 Which of the adjectives in the box would you use to describe any of the activities in either chart? Explain why.

a waste of time	enjoyable	entertaining	exciting	exhilarating
pointless	relaxing	rewarding	time-consuming	worthwhile

Listening

IELTS Listening Section 1: Form completion

1 Work in pairs. Discuss the following questions.
– Have you ever joined a gym? Why/Why not?
– What kind of activities can you do at a gym?

2 Look at the form below and decide what kind of answers you are looking for.

3 ⊙ 2.11 Now listen and complete the form below. Write NO MORE THAN THREE WORDS AND/OR A NUMBER.

> **Fitness Fanatics Health Club**
> **Gym Assessment Form**
> Name: Julie Ann Edmonson
> Age: (1) .... Contact number: 0798 674 5689.
> *(NB Best time to contact: between 6 and (2) .... pm)*
> Current level of exercise
> *Walks* (3) .... *steps most days.*
> *Current job involves a lot of* (4) ....
> **Exercise goals**
> (5) .... *maintenance and* (6) .... *exercise*
> *Plans to visit gym* (7) ....
> **Exercise classes suggested**
> *Zumba – on* (8) .... *at 6.30pm.*
> *Aqua aerobics- on Thursday at* (9) ....
> **Appointment for gym induction**
> Friday 24/5 at 7pm with (10) ....

Language focus

Expressing preferences

1 Look at the following extracts from the listening and choose the correct form. Listen again to check your answers.
1 Would you like *to lose/lose/losing* weight, or just get fitter?
2 I'm quite happy with my weight, but I'd like *to keep/keep/keeping* it this way.
3 Would you rather just *to use/use/using* the gym?
4 I'm not great at dancing, really, I prefer *to swim/swim/swimming*.
5 I'd rather *to come/come/coming* on Friday if that's possible?
6 I think I'd prefer *to have/have/having* a female trainer actually.

2 Look at the *Grammar and vocabulary bank* on page 157 to check you understand the rules, then complete the following sentences with the correct form of the verb.
1 Generally, I prefer .... (watch) television to .... (listen) to music.
2 John would like .... (play) tennis tomorrow, but Maia would rather .... (play) badminton.
3 I'd prefer not .... (stay) out too late tonight, I'm a bit tired.
4 What would you rather .... (do)? Go for a meal, or to the cinema?
5 I'd love .... (go) to that new Italian restaurant.
6 I'd rather you didn't .... (say) that.

1 Work in pairs. Discuss the first sentence of this text.

In 1930 the economist John Maynard Keynes predicted that by 2030 many of us would only be working for 15 hours a week, spending the rest of our time in leisure pursuits.

- Do you think this is likely to come true? Why/Why not?
- Do you think we are working harder now than in the past? Why/Why not?
- Do you think we have more or less leisure time now than in the past? Why/Why not?
  Do you think this varies depending on different parts of the world

2 Now read the rest of the text. Does the writer agree with Keynes' predictions?

Less time in the office but more time at work?

In 1930 the economist John Maynard Keynes predicted that by 2030 many of us would only be working for 15 hours a week, spending the rest of our time in leisure pursuits. In fact, the number of hours people work is likely to continue rising, with more European countries following the American model of a longer working week and fewer holidays. We may spend less time in the office in future, but mobile technology means that we will be expected to work on the train on the way to work, at home while we prepare an evening meal and even in bed.

However, perhaps surprisingly, it seems that we do in fact have a little more leisure time than 40 years ago, as a result of washing machines, online grocery shopping and so on. Of course, we also have to work harder to afford these labour saving devices!

Although we actually have more leisure time, most people believe the opposite to be true. This may be because we are trying to fit in so many more activities. Twenty years ago women participated in around six different leisure pursuits a year, today it's ten. There are more options around now, and people are more aware of them as globalization makes the world a smaller place. For example, experts anticipate a further growth in westerners becoming interested in more typically eastern pursuits such as Tai Chi, Yoga and Meditation.

Interestingly, it seems that people are spending relatively less on material goods and more on experiences. Rather than buying an expensive new car, people would rather spend the money on a weekend away in Paris, a cookery course, dance classes or a 'pampering' day at a beauty spa. There is a trend away from one holiday a year towards a number of shorter breaks, often long weekends. This pattern could, of course, reverse if current fuel subsidies are reduced making flying less affordable.

Shopping centres have recognized the trend towards experiences and increasingly you will find cinemas and restaurants in the mall, as well as shops. They now aim to provide a family day out rather than just a collection of shops. Westfield Stratford City in London, which opened on 13 September 2011, reflects this trend, and stated on its development website that 'Art and culture will be integral to the experience – from the striking architecture of individual retail districts and new retail concepts to cultural collaborations, events and installations that will enhance the next generation of retail space.'

The chart on the next page (Fig A) demonstrates the overall rise in spending over the last three decades, but also shows that spending on experiences continues to be in excess of spending on material goods. Experts predict this pattern continuing for the foreseeable future, notwithstanding global economic issues.

In fact, there is a theory that society is climbing towards the top of Maslow's hierarchy of needs. (Fig B). Having achieved our more basic needs, such as food, shelter and clothing, at the bottom of the pyramid, we now hope to achieve self-actualization at the top of the pyramid.

Another recent study showed the number of people choosing personal fulfilment as their number one wish more than doubled between 1986 and 2004 (Fig C). It seems that as we live longer we are all asking ourselves just how we can get the most out of life.

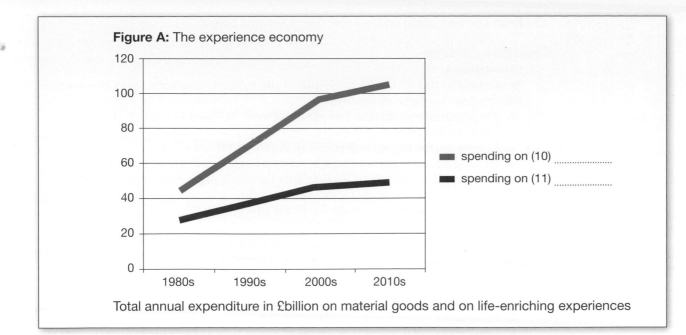

Figure A: The experience economy

spending on (10) ....

spending on (11) ....

Total annual expenditure in £billion on material goods and on life-enriching experiences

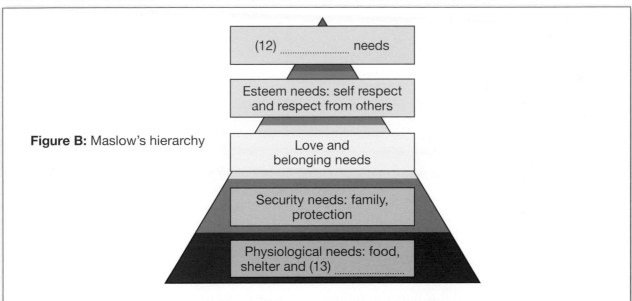

Figure B: Maslow's hierarchy

(12) .... needs

Esteem needs: self respect and respect from others

Love and belonging needs

Security needs: family, protection

Physiological needs: food, shelter and (13) ....

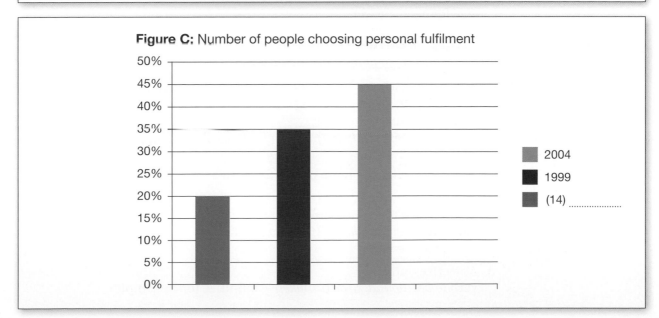

Figure C: Number of people choosing personal fulfilment

2004

1999

(14) ....

3 Read the text again and answer the questions below.

Multiple choice

Questions 1–3

According to the text, which THREE of the following factors affect the amount of leisure time we have nowadays?

A Technology means that people don't need to spend so much time on household tasks.

B People spend more time commuting to and from work.

C Globalization is increasing the pressure on people to work harder.

D Employers expect us to be available for work outside working hours.

E We have fewer days off work over the year.

F People are tending to sleep for fewer hours.

Summary completion

Questions 4–9

Complete the summary using the list of words A–Q below.

A family	**G** shopping	**M** security
B activities	**H** shopper	**N** increasing
C labour saving devices	**I** food	**O** longer
D fuel	**J** foreign	**P** developing
E shorter	**K** tourist	**Q** clothing
F cultural	**L** reducing	

Apparently, people are (4) .... the amount that they spend on material goods, choosing instead to spend the money on (5) .... Rather than taking one (6) .... holiday a year, people are tending to go away for long weekends. However, this trend is dependent on the price of (7) .... remaining subsidized.

Following the same trend, shopping malls look to provide an experience for the (8) .... , with cinemas and restaurants under the same roof and newer malls, such as the new Westfield Stratford City shopping centre, are now aiming to provide a space for (9) .... events as well as retail.

Labelling a diagram

Questions 10–14

Label the diagrams on page 117 with NO MORE THAN TWO WORDS from the passage for each answer.

Language focus

Expressions with future meaning

See *Grammar and vocabulary bank* on page 158.

1 Look at the following ways of talking about the future, then find examples in the text on page 116.

1 Verbs with future meaning
aim/decide/expect/hope/plan + infinitive (three examples)

....

anticipate/predict + noun or *-ing* form (two examples)

....

2 Modal verbs to express probability
may/might/could/should (three examples)

....

3 Adjectives/adverbs
verb *to be+ bound/sure/(un)likely* + infinitive (one example)

....

2 Rewrite the following predictions using some of the future expressions above, depending on how likely *you* think they are.

0 In ten years' time more people will work from home.

In ten years' time I anticipate more people working from home.

Do you? I think most people are unlikely to stop going into work. It will only be possible for certain kinds of jobs, won't it?

1 In the future we will have more leisure time.

....

....

2 Within a few years we will do all our shopping online.

....

....

3 By the cnd of the century people will be living on another planet.

....

....

4 In a few years we will pay for everything by mobile phone.

....

....

Vocabulary

The Internet

1 Look at the words and phrases in the box and use them to complete the word map.

| blog | chatting | instant messaging (IM) | laptop | mouse | screen |
| smartphone | | social networking site | tablet | texting | webpage |

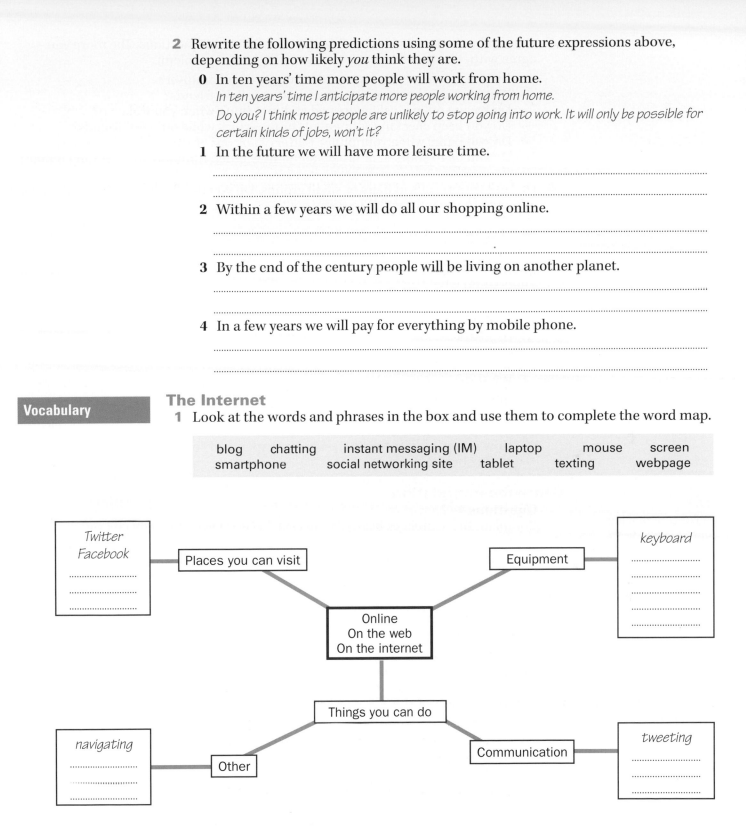

2 Add any other words and phrases that might be useful.

3 Are you hooked on technology? Answer the following questions. The more you agree with, the more likely it is that you may have a problem!

- Do you go online when you are feeling stressed or upset?
- Would you rather go online than read or talk to friends?
- Do you go online just before bed and first thing when you wake up?
- Do you keep checking your emails or messages while out with friends?
- Do you panic when your phone battery runs out or you can't get a signal?
- Do you lie to yourself or others about how much time you are spending online?

4 Discuss your results in pairs or small groups. Do you think it is really possible to be addicted to the internet? Why/Why not?

Listening

IELTS Listening Section 3

1 You are going to listen to Rob and Julie talking about internet addiction in a seminar with their tutor. Read the questions below before you listen and check you understand what you have to do.

Short answer questions

Questions 1–3

🔊 2.12 Listen and answer the questions below. Write NO MORE THAN TWO WORDS AND/OR A NUMBER for each answer.

1 What percentage of the secondary school students in the survey spent more than six hours a day online? ....

2 How old were most of the students when they were given their first computer?
....

3 How many hours a day do the students spend on social networking sites such as Facebook? ....

Sentence completion

Questions 4–7

Complete the sentences below. Write ONE WORD ONLY for each answer.

4 Heavy internet users tend to eat .... food.

5 Teenagers need to get enough sleep or it can affect their ....

6 You could also develop poor .... as a result of consuming too much caffeine.

7 A recent road accident was caused by someone .... a webpage.

> **TIP**
> Make sure that the word(s) you use to complete the sentence make grammatical sense and are taken straight from the listening, with no changes to the form of the word.

Matching

Questions 8–10

🔊 2.13 Listen to the second part. Which opinion does each person express about the internet? Choose your answers from the box and write the correct letter (A–F) next to questions 8–10.

> **A** Texting is having a negative impact on student's written English.
> **B** Students need to be taught how to use the internet for research.
> **C** Playing games online can be educational.
> **D** Copying things from the internet is plagiarism.
> **E** Social networking sites are harmless.
> **F** People should be banned from using the internet while driving.

8 Julie ....
9 The tutor ....
10 Rob ....

2 Which of the statements in exercise 1 do you agree or disagree with? Explain why.

3 Listen again. Which of the computer-related words in the word map on page 119 do you hear being used?

Part 2

1 🔘 2.14 Listen to Ravi in Part 2 of a Speaking exam answering question A below. Make notes about the key points he makes.

> **Part 2**
>
> **A** Describe a leisure activity which you enjoy doing.
>
> You should say:
> – what the activity is and how you do it
> – when and how often you do it
> – what equipment you need
>
> and explain why you enjoy it.

> **Part 2**
>
> **B** Describe a leisure activity which is popular in your country.
>
> You should say:
> – what kind of activity it is
> – what kind of people tend to do it
> – what equipment is needed
>
> and explain why you think it is popular.

2 Work in pairs. Choose one question each and prepare your own answer. Talk to your partner for 1–2 minutes.

3 With your partner, discuss the following question.
Do you think that people have more or less time for leisure now than in the past?

Part 3

4 🔘 2.15 Now listen to Ravi speaking on the same topic in Part 3 of his speaking exam. Which of the phrases in the box does he use?

as an example	for example	for instance
look at	for one thing	take

5 In the same pairs take it in turns to answer the following questions. Try to give examples to support what you are saying.

A Have leisure activities changed from when you were a child? How?
Do you think this change has been positive? Why/Why not?

B Do you think that people are more motivated to do leisure activities alone or with others? Why?

Do you think that people who are interested in the same sort of leisure activities are likely to get on well together? Why/Why not?

IELTS Writing Task 2: Describing problems and solutions

1 Look at the following Task 2 question and underline the key words.

Write about the following topic.

Cyberbullying, where new technologies such as the internet or mobile phones are used to bully and harass young people, is on the increase. Explain the causes and effects of this problem and suggest some possible solutions for individuals and schools.

Give reasons for your answer and include any relevant examples from your own knowledge or experience.

2 Read the following sample essay and find the paragraphs which deal with:
   – the causes of cyberbullying
   – the effects of cyberbullying
   – some possible solutions for individuals
   – some possible solutions for schools

1 *These days most people have access to the internet at home, and increasingly out and about, using smartphones and other mobile technology. While this has obvious advantages, it has also led to a growth in cyberbullying.*

2 *Whereas once bullying was confined to school or the way home from school, now bullies can attack at any time of the day or night, sending unpleasant messages or posting photographs of their victims on blogs and websites. In the past a bully might have told a dozen people your secret; now they can tell thousands. In a recent case, a boy who had made a silly video of himself found that the video had been posted on the internet by his classmates. Millions downloaded it and the embarrassment that resulted from this caused the boy to need psychiatric help.*

3 *The issue of cyberbullying is not going to go away, but there are some things which can be done to help tackle it. Firstly, individuals should try not to respond. A bully is always looking for a response, and if he or she doesn't get one, they may lose interest. However this does not mean that the victim should ignore what is happening. It is always a good idea to tell someone about what is happening so that they can support you if the bullying gets worse. Schools should also play their part. Anti-bullying policies in schools should include cyberbullying and all students should be aware of what this means and that it is unacceptable. If any bullying does occur the school should deal with it as strictly as any other kind of bullying.*

4 *In conclusion, cyberbullying is a serious problem and needs to be taken seriously by everyone involved.*

3 This kind of essay is a 'problem–solution' type essay, where a problem is explored and solutions offered. Read the essay again and list the problems (causes and effects) and solutions in the box below.

Problems	Solutions
Causes	
Effects	

4 Look at the *Useful language* box. Which of these expressions can you find in the essay opposite?

5 Rewrite the phrases in **bold** using words and phrases from the box.

1 The growth in mobile technology has **led to** more cyberbullying.

The growth ....

2 The embarrassment **caused** the boy to need psychiatric help.

As ....

3 The embarrassment that resulted from this **caused** the boy to need psychiatric help.

The embarrassment ....

4 The boy whose video was put online needed psychiatric help **because of** his embarrassment.

As ....

6 Now look at the following Writing Part 2 question. Make a list of problems and solutions in the same way you did with the first essay, but now using your own ideas.

Write about the following topic.

Research indicates that young people spend so much time watching television or going online that it is affecting their health. Explain the causes and effects of this problem and suggest some possible solutions.

Give reasons for your answer and include any relevant examples from your own knowledge or experience.

Problems	Solutions
Causes	
Effects	

7 Write a plan, using the following framework if helpful.
- Introduction: state the problem you are going to discuss in your own words.
- Causes of the problem.
- Effects of the problem (these two may be separate or in the same paragraph).
- Solutions for the individuals.
- Solutions for the wider society.
- Conclusion: summing up your main point.

8 Now write the first draft of your essay.

9 Read the sample answer and answer these questions.
   1 What does the writer think are the *causes* of the situation? Which paragraph?
   2 What does the writer think are the *effects* of the situation? Which paragraph?
   3 What does the writer think are the *solutions* of the situation? Which paragraph?

Young people are spending more and more of their time watching television or on the internet and research suggests that this is having a negative effect on their health. In this essay I would like to consider what may have led to this situation and look at some possible solutions.

Probably the largest factor is the huge increase in the amount of time that people are spending on the web. Almost everyone has access to the internet and people are now using it not just to send emails or research information, but to socialize on websites such as Twitter and Facebook and to shop. Another factor affecting younger children is that parents tend to be more worried about letting them play unsupervised and prefer to have their children stay at home.

However, spending so much time watching TV or on the internet means that children and young people are simply not getting enough exercise. This leads to greater levels of obesity and can cause diabetes and other health problems.

Parents and schools have a responsibility to make sure that young people are being encouraged to take enough exercise. Part of any young person's free time should be spent walking, dancing, cycling or playing sports and these activities need to be made as attractive as time spent online. More youth groups should be set up where young people can socialize and take part in healthier activities.

In conclusion, I believe that young people often spend too much time online because they don't feel that there are any interesting alternatives. If these alternatives were provided, we might see a change in behaviour and an improvement in their health.

10 Compare the sample answer with your first draft. Rewrite your answer, using the following checklist.
   – Check that the structure of your draft follows the pattern given.
   – Check for correct grammar and spelling.
   – Include any other useful ideas or phrases you found in the sample answer.

See *Grammar and vocabulary bank* on page 158 for synonyms you can use in your essay.

Negative prefixes

1 How do you know that all these words are negative?

impossible	inconceivable	unlikely

TIP
Understanding the meaning of prefixes can help you guess the meaning of new words.

2 Look at the table below. Write the prefixes next to their meanings and add an example for each.

anti-	dis-	il-	micro-	mis-	pre-	re-	trans-

	not, or to reverse an action	
	again or back	
	across	
	against	
	wrong or badly	
	not (with some words beginning with l)	illegal
	before	
	small	

3 These prefixes indicate a number. Write them in the correct box.

bi-	dec-	mono-	quadri-	tri-	uni-

1	2	3	4	10
mono				

4 Complete the sentences using the adjective in brackets plus an appropriate prefix.
   1 It appears that the politician was .... and lied about what he had done. (honest)
   2 Sorry, but that point is completely .... to what we are talking about. (relevant)
   3 If children .... , they should be told off. (behave)
   4 I don't like him much because he's so .... (polite)
   5 Stealing is simply .... (moral)
   6 I am .... what to do now. (certain)

5 Guess the meanings of these words. Then check your answers in a dictionary.
   1 unicycle   *like a bicycle with only one wheel* ....
   2 mismanage   ....
   3 microbiology ....
   4 monorail   ....
   5 prepackaged ....
   6 transnational ....
   7 monochrome   ....
   8 microfilm   ....
   9 misjudge   ....
   10 quad bike   ....

Reading

1 Look at the word cloud above. A word cloud is made from all the words in a text. The more often a word appears in a text, the bigger it is in the word cloud. The text you are going to read includes all these words.
– **Which words are the biggest?**
– **Why do you think different is the biggest word?**

2 Now read the text and answer questions 1–13. You should spend about 20 minutes on this task.

The Global Product – the world as a single market

A For businesses, the world is becoming a smaller place. Travel and transportation are becoming quicker and easier, communications can be instantaneous to any part of the world and trade barriers are breaking down. Consequently, there are tremendous opportunities for businesses to broaden their markets into foreign countries. The challenge facing those promoting products globally is to determine whether marketing methods should be the same across the world or if they should be adapted to different markets based on specific cultural factors.

B Many theorists argue that, with the 'shrinking' of the world, global standardization is inevitable. Over time, and as economies develop, it has been suggested that consumer buying patterns will blend into one another and national differences may disappear. Kellogg, the American breakfast cereal producer, has been very influential in challenging consumption patterns in countries outside the United States. In France, for example, breakfast cereals were almost unheard of, and market research suggested that the market was closed to companies like Kellogg. However, today, there is a demand for breakfast cereals across

France. Nevertheless, the standardization of products for worldwide consumption in this way is rarely the most effective strategy as is evident from an analysis of the following key aspects of global marketing.

C First of all, it is considered better business practice by many large, established companies to change their products from one country to the next. Take the example of Coca-Cola®. The recipe for this drink is changed to suit local tastes – the brand in the US is much sweeter than in the UK, whilst in India the product's herbs and flavourings are given more emphasis. In terms of the car industry, it would be too expensive for manufacturers to develop and build completely different vehicles for different markets yet a single, global model is likely to appeal to no one. In response to varying needs, Nissan, for example, sells in 75 different markets, but has eight different chassis designs. The Ford Mondeo was designed with key features from different markets in mind in an effort to make its appeal as broad as possible. The best policy, as far as most multi-national companies are concerned, is to adapt their product to a particular market.

D Secondly, it is important to consider whether a product should be launched simultaneously in all countries (known as a 'sprinkler launch') or sequentially in one market after another (a 'waterfall launch'). In practice, most companies producing consumer goods tend to launch a new product in one or two markets at a time rather than attempt to launch a product across a range of countries at a single time. Many high-tech products such as Blu-ray™ players reach the market in Japan before reaching the UK. Hollywood films are often seen in the United States weeks or months before they arrive in other countries.

E The advantage for firms is that it is easier to launch in one market at a time. Effort and concentration can be focused to ensure the best possible entry into the market. Moreover, for technical products especially, any initial problems become apparent in a single market and can be corrected prior to launch elsewhere. Even though this method can be time-consuming, it is usually a safer approach than a simultaneous launch. Despite this, in certain highly competitive markets such as computer chips, companies such as Intel® tend to launch their new products internationally at the same time to keep the product ahead of its competitors.

F The final consideration when planning to enter a global market, rather than assuming the product will suit all markets, is to take cultural differences into account. Prices have to be converted to a different currency and any literature has to be translated into a different language. There are also less tangible differences. It is quite possible that common practices in one country can cause offence and have grave consequences for business success in another. In one situation in China, a Western businessman caused offence to a group of local delegates because he started to fill out the paperwork immediately after shaking hands on a deal. Completing the legal documents so soon after the negotiations was regarded as undermining the hosts' trust. Knowledge about such cultural differences is absolutely vital.

G Therefore, if a company is attempting to broaden its operations globally, it must take the time to find out about local customs and methods of business operation. Equally important is to ensure that such information is available to all necessary workers in the organization. For example, in order to attempt to avoid causing offence to passengers from abroad, British Airways aims to raise awareness of cultural differences amongst all its cabin crew.

H It can be concluded that global standardization of products to 'fit' all markets is unlikely to be the most viable option. Marketing methods employed will depend on many factors, such as the type of product, the degree of competition, the reputation of the firm and/or the brand, the state of the economy into which the product is to be launched and how and when to launch. In short, the key to marketing success on a global level is to have sufficient information on how cultural differences are likely to affect the marketing of a product and then allow the appropriate decisions to be made.

Matching headings to paragraphs

Questions 1–7

Choose the most suitable headings for paragraphs B–H from the list of headings below. There are more headings than paragraphs so you will not use all of them. The first has been done as an example.

List of headings	
i	Launching a new soft drink product
ii	The main benefits of the single market launch
iii	Researching cultural differences and providing information
iv	The lack of cultural differences in the world today
v	Examples of launching a product in one market at a time
vi	The emergence of global marketing and its challenges
vii	The world as a single market: a successful case
viii	Specific cultural differences to consider
ix	Different markets, adapted products
x	Success in the global market – key factors

0	Paragraph A	*vi*	4	Paragraph E ....
1	Paragraph B		5	Paragraph F ....
2	Paragraph C		6	Paragraph G ....
3	Paragraph D		7	Paragraph H ....

Note completion
Questions 8–11
Using the information in the passage complete the notes using NO MORE THAN THREE WORDS.

Global marketing

World getting smaller – chance for businesses to 8 .... globally. Companies treating world as single market with standardized product not always appropriate.

Therefore, factors to take into account:

A. Adapt the product to specific markets
eg Coca-Cola®, 9 .... , Ford (Mondeo)

B. Compare different ways to launch the product
10 .... launch or 'Waterfall' launch
All countries at same time   One or two countries after another
Example: Intel®   Example: DVD players and
*   11 .... movies.*

C. Consider cultural differences
Acquire knowledge and raise awareness about common business practices and local customs.

Multiple choice
Questions 12–13
Choose the appropriate letters A–D.

12 According to the writer
- **A** all types of company adapt their products to different markets.
- **B** having the same product for different markets can never be successful.
- **C** car manufacturers are unlikely to develop totally different models for different parts of the world.
- **D** it is better to launch a product in different markets at the same time.

13 The writer concludes that
- **A** marketing strategies depend mainly on the product type.
- **B** successful promotion of a product depends on being informed about cultural differences.
- **C** the launch of a product is not particularly significant.
- **D** companies can gain global success by setting up offices all over the world.

Formal and academic language

The language in this article is quite formal and academic. Look at the text again and find a more formal word or phrase that means the same as the more informal words and phrases given below.

1 decide (para A) ....
2 trying to sell (para A) ....
3 as we can see ... (para B) ....
4 to get as many people to like the product as they can (para C) ....
5 at the same time ... (para D) ....
6 before (para E) ....
7 serious (para F) ....
8 trying to sell its products around the world (para G) ....
9 the best choice (para H) ....

1 Look at the following nouns related to the topic of advertising and match them to their definitions.

1 brand		A	a design that is the official sign or a company or organization
2 logo		B	an advertisement on television or radio
3 slogan		C	a product that a particular company makes
4 billboard		D	a short phrase that is easy to remember, used in advertising or politics
5 commercial		E	the process of people telling each other about something
6 jingle		F	a big sign next to a road used to advertise something
7 word of mouth		G	a short song used in radio or television advertisements

IELTS Speaking Part 2

2 Look at the following question and make some notes of key points. Consider what advertising related vocabulary you could use. Then talk about it to your partner for 1–2 minutes.

Part 2

Describe a memorable advertisement.

You should say:
– what the advertisement was for
– how the advertisement tried to market the product
– whether you thought it was effective or not

and explain why you found it memorable.

IELTS Speaking Part 3

3 Now take it in turns to answer one of the following pairs of questions.
– What factors do you consider makes an advert particularly effective?
– Do you think that people are less easily taken in by advertising these days? Why/Why not?

– Why do you think that certain brands become successful worldwide?
– Do you think that there should be rules and restrictions on advertising? Why/Why not?

Reading

1 Look at the cartoons. How are the people in them trying to encourage or persuade others to buy something?.

2 Read the definitions below. Do you think that these cartoons are examples of guerrilla marketing or stealth marketing? What is the difference? Do you find both equally (un)acceptable?

> **guerrilla marketing** using energy and imagination to get people talking about a product.
>
> **stealth marketing** marketing a product in such a way that people do not realize they are being sold to.

3 Now read the following article. What examples can you find of stealth marketing and guerrilla marketing?

See *Grammar and vocabulary bank* on page 159 for phrasal verbs related to this text.

4 Read the text again and answer the following questions.

Yes, No, Not given

Questions 1–5

Do the following statements reflect the opinion of the first expert, Maria Clarke?

Write

YES (Y) if the statement reflects the opinion of the expert.

NO (N) if the statement contradicts the opinion of the expert

NOT GIVEN (NG) if it is impossible to say what the expert thinks about this.

1 Guerrilla marketing is more dishonest than stealth marketing. ....
2 Advertisers should be made to indicate if something is actually an advertisement. ....
3 It might be easier for companies to manipulate teenagers than adults ....
4 Before teenagers are hired to do marketing, their parents should be consulted.
   ....
5 The government is not doing enough to protect people from being manipulated. ....

Selling by stealth?

It seems that traditional marketing campaigns just aren't working as they used to do. A recent study showed that just 18% of US television campaigns actually increased sales – and in some cases sales actually dropped. Into this gap has come some new forms of marketing such as 'stealth' or 'guerrilla' marketing. But are they ethical? Here two experts kick off the debate.

No, says Maria Clarke

It is true that there are degrees of deception involved in guerrilla or stealth marketing. Both of them aim to create a 'buzz' around a product, creating interest so that people will talk about the product to their friends. With stealth marketing, I believe that the deception almost amounts to fraud as people are paid to pretend to like a product and encourage others to buy it. With guerrilla marketing, the aim is simply to get people talking about a product by doing something unusual and creative. All very well, you may think, but people are still being deceived. It should always be clear whether something is an advertisement or not. Nothing infuriates me more than coming across a double page 'advertorial' in my glossy magazine, written to look like a normal article, but actually aimed at selling me something. But according to British law, the magazine must state somewhere on the page that it is actually an advertisement, so that, if I look closely enough, I realize I'm being sold to. Not so with many of these campaigns. One of the first, and most famous examples of guerrilla marketing took place in 2002. A company which manufactured mobile phones paid a group of actors to pretend to be tourists at various attractions, asking other visitors to take their photos using a new cameraphone produced by the company. The actors would then engage those who helped them in a conversation about the camera, pointing out all its features. Is this honest?

Even worse, companies are often specifically targeting young people, who may be more impressionable. In America, a well-known company recruited 230,000 teenagers to sell products to their friends. They told them that they didn't have to let their friends know they were working for the company, it was their decision. In this way, they are, in fact, encouraging these young people to lie to those closest to them and to manipulate other people as a source of income.

We mustn't let the advertising companies get away with it. The Government needs to look into these practices straightaway and bring in new laws to control these unscrupulous marketeers.

Maria Clarke works for Marketing Alert, an organization set up to monitor advertising and marketing rules.

Yes, says Henry Goodison

People who work in advertising have always been creative. The newer forms of advertising, sometimes called 'stealth' or 'guerrilla' marketing, are simply new ways of being creative, creating scenarios using actors or something unusual for people to notice. Incidentally, I prefer to use the term 'buzz' marketing as the other terms do have rather negative connotations.

As the head of an advertising agency, I have to come up with new and exciting ways to promote products. For example, we recently created a campaign where actors dressed up in dog costumes on the underground to promote a new brand of dog food. Where's the harm in that? People were entertained, not deceived.

There is a reason why people aren't responding to traditional advertising these days and it's because it is often extremely dull. A good advertising campaign gets people talking, sending each other videos on YouTube, it really does create a buzz of interest.

Word of mouth is very important to the industry these days, but this isn't about paying people to pretend to like things, we don't need to do that. It's about encouraging those people who like your product to tell others about it. Everyone likes to get a recommendation from a friend. Sometimes our methods can be a little bit sneaky, but so can traditional advertising. All those classic 50s adverts, that tried to make women feel terribly guilty if they didn't have a sparkling clean kitchen floor – isn't that manipulation?

It's simply nonsense to say that there's something worse about buzz marketing. The Government shouldn't be getting involved. Just let the advertising industry get on with informing and entertaining – it's what we do best.

Henry Goodison is the Director of BuzzBuzzBuzz , an advertising agency.

Questions 6–9

Do the following statements reflect the opinion of the second expert, Henry Goodison? Write YES, NO or NOT GIVEN.

6 Using the terms 'stealth' and 'guerrilla' marketing gives a bad impression. ....

7 People are bored with the classic forms of advertising. ....

8 Stealth and guerrilla advertising bring in more money than more traditional adverts. ....

9 Traditional advertising was not as manipulative as these new forms. ....

Sentence completion

Questions 10–13

Complete each sentence with the correct ending, A–G below.

10 Stealth marketing is different from guerrilla marketing because ....

11 Advertising campaigns have had to become more creative because ....

12 Guerrilla marketing is seen as being imaginative because ....

13 Word of mouth is valuable to companies because ....

> A people tend to believe their friend's recommendations.
> B it is easy to recruit teenagers by giving them financial rewards.
> C people don't know they are being sold to.
> D it often uses actors or unusual objects.
> E people should know when they are being sold to.
> F old-fashioned adverts aren't working as well nowadays.
> G it doesn't have to be paid for.

5 Whose arguments do you most agree with? Why?

Language focus

Modals of obligation and prohibition

1 These sentences from the reading texts all contain modal verbs.

0 It *should* always be clear whether something is an advertisement or not.

1 ... the magazine must state somewhere on the page that it is actually an advertisement.

2 They told them that they didn't have to let their friends know they were working for the company, it was their decision.

3 We mustn't let the advertising companies get away with it.

4 The Government needs to look into these practices straightaway ...

5 ... I have to come up with new and exciting ways to promote products.

6 ... but this isn't about paying people to pretend to like things, we don't need to do that.

7 The Government shouldn't be getting involved.

Put the modals from the sentences above into these categories.

Obligation			Prohibition	
strong	weak	lack of obligation	strong	weak
	should			

2 Look at the sentences again. What form of the verb follows *must* and *should*? What form of the verb follows *have* and *need*? Check your ideas in the *Grammar and vocabulary bank* on page 158.

3 Work in pairs. How are these modals expressed in the past? Fill in the table, then check your answers in the *Grammar and vocabulary bank* on page 158.

Present time	Past time
should	*should have* + past participle
have to	
must	
mustn't	
need	
don't need to	
don't have to	
shouldn't	

4 Complete the following sentences with an appropriate modal in the correct tense.
  1 I'm sorry you failed your exam, but you really .... (work) harder recently.
  2 You .... (wear) your uniform whenever you are at work. It isn't optional.
  3 Please turn your mobile off. You .... (use) mobiles in class, it's not allowed.
  4 When I was at school we .... work) much harder than kids do nowadays.
  5 It wasn't raining so I .... (bring) my umbrella.

5 Here are some other lexical expressions to express prohibition and obligation.

Prohibition	Obligation (weak)
... is banned	*is/are expected to ...*
... is forbidden	*is/are supposed to ...*
... is not allowed	*It is ... responsibility to ...*
There is a ban on ...	*... are responsible for + -ing ...*

Write about five rules in your country.

You should carry your driving licence with you, but you don't have to.

There is a ban on smoking in public places.

6 ⊙ **2.16** Listen to a tutor giving feedback on a student's work. Write down any examples you hear of language to talk about obligation/lack of obligation or prohibition.

Obligation	
Lack of obligation	
Prohibition	

IELTS Writing Task 2: Arguments for and against a viewpoint

1 Look at this Writing Task 2 question and underline the key words.

Some people feel that some of the newer methods used in advertising are unethical and unacceptable in today's society. Others believe that this viewpoint is an over-reaction.

Discuss both these views and give your own opinion.

Give reasons for your answer and include any relevant examples from your own knowledge or experience.

2 Look back at the reading text on page 131 and make a list of arguments for each of the two views in the question. Also add some of your own ideas.

Some of the methods used in advertising are unethical and unacceptable.	To say methods are unethical and unacceptable is an over-reaction.
People are being deceived because they don't know if something is an advert.	*New forms of advertising are just new ways of being creative.*

3 In this kind of essay, you generally present two points of view before giving your own opinion. When giving these views, therefore, you will often use impersonal statements. Use the statements in the box to make the arguments in exercise 2 more impersonal.

Some people claim that people are being deceived because they don't know if something is an advert.

> It is sometimes thought that   It is widely believed that
> Many people find (that)   Perhaps the majority of people would agree that
> Some people claim (that)   Those who feel ... might argue that

> **Strategy**
>
> In an essay like this you are expected to present the two different viewpoints and then give your own opinion. It is a good idea to structure the essay in this way:
>
> Paragraph 1: introduction
> Paragraph 2: viewpoint 1
> Paragraph 3: viewpoint 2
> Paragraph 4: your opinion and conclusion.
>
> It is fine to use more than one paragraph for presenting each viewpoint, but in practice, with only 250 words, you are unlikely to need more than five paragraphs in total.

4 Using the structure suggested in the strategy box, decide which of the following words and phrases could be used to start each paragraph.

> Having said that   However   In my view   In recent years
> On the one hand   On the other hand   On balance, I would say that
> Over the last few years   Personally

5   Now write a first draft of your essay. Read it and check that:
   – it follows the suggested structure
   – you have checked and corrected any spelling and grammar mistakes.

6   Read the model answer below and compare it with your answer.

In recent years there has been a move towards new and different kinds of advertising, aimed at creating word of mouth. While some people see this as a positive move, others consider it almost immoral for people not to be aware that they are being marketed to.

Those who feel that these new forms of marketing are unethical argue that there is never any excuse for advertising companies to try and deceive the public. Some of the advertising campaigns carried out in recent years have involved people pretending to be members of the public when they were in fact actors, which is certainly a deception.

Many people are also particularly concerned about the use of teams of young people who are asked to promote products to their friends and family, often without mentioning that they are being paid to do this.

However, those working in advertising might claim that advertising has always been about manipulation, and that these new approaches are not any worse than previous campaigns. They are also often highly entertaining and creative, which, advertising executives argue, makes this kind of advertising more attractive to the general public, rather than less. Finally, they argue, this kind of advertising seems to be much more effective that the traditional kind.

Personally, I think that it probably is an over-reaction to consider newer forms of word-of-mouth advertising as immoral. While I would not be happy for my teenage children to promote products to their friends, I consider that it is up to parents to teach their children about how advertising works, and how to avoid being manipulated. Similarly, we need to take some personal responsibility for not being taken in.

TIP
Remember in IELTS Writing Task 2 you have 40 minutes and need to write a minimum of 250 words.

7   Now write your own answer to the following question, using the same structure. When you have finished, compare it with the model answer on page 164.

Recent changes in the law in the UK mean that adverts for food products high in fat, salt and sugar will no longer be shown alongside programmes popular with those aged under 16, even if the programme itself is aimed at adults.

Some people feel that this is an excellent idea, others feel that the government has gone too far.

Discuss both these views and give your own opinion.

Give reasons for your answer and include any relevant examples from your own knowledge or experience

IELTS Listening Section 3

1 You are going to listen to two students preparing a presentation on 'The Marketing Mix'. The four elements of the marketing mix, or marketing strategy, are *product, promotion, place* and *price*. What do you think might be involved in each of these?

2 ⓞ 2.17 Look at the questions and try to guess what kind of answer you are looking for in each case. Now listen and complete questions 1–10.

Classification

Questions 1–4

Which student will cover the following topic areas in the presentation? Write the correct letter A, B, C next to questions 1–4.

A Kate   1 Product ....   3 Place ....
B Tom   2 Price ....   4 Promotion ....
C Isabelle

Table completion

Questions 5–10

ⓞ 2.18 Listen to the second part and complete the table. Write NO MORE THAN TWO WORDS for each answer.

Topic	Key points
Product	Can be (5) .... or service. Need to think about design, (6) .... , and a brand name.
Price	The price set depends on the (7) .... and the target market but it needs to be (8) ....
Place	Can be sold wholesale or directly to shops or (9) ....
Promotion	About (10) .... your potential customers and persuading them to buy.

3 Work in pairs or small groups. Think of a well-known product and answer the following questions.
  – What are the important things about it? Do you like the brand name?
  – What target market is it aimed at? How does the price reflect this? How does it compare price-wise with other similar products?
  – Where is it sold? Could it be sold successfully anywhere else in the world?
  – How is it promoted? What adverts have you seen? Did they work well?

4 Now use the information from your discussion to make a short presentation about the product and how it is marketed to another group or to the whole class.

 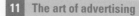

Understanding verbs in essay titles

When writing essays or assignments it is important to understand the verbs that tell you what to actually do in the question.

1 Look at the examples below in italics and answer the questions. Use a dictionary to check the meaning of any unknown words.

Compare and contrast traditional adverts and newer forms of advertising.

Discuss the arguments for and against newer forms of advertising.

Describe how stealth marketing works.

Explain why more traditional forms of advertising are becoming less effective.

Identify the key advantages of selling direct to the customer online and justify your opinion.

Evaluate the effectiveness of stealth marketing.

   1 What is the difference between *compare and contrast* and *explain*?
   2 What is the difference between *evaluate* and *describe*?
   3 What is the difference between *identify* and *discuss*?
   4 How should you *justify* an opinion?

2 Look at these essay extracts. Which is an example of:
   – comparing and contrasting?
   – justifying an opinion?
   – evaluating?
   – describing?

1 *I do not believe that advertisements are harmless. In fact, advertisements can encourage people to spend more money than they can afford or to buy products which are not actually good for them.*

2 *On balance, I think that the recent changes to the advertising regulations have been quite successful in reducing children's exposure to pressure from the fast food companies.*

3 *Complaints about adverts for food and beauty products fell last year, but complaints about holiday advertisements reached an all time high.*

4 *Charities and pressure groups often use quite shocking or hard hitting images in their advertising to create the maximum impact.*

Collocations

3 Choose the best adjective to collocate with each noun in **bold**. Use the *Macmillan Collocations Dictionary* to help you.

   1 Obesity is becoming a *major/valuable* **problem** in some areas of the world.
   2 Banning fast food adverts would be a *fundamental/significant* **achievement**.
   3 People have a *major/fundamental* **right** not to be deceived by big corporations.
   4 There is *an important/a major* **distinction** between stealth marketing and guerrilla marketing.
   5 There are *valuable/significant* **lessons** to be learnt from experience.
   6 There is a *fundamental/significant* **trend** towards word of mouth advertising.
   7 Whether advertising should be aimed at children is *a significant/an important* **question** to consider.

12 Success and achievement

1 Look at these pictures of successful people. What type of success does each one represent? How have they achieved their success? Which type of success would you most like to achieve?

2 How do you feel about examinations? Look at these statements. Tick the ones that apply to you.

1 My future will be ruined if I fail/don't get the grades I want. ☐
2 I am not lucky with exams. ☐
3 I'm just no good at exams. Some people are, I'm not. ☐
4 Exams get more difficult as you work your way up. ☐
5 I haven't covered the syllabus, so I won't pass. ☐
6 The exams will expose me as a phoney, or stupid. ☐

3 Work in pairs and discuss your answers.

4 Now read the passage and answer questions 1–13.

Dispelling irrational beliefs about exams

Here are six common beliefs that are held about exams and their outcome, all of which have some elements of false assumption or irrationality about them.

My future will be ruined if I fail/don't get the grades I want.

Examinations are an important way in which professional groups in our society select their membership. Success in them does open doors to particular jobs and careers. Lack of success will mean certain jobs and careers are not immediately open to you, at least at the level of entry you originally intended. Some may be closed altogether.

However, happiness, wealth, peace of mind, a rich experience of life, meaningful status in the eyes of others, a worthwhile career, a useful job and a sense of purpose and self-belief as a human being do not depend upon examination results. The world is teeming with people who have found that to be the case whether they have passed examinations or not.

I am not lucky with exams.

Some people do appear luckier than others at games of chance, with acquiring money, in making relationships, or in achievements. There is certainly an aspect of chance involved in which questions appear on the examination paper, compared to those you have chosen to revise.

However, examination technique can be learned very effectively by anybody, and the element of luck reduced to a minimum. Practising what you have to do in the examination room is the key, as Arnold Palmer, one of the most successful golfers of all time is quoted as saying: 'The more I practise, the luckier I get.'

I'm just no good at exams. Some people are, I'm not.

There are two elements in this view. One is that your past performance will determine any future attempts. The other is that in comparing yourself with others, you find your performance inadequate. The answer to the first element is that the past frequently is escapable. By buying this book and reading this page, you have set out to become 'good at exams'. Other people are largely irrelevant. They do not depend for their success upon your lack of success or vice versa.

Exams get more difficult as you work your way up.

Difficulty is a relative word. What is difficult at one age is not at another; what is difficult when you are inexperienced in an activity is not when you are experienced; what is difficult to one person is not for another; what is difficult on one day is not on another.

Certainly, examinations demand more specialist knowledge, understanding and expertise, as you move through their different levels. They may become more technical, involve more abstract ideas and concepts, involve you in greater specialization and more specialist jargon. This does not mean they become more difficult.

I haven't covered the syllabus, so I won't pass.

It isn't irrational to fear that you haven't revised or understood enough of the subject you have studied to pass a course. It may be true that if you have studied and revised little of the course you have left yourself at risk of failing to accumulate sufficient marks to pass it. It may be that you will need some luck in the choice of questions that appear in the exam paper.

However, it is irrational to believe that if you haven't covered the syllabus you are inevitably going to fail the course. Few courses, teachers or students 'cover the syllabus' in the sense of paying full and equal attention to all parts of it. Examiners do not expect you to have done so. They accept that there are bound to be areas where you are under-prepared, unclear or uninformed. They want to see you demonstrate what you do understand and what you have prepared.

Even when you are struggling to find enough questions to answer, you will find that many have some kind of link or association with your course content. You will normally find some links which you can build up into an answer.

The exams will expose me as a phoney, or stupid.

You may experience the common fear in many students that the exams will expose them as inadequate, lacking in even basic know-how or understanding. There is a further underlying fear – that the exams will expose your lack of ability to be tackling that level of study, whether it be GCSE or post-graduate qualifications. The fear can be further intensified by fantasies of the judgement by examiners, tutors, family and friends. Examiners can be seen as poised with red pens to expose your ignorance and misunderstanding. You may feel that family and friends see you as stupid, or that tutors will reject you, as they feel let down or fooled.

The focus on ability is largely irrelevant. The vast majority of people who set off on a course of study are quite capable of successfully completing it. It is practical life circumstances, false beliefs and negative attitudes, which, coupled with poor study techniques, may cause problems – not lack of ability.

Yes, No, Not given

Questions 1–8

Do these statements reflect the views of the writer in the reading text on page 139?

Write

YES (Y) if the statement reflects the views of the writer.

NO (N) if the statement contradicts the views of the writer.

NOT GIVEN (NG) if it is impossible to know what the writer thinks about this.

1 If you fail an exam, it may be impossible to get the job that you want. ....
2 Many people who have not passed exams have had satisfying careers. ....
3 Practice is not as important as luck. ....
4 A large percentage of people who fail an exam, fail again when they re-take it. ....
5 It is unhelpful to compare yourself with others. ....
6 Exams become more difficult at higher levels because of the greater technical skill or knowledge required. ....
7 Examiners expect you to have thoroughly studied the syllabus. ....
8 Time management is an important factor in exam success. ....

Summary completion

Questions 9–12

Complete the summary using words from the box. You will not need to use all the words.

ability	developing	disappointed in	experience
furious with	increase	ineffective	reveal

Many students are worried that exams will (9) .... their lack of intelligence, or inability to be studying at a particular level. They can also imagine that examiners will deliberately judge them harshly or that teachers, friends and family will be (10) .... them.

In fact, (11) .... is not usually the problem. Most people who start a course are able to complete it successfully. More often, problems are caused by the student's negative attitude, (12) .... learning strategies or simply the circumstances of their life at the time.

Multiple choice

Question 13

What is the main purpose of the writer of this article?

A to explain the importance of exam success
B to advise students about how to revise for exams
C to reduce students' anxieties about exams
D to compare and evaluate different exam techniques

Listening

IELTS Listening Section 2: Multiple choice

1 You are going to listen to someone talking about how his British education has contributed to his success.

Questions 1–5

(○) 2.19 Choose the correct letter, A, B or C.

1 The talk will include information about
A a student's sporting achievements
B a student's high grades on a course
C a student's career

2 The happiest events he remembers from university are
A social occasions
B visits to other places
C lectures

3 What does the speaker say can lead to a higher position and a good job in his country?

   A a traditional education

   B a degree from a British university

   C getting a British passport

4 What subject did the speaker study when he arrived in the UK?

   A Politics

   B Economics

   C Crime studies

5 What does the speaker say is important when choosing an area of study?

   A Whether it will help you get a job.

   B Whether you can afford to pay for the course.

   C What course your parents want you to do.

Sentence completion

Questions 6–10

🔘 **2.20** Listen to the second part of the talk.

Complete the sentences below using NO MORE THAN THREE WORDS for each answer.

6 After returning to his own country the speaker applied for a job with the

....

7 Employers in Pakistan prefer graduates who have ....
at tertiary level.

8 The experience of studying abroad also demonstrates independence and

....

9 He later returned to England and gained a Master's Degree in

....

10 Last year he went back to Pakistan to become ....
of an education project.

2 Look at these extracts from the Listening. Is the underlined word in each extract a noun or a verb?

When I graduated in Politics ...   noun/verb

... there were other reasons why employers favour graduates ...   noun/verb

Now decide if the missing word in each extract from the listening is a noun or a verb, then complete with a suitable word from the box. Look at the audioscript on pages 174–5 to check your answers.

balance	talk	value	visit

1 We open this afternoon with a short ....
from one of our success stories.   noun/verb

2 It's very nice to be back to .... the university.   noun/verb

3 I think that it's very important to .... what you think
will make you employable, with what you're interested in.   noun/verb

4 Employers .... that, I think.   noun/verb

IELTS Writing Task 1

Summarizing information

1 Discuss the following in pairs.
- – How successful has your country been at the Olympic® Games in recent years?
- – Which sports does your country have most success in?
- – Are there any Olympic athletes that you particularly admire?

2 Read this Task 1 question.

The graph shows the number of medals won by four different countries at six consecutive Olympic Games from 1988–2008.

Summarize the information by selecting and reporting the main features, and make comparisons where necessary. Write at least 150 words.

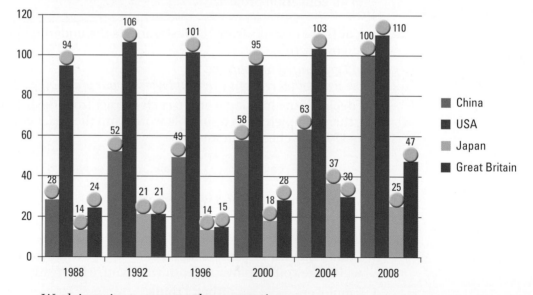

Work in pairs to answer these questions.

1 Does each country generally show an upward or downward trend in the number of medals won?

2 Which countries show the most significant changes over the time period?

3 Which countries show smaller changes?

4 Are there any years when there was a big change in the number of medals won compared to the previous Olympics?

3 Now complete the Writing task. You should spend no longer than 20 minutes planning, writing and checking your answer. When you have finished, compare your answer with the model answer on page 164.

1 Which of the nouns in the box collocate with which verbs (1–5)?

a competition	an exam	a goal	a medal
a prize	a qualification	a race	success

1 to enter ....
2 to win ....
3 to pass ....
4 to gain ....
5 to achieve ....

2 Now match the adjectives with the nouns in the box to make adjective–noun collocations.

achievement	competition	exam	qualification	success

1 practical ....
2 professional ....
3 sporting ....
4 great ....
5 academic ....

3 Complete the questions in an appropriate way using collocations from exercises 1 and 2. There is more than one possible way to complete them. Work in pairs. Ask and answer the questions, giving extra information where necessary.

1 Have you any .... qualifications?
2 Have you ever won a .... ?
3 What .... would you like to achieve in the future?
4 What is your greatest .... ?

See *Grammar and vocabulary bank* on page 159 for more on umbrella nouns and collocations

Speaking

IELTS Speaking Part 1

1 In Part 1 of the Speaking exam you will be asked to talk about familiar topics.

Write questions the examiner might ask about each of the following topics. Work in pairs. Take it in turns to roll a dice. Your partner will ask you questions on the topic with that number. When it is your turn, ask the questions you have written.

1 Home country/city	**2** Friends/family	**3** Free time/interests
4 Study/work	**5** Holidays and travel	**6** Future plans

TIP
Remember to add some details to your answers.

IELTS Speaking Part 2

2 ⊙ 2.21 Listen to a student doing this task. Which of the collocations from the *Vocabulary* section does she use?

Part 2

Describe a particular situation or event in which you were successful, eg an exam, a sporting event, a compotition, etc.

You should say
– what the situation/event was
– when and where it happened
– what preparation was involved

and also say how you felt about achieving this success.

3 Spend one minute preparing your talk on the same topic. Work in pairs. Take it in turns to speak for 1–2 minutes on this topic. When the time is up, ask one of these questions.

– Do you think you will achieve more success in the future?
– Would you like to achieve more success in the future?

Give feedback to your partner on their performance.

IELTS Speaking Part 3

4 Work in pairs. Look at these Part 3 questions.

– How is success measured in today's society?
– How important are non-academic achievements such as in sport or music?
– Can you name a successful person you admire and say why?
– Do you think money equals success?
– Are exams the best way to assess someone's ability?
– Do you think there is too much pressure on young people to achieve academic success?

Choose a possible opening phrase for each question and then give a full answer.

Useful language

Um. Let me think. Yes, one person who ...
Not at all. In my view ...
Absolutely. When I was at school ...
In different ways, for example ...
Very important in my opinion ...
Good question. Not always because ...

5 Give feedback to your partner on their performance.

Talking about ability

1 Look at these sentences from the listening on page 144
   a I couldn't dance or sing.
   b I finally managed to come up with one.
   c I was able to meet one of my favourite writers.
   d I hope I'll be able to use my talent in my future career.

   Which of the verb forms is used

   1 to talk about a general ability in the past? ....
   2 when it is not possible to use *can*, eg after another modal or auxiliary verb?
   ....
   3 to refer to ability on one particular occasion in the past? (two examples)
   ....
   4 to give the idea that the task was difficult to complete? ....

2 Which of the verb forms are:
   1 followed by the infinitive with *to*? ....
   2 followed by the infinitive without *to*? ....

3 Complete the sentences by choosing the most appropriate form.
   1 I'd like to *be able to/can* help you but I don't have time.
   2 At the age of ten he *managed to/could* already speak three languages.
   3 Despite feeling ill, she *managed to/could* complete her assignment.
   4 *Could you/Were you able to* finish that report?
   5 If I start saving now, I might *can/be able to* afford to go on the trip.

4 Make notes on the following.
   – something you could do as a child
   – something you couldn't do when you were younger but can do now
   – something you weren't able to do the first time you tried but managed to do later
   – something you hope to be able to do by the end of the year
   – something you would like to be able to do in your future career

5 Exchange ideas with your partner.

IELTS Writing Task 2: Giving opinions and examples

1 Read this question and underline the key words.

   Many people judge success solely by money and material possessions. However, success can be achieved or measured in other ways.

   What are your opinions on this topic?

   Give reasons for your answer and include any relevant examples from your own knowledge or experience.

   Write at least 250 words.

2 Discuss these questions in pairs.
   – How do people judge success in terms of money and material possessions? Give examples.
   – What other ways can people achieve or measure success? Give examples.
   – In your opinion, what types of success do you consider to be the most important?
   – How would you organize your answer?

3 Now write your answer. You should spend no more than 40 minutes planning, writing and checking your answer. When you have finished, compare your answer with the model answer on page 164.

Test your knowledge ...

| START ➤ | Speak for one minute about a traditional food from your country. (1) | Name three different types of crime, criminals and verbs. (4) | What are the disadvantages of increased tourism? (3) | ➤ |

Work in groups of three or four. There are four different types of question: Vocabulary, Grammar, Speaking Part 2 and Speaking Part 3, and all of these test your knowledge of previous units (shown in brackets after each question).

Take it in turns to roll a dice and move around the board. When you land on a square you should answer the question or do the task. You can check your answer by looking back at the relevant unit. If you get the answer right, stay on that square ready for your next turn, If you get the answer wrong you must go back two squares.

Give four different rules for using the definite article (*the*). (3)	Speak for one minute about a place you like visiting. (3)	Describe the size, shape, colour and material of something in the classroom. (7)	Why is success so important in society today? (12)	➤
How do you think ways of spending leisure time will change in the future? (10)			
Give three words or phrases relating to advertising. (11)	Speak for one minute about something you do to help the environment. (2)	Give four different ways to express purpose. (7)	Do you think all criminals should be sent to prison? (4)	

➤	Name four state verbs. How are they different to other verbs? (2)	Speak for one minute about an interesting journey you have made. (3)	Give two nouns and an adjective from the word family *employ*. (5)	Discuss the significant changes that have taken place in the workplace in the last 25 years. (5)

			Make this sentence more academic: *Loads of people speak English all over the world.* (6)

➤	Make this sentence passive: *Europeans first drank coffee in the 15th century.* (6)	➤ FINISH		Speak for one minute about a something you do to keep healthy. (8)

Name three verbs to describe upward trends and three verbs to describe downward trends. (3)

◄	What does the prefix *mis-* mean? Give two words with this prefix. (10)	Speak for one minute about a sport you enjoy playing or watching. (10)	Think of a verb which can be followed by both the infinitive and *-ing* form. What is the difference in meaning? (9)	How can global problems such as poverty and disease be addressed? (6)

IELTS Listening Section 3
Listen to a discussion between a tutor and two of his students about preparing for IELTS.

Note completion
🔊 **2.22 Questions 1–5**
Listen to the first part and complete the notes below. Use NO MORE THAN THREE WORDS for each answer.

> ### Advice and tips for IELTS Listening
>
> First piece of advice: read **1** ....
>
> Look at the whole section to establish the **2** ....
>
> Predict the kind of information required in answers:
> - eg name of a person
> - place
> - date
> - **3** ....
>
> Grammar
> What part of speech is needed? eg
> - a noun
> - a verb
> - **4** ....
>
> While listening, make a note of answers and stay focused.
>
> In the transfer time remember to **5** ....

Table completion
🔊 **2.23 Questions 6–10**
Listen to the second part and complete the table below. Use NO MORE THAN THREE WORDS for each answer.

IELTS	Problems mentioned by tutor	Problem mentioned by students	Advice given
Reading	(6)	academic vocabulary	Do more practice papers. Work out meaning. Don't stop or get blocked if you see (7) ....
Speaking	not having enough to say in Parts 2 and 3	none mentioned	Practise each part of the test and choose common topics eg health, travel, education (8) ....
Writing	(9)	(10) using .... in written work	Look at errors and corrections made in previous writing tasks.

Self-evaluation

Assess what you can do to develop your skills.

Area of focus	I do this	I need to do this more	What will I do? Specific target or example.
I need to practise my speaking skills at every opportunity – inside and outside class.			
I will record myself talking about a particular topic then evaluate my performance.			
In class, I will give my opinion and views on different topics more often.			
I will give a presentation in class.			
I will join a club or society in order to meet more English speakers.			
I will listen to the news in English at least once a day.			
I will use some audio resources (eg online, from a library) to practise my listening skills.			
I will listen carefully to what my teacher or classmates say, then ask more questions.			
I will ask my teacher which area of pronunciation I need to focus on most and practise this area.			
I will try and attend more 'live' talks or lectures in English.			
I will read an item of news in English at least once a day.			
I will keep a record of and learn vocabulary relating to different topics.			
I will improve my reading speed by doing more timed reading tasks.			
I will analyse questions and answers in a particular text.			
I will review strategies to help me improve my reading skills.			
I will look at model answers for IELTS and make a note of standard phrases I can use to develop an academic writing style.			
I will use a grammar book or online resources to focus on key areas I need to improve.			
I will write more regularly and ask my teacher, friends, classmates or colleagues to check my work.			
I will look at previous IELTS Writing questions and plan possible answers using word maps.			
I will do writing tasks under timed conditions including planning, drafting and checking.			

Grammar and vocabulary bank

Unit 1 Forming questions

If there is an auxiliary verb *be/have* or a modal verb, reverse the order of the subject and the auxiliary.

I can speak Chinese.
Can you speak Chinese?

If there is no auxiliary, use a 'dummy' auxiliary *do/does/did*.
I live with my grandmother.
Who do you live with?

Complete the questions.

0	You can swim	*Can you swim?*
1	You have been to England.	Have _____ ?
2	Jill is living in Hong Kong.	Is _____ ?
3	Peter went to Australia two years ago.	When _____ ?
4	He writes books.	What _____ ?
5	She travels to school by bike.	How _____ ?

Countable/uncountable nouns

Countable nouns are nouns which can be counted. They have both a singular and plural form.
one student, two students; a woman, three women

Uncountable nouns are nouns which cannot be counted. They do not have a plural form.
love, advice, salt, money

Correct the mistakes in the following sentences. Why are they incorrect?

0 I would like some informations about the course.
I would like some information about the course.
'Information' is an uncountable noun and does not have a plural form.

1 Oh, no! Not more homeworks!
_____

2 There have been a lot of price rise in the last few years.
_____

3 Every advice I get just makes me more confused.
_____

4 I don't have much dollars in cash, but I can write you a cheque.
_____

5 Can you bring my luggages, please?
_____

Quantifiers

A lot of is followed by a plural countable noun and verb or an uncountable noun and singular verb.

A lot of students study overseas.
Students have to spend a lot of money on accommodation.

The majority of is followed by a plural noun and verb.
The majority of overseas students enjoy living in the UK.

The number of is followed by a plural noun and a singular verb.
The number of students studying overseas has increased in recent years.

Much is generally used in questions and negative sentences with uncountable nouns.
There isn't much cheap accommodation in town.

Many is used with countable plural nouns.
There are many different courses to choose from.

A number of is followed by a countable plural noun and a plural verb.
A number of universities offer foundation courses for international students.

You can add adjectives to *a number of* to show how large or small the number is.
a large number of people; a small number of countries

Most, several and *some* can be used with a plural noun or with *of* + *the* + noun. The second use is more specific in meaning.
Some subjects are more popular with international students than others.
Some of the students (in the class) chose to study Science.

Parts of speech: nouns and adjectives

Complete the sentences by choosing the correct alternative (the noun or adjective appears in the *Reading* section on pages 6 and 7).

0 Students living overseas for the first time can suffer from *lonely/loneliness*.
1 It can take some time to adapt to a *different/difference* culture.
2 Living overseas can help you become more *independent/independence*.
3 Students often miss the *comfortable/comfort* of their own homes.
4 Language barriers can cause *significant/significance* problems.
5 Studying overseas offers many *possibles/possibilities*.

Unit 2 Subject–verb agreement

Always check that the verb you use agrees with the subject. These quantifiers are followed by a singular verb.
every/everyone, each, no one, either/neither, another

These quantifiers are followed by a plural verb.
all, both, many, several, some, a lot of

Remember that some nouns are uncountable and therefore followed by a singular verb.
agriculture, energy, (the) environment, technology, poverty, trade, transport, travel, waste, water

These nouns are also uncountable in English, though not in all other languages.
money, politics, progress, research, traffic

Also note that *police* is plural, while *government* is singular.

Some phrases are always followed by singular verbs, some by plural verbs, and some can be followed by both.

Underline the best alternative.

0 Everyone *live/lives* between 2 and 10 miles from the college.
1 Most of the teachers *travel/travels* to college by car.
2 None of the teachers *cycle/cycles* to work.
3 Some teachers *travel/travels* to work by bus.
4 One of the teachers *use/uses* the train.
5 Nobody *is/are* late for college.
6 Every member of staff *has/have* a car park permit.

Present simple vs present continuous

1 What is the difference between these pairs of sentences?

1 a The sun rises in the East.
   b The sun is rising in the East.
2 a He lives with his mother.
   b He is living with his mother.
3 a I start work at 9am.
   b I am starting work at 9am this week.
4 a That old fish smells terrible.
   b He was smelling the roses when he sneezed.

2 Are these sentences right or wrong? Correct them if necessary.

0 Degrees are often requiring full-time study.
Degrees often require full-time study.

1 I usually arrive early for class.
....

2 He is knowing Toronto very well.
....

3 Come on. We wait for you.
....

4 I am agreeing with you.
....

5 I am having a big house.
....

Collocations

Words that are often used together are called collocations. Complete the gaps in the diagram using the words in the box.

~~accident~~	air	~~busy~~	fumes	heavy	jams
lights	main	rage	safety	users	~~works~~

Check that you know whether the word comes before or after the word in the box.

1 *Traffic accident*   2 *Busy road*   3 *Road works*

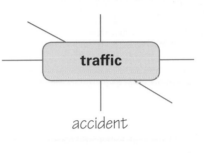

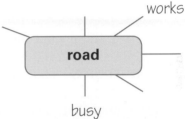

Unit 3 Articles

Complete the gaps using an appropriate article.

Articles are often **0** _a_ difficult area for students of English as **1** .... foreign language. **2** .... most important thing to remember is that **3** .... definite article is used where both people in **4** .... conversation know what they are referring to. For example, **5** .... first time something is mentioned, there is no shared knowledge, so we use the indefinite article **6** .... / .... **7** .... second time something is mentioned, however, both people have shared knowledge of it, so we use **8** .... definite article **9** .... This is true when **10** .... noun is unique, eg **11** .... *Sun*, or **12** .... *Taj Mahal*. As there is only one of these things, both people know which one they mean, so we use **13** .... definite article.
There are **14** .... few other rules. The indefinite article is used in some fixed expressions such as **15** .... *lot* and **16** .... *few*, and to mean 'per', eg *70 miles* **17** .... *hour*.
Another common use of the definite article is in superlatives, eg **18** .... *best tea in the world*.
Finally, be careful with geography. Most place names and names of people do not need an article, but expressions like **19** .... *Republic of Indonesia*, that follow the pattern of *The Republic/Kingdom/State*, etc. *of…* need **20** .... definite article.

Synonyms

1 Look at the words in the box. They all have a similar meaning to *trip* but are used in slightly different ways. Match the words with the definitions.

~~crossing~~	drive	expedition	flight
	outing	tour	voyage

0 A short trip across water. *crossing*
1 A long trip to a distant place, possibly with some danger, often for a scientific reason. ....
2 A trip by car. ....
3 A trip by plane. ....
4 A long trip either by sea or in space. ....
5 A short trip (usually for the day) made by a group of people. ....
6 A trip to a series of different places. ....

2 Now replace *trip* in the following sentences with a more specific word. Remember to change the article if necessary.

0 They went on a *trip* to the science museum.
They went on an outing to the science museum.

1 Did you have a good *trip*? No, I hate flying.
....

2 The rough weather made her seasick for the entire *trip*.
....

3 He's trying to raise money for a *trip* to the Sahara Desert. They're going to look for a new species of desert cactus.
....

4 As travel becomes more affordable, a world *trip* is available to more people.
....

5 My *trip* to work only takes 20 minutes, provided the traffic isn't too bad.
....

6 Before air travel, people had to make the long *trip* across the Atlantic by ship.
....

Collocations

For each of the sentences choose two possible collocations.

0 This hotel mainly caters for *budget/business* travellers.
1 We can offer discounts on car hire to .... travellers.
2 Extreme holidays appeal to .... travellers.
3 I have travelled .... in Europe and Asia.
4 I don't like travelling .... – I prefer to go on a package holiday in my own country.

Unit 4 Defining relative clauses

Relative clauses give extra information about a person or thing in the main clause. They come immediately after the noun that they describe.

Defining relative clauses give information which is essential to the meaning of the main clause.

* No commas are needed at the beginning or at the end of the clause.
* *That* can replace *who* for people or *which* for things.
* If the relative pronoun refers to the object, it can be left out.

Complete each of the spaces below with an appropriate relative pronoun. Choose from *that/which/who/whose/where/none needed*. Some will have more than one possibility.

0 Burglary is one of the most common crimes *that/which/–* people commit.
1 Insurance premiums are often reduced in streets .... a Neighbourhood Watch Scheme has been set up.
2 If you make an insurance claim, you will need the crime reference number .... the police give you.
3 Many crimes .... the police investigate are never solved.
4 It often takes a long time for people .... houses have been burgled to fully recover.
5 Unfortunately, people .... have been burgled once are statistically more likely to be burgled again.

Present perfect vs past simple

The present perfect links past events and situations with the present. It is usually used:

* to talk about past experience in a general way, eg *I've eaten crab*.
* to talk about recent events, eg *Three children have been rescued from a river*.
* to talk about actions or situations which began in the past, but continue to the present, eg *I've known him for a year*.
* to talk about a past action that has a clear result in the present, eg *I've cut my finger*.
* with time expressions such as: *ever, recently, yet, for* and *since*.

The past simple is used to describe events or situations which:

* are complete and which happened at a specified time, eg *I left home in 1998*.
* are complete and happened over a period of time in the past, eg *I went to the gym every day for 10 months*.
* with time expressions such as *last week, in 1998, three weeks ago,* etc.

Underline the best alternative. If both are possible, what is the difference?

0 I _completed_/have completed my English assignment last night.
1 I _didn't go/haven't been_ to America yet.
2 I _have lived/lived_ here since 2008.
3 I _graduated/have graduated_ from Warwick University in 2006.
4 I _studied/have studied_ in Beijing for six months.
5 I _have made/made_ some cakes. Would you like one?
6 I _have been/went_ to Singapore many times when I lived in Asia.
7 My brother _has lived/lived_ here for two years.

Collocations

Look at the possible collocations with _crime_ and use the phrases to complete the sentences below.

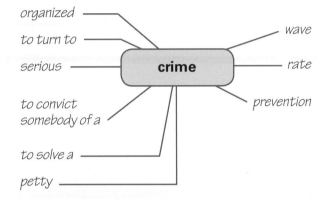

0 The court _convicted her of a crime_ she hadn't committed.
1 Rather than building more prisons, we should focus on ....
2 Young people who cannot get work may .... in desperation.
3 The blackout in the city caused a .... as criminals took advantage of the confusion.
4 The FBI has a large section dedicated to fighting ....
5 The government insists that the .... is falling as a result of its policies.
6 The police need to spend less time on ...., such as shoplifting, and more on ....
7 Regardless of what is shown in detective films, it usually takes the police less than 24 hours ....

Unit 5 Future forms

There are four common ways to express the future in English: _going to_, _will_, the present continuous and present simple tenses.
- Use _going to_ for plans and intentions.
- Use _will_ for predictions, future facts, promises, threats and for decisions made at the time of speaking.
- Use the present continuous for arrangements. It is very similar to _going to_, but is usually at a specific time or place or with a specific person.
- Use the present simple for timetabled or regular events.

Underline the best alternative. If both are possible, what is the difference in meaning?

0 If Wednesday's a problem _we'll meet/we're meeting_ on Tuesday.
1 I am _going to take/taking_ the IELTS exam in June.
2 You are _going to fail/failing_ your exam, unless you start working harder.
3 Online shopping _increases/will probably increase_ in popularity over the next decade.
4 Can you open the window? Actually don't worry, _I'll do/I'm going to do_ it.
5 _I'll try/I'm trying_ not to be late for class again.
6 The exam _starts/will start_ at 2 pm. Don't be late!

Comparatives and superlatives

We use comparatives to compare one thing or person to another.
Manchester is a larger city than Oxford.

We use superlatives to compare one thing or person with a whole group.
London is the largest city in the UK.

Look at the rules and examples and complete the table.

Adjective	Comparative	Superlative
rich	_richer (than)_	_the richest_
cold		

Rule One-syllable: + -_er_/-_est_

Adjective	Comparative	Superlative
late	_later (than)_	_the latest_
safe		

Rule One-syllable ending in -_e_: + _r_/_st_

Adjective	Comparative	Superlative
hot	_hotter (than)_	_the hottest_
fit		

Rule One-syllable ending in one vowel + one consonant: double consonant + _er_/_est_

Adjective	Comparative	Superlative
dirty	dirtier (than)	the dirtiest
easy		

Rule Two-syllable ending in -y: ɏ +ier/iest

Adjective	Comparative	Superlative
difficult	more difficult (than)	the most difficult
intelligent		

Rule Two or more syllables: more/most + adjective

Adjective	Comparative	Superlative
good	better (than)	the best
bad		

Rule Irregular adjectives

Work vocabulary

Complete the text with a suitable form of the verbs from the box.

> apply for (a job) be offered (a job)
> be/get promoted be made redundant
> ~~be sacked~~ resign retire retrain

My first job was delivering newspapers when I was at school but I had to get up at 5am and I
0 _was sacked_ for being late every morning! After I left school I got a job in a factory but six months later the firm closed and I
1 .... I then worked in a fast food restaurant but I hated it, so after a couple of months there I **2** .... I then decided to **3** .... so I went to college and took some computing courses. I passed my exams and spent the next few months
4 .... jobs. I had more than twenty interviews before I was successful and I
5 .... with a local company.
I started as a junior office assistant and have already
6 .... twice. I hope to become office manager before I **7** ....

Unit 6 Non-defining relative clauses

Non-defining relative clauses give extra information about a person or thing in the main clause. This information is not essential to the meaning of the main clause.

- Commas are required before and after the relative clause.
- *That* cannot replace *who* for people or *which* for things.
- The pronoun cannot be omitted.

Combine the two sentences using a relative clause.

0 The computer virus has caused millions of pounds worth of damage around the world. The computer virus is believed to have originated in Texas.

The computer virus, which is believed to have originated in Texas, has caused millions of pounds worth of damage around the world.

1 Tourists are vital to the Thai economy. Tourists mainly visit Bangkok and the islands.

....

2 FairTrade products are increasing in popularity in the West. FairTrade products are often more expensive.

....
....

3 The president of the charity has resigned. The president has been in office for seven years.

....

4 The internet has made communication much quicker. The internet is widely available in most parts of the world.

....
....

The passive

Complete the text with passive verbs in the present tense.

Chocolate **0** _is made_ (make) from up to 12 different types of cocoa beans. First the beans
1 .... (sort) by hand before being roasted. Each type of bean **2** .... (roast) separately, which is time consuming but important. Next, the beans **3** .... (load) into a machine called a 'winnower', which removes the hard outer shells of the beans. After this the beans
4 .... (mash) into a thick paste and sugar and vanilla **5** .... (add).
This paste **6** .... (call) the 'chocolate liquor'. Then the chocolate liquor **7** .... (heat) for up to 72 hours to make sure the liquid
8 .... (blend) evenly. Following this, the liquor **9** .... (temper) for several hours – repeatedly heated and then cooled.
Finally, the chocolate **10** .... (allow) to cool and harden before being packaged.

Verb + noun collocations

Complete the sentences with a suitable verb from the box below.

| cut | do | earn | go | reach | ~~lose~~ | make | put | take |

0 Many shops _lose_ business due to poor service.

1 It is difficult for farmers like the Menzas to .... a profit.

2 It was a pleasure to .... business with you.

3 The two sides finally .... an agreement.

4 They decided to .... into business together.

5 Competition from cheaper imports forced them to .... their prices.

6 Loan sharks .... advantage of the desperate farmers.

7 She doesn't .... much money, but she enjoys the work.

8 He .... all his money into the business.

Unit 7 Phrasal verbs

A phrasal verb is made up of two or more parts: a verb, plus a preposition or an adverb. It is easy to guess the meaning of some phrasal verbs from the words used, eg *take off your jacket, sit down, go away, get up*.

Other phrasal verbs are less easy to guess from the words used.

The plane took off. (left the ground)

You should give up smoking. (stop)

I get on with my colleagues. (have a good relationship with)

With some verbs the preposition or adverb can go before or after the object.

He took off his jacket. OR *He took his jacket off.*

When you use a pronoun (*it, them, him, her* etc) to replace the noun, the preposition or adverb must go after the pronoun.

He took it off NOT *He took off it.*

Complete the sentences using the phrasal verb in brackets and a suitable pronoun.

0 If you don't understand a word you can _look it up_ in a dictionary. (look up)

1 Here's the application form. Make sure you .... in black ink. (fill in)

2 I've dropped some papers. Can you help me ....? (pick up)

3 When you've finished using the computers can you .... please? (switch off)

4 Peter's a heavy sleeper. Can you .... at 8am please? (wake up)

5 It's a difficult problem but I'm sure we can .... (work out)

Dependent prepositions

Complete the sentences with suitable dependent prepositions. Use a dictionary to help you.

0 The popularity of texting has resulted _in_ a decline in language skills.

1 People who eat too many TV dinners may suffer .... obesity and other health problems.

2 Many people feel that it is dangerous to rely too heavily .... electronic money like credit cards.

3 Modern MP3 players developed .... the Sony Walkman.

4 Purchasers are not always convinced .... celebrity endorsement of products.

5 The invention of the bar code succeeded .... making shopping quicker and more convenient.

Synonyms

These verbs are all synonyms of *make*, but have a more specific meaning.

| create | design | develop | manufacture | invent |

1 Use your dictionary to answer these questions. Which word(s):

1 can be used to describe things made in factories?

....

2 is/are often used to describe making something new, or making something for the first time? (two words)

....

3 can also mean to improve something?

....

4 often include(s) the idea of deciding how something will look as well as how it will work?

....

2 Complete the sentences with a appropriate form of one of the verbs.

0 The light bulb _was invented_ by the American scientist, Thomas Edison.

1 He works in a factory which .... computer hardware.

2 Our house .... and built by a famous local architect.

3 Many Asian countries started to .... their economies in the second half of the 20th century.

4 The opening of a new factory last year .... 200 new jobs in the local area.

Collocations: *make* and *do*

1 Decide if the words or phrases in the box are preceded by *make* or *do* and then put them in the appropriate column.

> a course   a choice   a decision   a degree
> a list   a loss   a mistake   a speech
> an appointment   an exercise   an experiment
> housework   money   progress
> research   some work

Make	Do

2 Fill in the gaps in the sentences with make or do in the appropriate form.

0 She was nervous of .... speeches in public.
1 He was no good at ...*making*... difficult decisions.
2 I believe that men and women should .... equal amounts of housework.
3 I'd like to .... a million dollars by the time I'm twenty!
4 I can't .... my homework if people .... a noise.
5 My spoken English has really improved but I still .... lots of spelling mistakes in my writing.

Unit 8 Conditionals
Real conditionals

A real conditional is used to talk about a possible situation and its likely outcome.
We use a zero conditional to talk about something that is definite or always true.
If you heat ice, it melts.
If + present simple + present simple

We use a first conditional to talk about something which is likely but not definite.
If it rains tomorrow, I'll take an umbrella.
If + present simple + will + infinitive

We can replace *will* with another modal verb (*may, should, might*).
If it rains tomorrow, I might go to the cinema.

We can replace *if* with *when* to show something always happens or is more definite.
When I am tired, I yawn. (zero)
When I see him I'll tell him. (first)

Unreal conditionals

We use a second conditional to talk about an unreal, unlikely or imaginary situation and its outcome.
If I won the lottery, I would travel around the world.
If she worked harder, she might pass her exams.
If + past simple + would (or other modal verb) + infinitive

Decide if these sentences are real or unreal and then <u>underline</u> the correct alternative.

0 If I get a good score in IELTS, I *go/might go/would go* to Cambridge University. ...*real*...
1 If the government does not do something about pollution, our health *will suffer/suffers/suffered*.
....
2 If I had more time, I *would be able/will be able/can* to study more. ....
3 The population will continue to grow if nothing *is done/was done/does* to prevent it. ....
4 When you are hot, you *sweat/would sweat/should sweat*. ....
5 More people would join the nursing profession if salaries *would be/were/are* higher. ....
6 You should have your eyes tested if you *had/have/will have* a lot of headaches. ....

Dependent prepositions
Complete the paragraphs with suitable dependent prepositions. Use a dictionary to help you.

Many people see therapies such as acupuncture as a sensible alternative **0** ...*to*... conventional medicine. People who are allergic **1** .... pollen, for example, may suffer **2** .... allergy symptoms for several months of the year. They prefer not to take drugs for this length of time and believe that acupuncture provides a cure **3** .... most of their symptoms.
Others disagree **4** .... this view. According to Professor Ernst, there is no scientific support **5** .... most of the claims made by alternative therapists. 'I'm not convinced **6** .... the so-called scientific explanations therapists give. When the therapies work it's simply because people believe **7** .... them.'

Collocations
Complete these sentences by making collocations. For some sentences there is more than one possible answer.

1 Seeing a doctor is a conventional way *of diagnosing/to diagnose* an illness.
2 The medicine relieved the .... of her cold.
3 Paracetamol is a drug taken .... pain.
4 Blood tests are often used to diagnose ....
5 The doctor .... antibiotics for his chest infection.

Unit 9 -ing form and infinitive

Some verbs are followed by an -ing form, eg *avoid, consider, imagine, involve, mind, practise*

Some verbs are followed by an infinitive, eg *agree, decide, fail, hope, promise, refuse, want, wish*

Some verbs can be followed by an -ing form or an infinitive, eg *begin, forget, remember, stop, try*

The meaning of these verbs may change (see page 108).

Note that a preposition is always followed by an -ing form.
I learn by doing.
I'm keen on writing.

<u>Underline</u> the best alternative.

0 I would like <u>*to do*</u>/*doing* VSO next year.
1 Do you mind *to help*/*helping* me with my homework?
2 I enjoy *to learn*/*learning* new words.
3 He avoids *to do*/*doing* his homework if he can.
4 He decided *to take*/*taking* the exam early.
5 Two months before the exam, she began *to study*/*studying* hard.
6 Did you remember *to lock*/*locking* the door?

Word formation

Complete the following sentences using the correct form of the word in brackets.

0 Passing his exam with 98% was a fantastic <u>*achievement*</u> (achieve)
1 As a result of cuts in spending, ... standards are dropping. (education)
2 After seven years of study, she finally .... as a doctor. (qualification)
3 In his job he had gained a good deal of .... and experience. (know)
4 Not everyone has the .... to play a musical instrument. (able)
5 When I was at school, I had to .... a lot of facts and figures. (memory)
6 The teacher said she was of above average .... (intelligent)

Hedging

Hedging, or cautious language, is a common feature of academic writing. The following are all common ways of hedging.

Phrases
Many people believe/assume that ...
It appears/seems that ...
It is often the case that ...

Modal verbs
can, could, may, might

It may be true that ...
The answer might be to ...

Adverbs of frequency
often, sometimes, usually

It is often assumed that ...

Adverbs
possibly, probably

It is probably true to say that ...

Unit 10 Expressing preferences

would like, *would prefer* and *would rather* can all be used to express a preference. However, the structures are slightly different.

would rather + *do* something
would rather + someone else + *did* something (past tense for hypothetical use)
would like/*would prefer* (someone) + *to do* something
prefer + *doing* something (for a general preference)

Choose the correct option(s) in each sentence.

0 He'd rather <u>*study*</u>/*studying*/*to study* law than engineering.
1 I'd like *going*/*to go*/*go* to university in Australia.
2 If it's OK with you, I'd rather *not go*/*not going*/*not to go* out tonight.
3 I prefer *wearing*/*wear*/*to wear* flat shoes.
4 I'd prefer him *coming*/*come*/*to come* next weekend.
5 I'd rather you *not smoking*/*didn't smoke*/*not to smoke* in here please.

Expressions with future meaning

Verbs with future meaning
aim/decide/expect/hope/plan + infinitive
I expect to go to university next year.

anticipate/predict + noun or *-ing* form
The government predicts a rise in the number of students over the next five years.

Modal verbs to express probability
may/might/could/should
You should send in your application soon if you want to be sure of a place on the course.

Adjectives/adverbs
to be + bound/sure/(un)likely + infinitive
You're bound to feel a little nervous before your Speaking exam.

Rearrange the words to make sentences.

0 plan to doctor a I become
I plan to become a Doctor

1 to in a I finish studies year aim my
....

2 might do I PhD eventually a
....

3 course will my soon I new start
....

4 eventually to I my am in father's company work likely
....

5 my hope gradually I improve English to
....

6 anticipate staying I three here at least years
....

Synonyms
Choose two alternative words or phrases from the box to complete each gap in the text.

increasing amounts	consider	discuss
effect impact	indicates	more and more
situation	state of affairs	suggests

Young people are spending **1** .... of their time watching television or on the internet and research **2** .... that this is having a negative **3** .... on their health.
In this essay I would like to **4** ....
what may have led to this **5** .... and look at some possible solutions.

Unit 11 Modals of obligation and prohibition: past and present
Modal verbs such as *must* and *should* are followed by a bare infinitive.
Need, have, ought use a full infinitive.
When these modals are used in the past there are some important changes to note.

Present time	Past time
should	*should have* + past participle
have to	*had to*
must	*had to*
mustn't	*was/weren't allowed to*
need	*needed*
don't need to	*didn't need to/needn't have*
don't have to	*didn't have to*
shouldn't	*shouldn't have* + past participle

- *Must* and *have to* are interchangeable in most cases. *Have to* can be used to express obligation from a third party.
  I have to get to work early, or my boss will give me the sack.
- *Should* and *ought to* have the same meaning, but *should* is much more common. *Ought to* can sound slightly more formal.

Rewrite these sentences in the past.

0 The world's resources should be more equally distributed.
The world's resources should have been more equally distributed.

1 People must be treated equally regardless of gender.
....

2 You don't need to hand in your essay until after the summer.
....

3 You don't have to book your train seat in advance.
....

4 You have to arrive at least an hour before your flight.
....

5 Higher taxes shouldn't be imposed on those with lower incomes.
....

6 People ought not to throw litter on the street.
....

Phrasal verbs

1 Match the phrasal verbs in box A with their synonyms in box B.

A

> aim at (something)   come up with (something)
> get away with (something)   get on with (something)
> kick off (something)   look into (something)

B

> continue   create   intend   investigate
> start   succeed in not being punished

2 Now complete these phrases with the appropriate phrasal verb, in the correct form.

0 Just let the advertising industry _get on with_ informing and entertaining – it's what we do best.

1 ... written to look like a normal article, but actually .... selling me something.

2 Here two experts .... the debate.

3 The government needs to .... these practices straightaway.

4 We mustn't let the advertising companies .... it.

5 We have to .... new and exciting ways to promote products.

Unit 12 Umbrella nouns

Umbrella nouns (or general nouns) are widely used in academic English:

- to help link ideas in a text and avoid repetition.
- to avoid using vague non-academic words like *thing*.

There is a general lack of awareness in some countries about health. This ~~lack of awareness~~ situation can result in increased incidence of some diseases.
Two ~~things~~ subjects that will be discussed in today's talk are revision techniques and time management.

The words *situation* and *subjects* are *umbrella nouns* and have been used to replace the crossed out words.

Choose an appropriate umbrella noun from the box to complete the sentences below. Use the plural form if necessary.

> ~~factor~~   problem   question   situation   subject   trend

0 Safety is one of the most important _factors_ when designing new cars.

1 Recent developments in genetics raise important moral and ethical ....

2 The country has suffered economic problems for many years but the .... has improved recently.

3 The research project succeeded despite a number of .... including a lack of government funding.

4 Pass rates for science subjects have increased in recent years and it is expected that this .... will continue.

5 Immigration is both complex and controversial and this .... will be discussed in more depth in next week's lecture.

Collocations

All these words can collocate with the word *exam*. Use them to complete the word map.

> do   fail   final   mark   nerves   oral
> pass   paper   practical   set   sit   ~~take~~

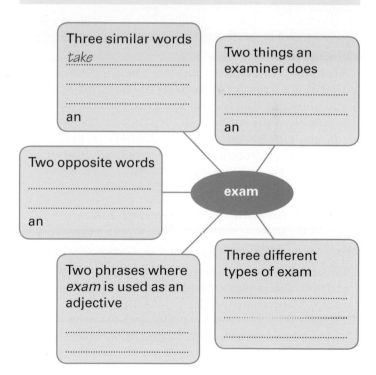

Three similar words
take
....
....
an ....

Two things an examiner does
....
....
an ....

Two opposite words
....
....
an ....

exam

Three different types of exam
....
....
....

Two phrases where *exam* is used as an adjective
....
....

Writing

Unit 1
Model answer for Task 1 on page 13 (Figure 1)

The graph shows the number of applications and acceptances at universities in the UK in the period 1994–2009. During this period student applications increased and the number of acceptances had a similar trend.

In 1994 there were just over 350,000 home applicants and this figure remained constant for two years. In 1996 there was a sharp increase to about 400,000 followed by a slight dip before numbers began to rise again. This trend was repeated in 2005. From 2006 the number of applicants increased sharply reaching 550,000 by 2009.

The number of acceptances followed a very similar trend yet the numbers are about 100,000 fewer than applicants. In 1994 the figure was about 250,000 and this rose to just over 400,000 by 2009.

From 1994 to 2009 there was an overall increase of about 200,000 home applicants for British universities while the number of acceptances was slightly lower at approximately 170,000 over the period.

(155 words)

Comments

This answer begins with a clear opening statement that is not exactly the same as the description in the question. The second sentence tells the reader generally what happens in the chart (... *student applications increased and the number of acceptances had a similar trend*). After this general point the descriptions become more specific.
The answer is well organized and clear.

Opening paragraphs for Figures 2–4

Figure 2
The pie chart shows the most popular countries for students to study overseas at university level in 2006. The preferred destination was the United States followed by the UK.

Figure 3
The bar chart provides information about which countries overseas students to the UK came from in 2008–9. The data show that more students came from China and India than other countries.

Figure 4
The table shows the university subjects which were studied by international students in the UK in 2009–10. By far the most popular subject was Business and administrative studies followed by Engineering and technology.

Unit 2
Model answer for Task 2 on page 27

Nowadays, most people are aware of the threat of climate change and are willing to make small changes to the way they live. However, for the majority of people this does not include such things as giving up their car or giving up flying abroad.

Small changes can certainly be valuable. If everyone always switched off lights when leaving a room, for example, this could have a significant impact on our energy use. People could also recycle more often or use rechargeable batteries.

That said, it is becoming more and more obvious that small changes are probably not enough. Many families now own two cars and use them for even the shortest journeys. The impact of this on the environment is enormous. The government has made some steps towards dealing with this problem by encouraging people to buy cars with lower emissions, but they also need to encourage the use of public transport. At the moment it is often more expensive as well as more inconvenient to travel by bus or train, and this needs to change.

Flying is another area where behaviour needs to change. It is predicted that 30% of our greenhouse gas emissions by 2050 will come from aeroplanes, if the current demand continues. Many people fly on business, but, surely, meetings could now be held using Skype and videoconferencing? The government should raise taxes on fuel for aircraft, which they currently subsidize, to encourage people to restrict their flying.

In conclusion, I would say that, where possible, the government should do more to encourage people to reduce their carbon footprint, rather than force them. However, they should also use any taxes on fuel to improve public transport, to make it easier for people to leave their cars at home or even give them up entirely.

(299 words)

Comments

This answer tackles the question well. It has been well-planned and is organized into five clear paragraphs with an introduction, main body and conclusion. In the conclusion, it is clearly stated how far the writer agrees with the statement. There is plenty of good vocabulary related to the topic (*fuel, lower emissions, carbon footprint*) and good use of linkers (*however, that said*). There is no penalty for writing *more* than 250 words, but be careful not to spend too long on one task.

Unit 3
Model answer for Task 1 on page 37

The table shows figures for the number of visits by UK residents to five different countries from 2004 to 2008. Spain was by far the most popular of the destinations while Egypt had the fewest visitors out of the places shown.

Spain and USA were the most popular countries to visit and numbers increased slightly at different times. However, by 2008 the number of visitors to these places had actually decreased over the period from 13,883,000 to 13,819,000 for Spain and by 164,000 for the USA.

The most notable increase in the number of UK visitors was to Poland as the figure increased five times from about 300,000 in 2004 to 1,578,000 in 2008. Numbers to Egypt almost doubled while visitors to India also rose significantly with the figure increasing from 657,000 to 956,000.

The chart shows that the most popular destinations such as Spain and USA remain popular even though there has been a slight drop in numbers while countries such as Poland, Egypt and India have become much more popular in recent years.

(174 words)

Comment

There is a clear opening statement which provides information about the most and least popular destinations. More detailed information is given in paragraphs 2 and 3 with specific figures mentioned. The concluding paragraph summarizes the overall trends.

Unit 4
Model answer for Task 2 on page 49

One of the most serious problems that schools face today is bad behaviour and poor discipline. Pupils often break the rules and are aggressive or rude, often showing a complete lack of respect for teachers. Such behaviour can have extremely negative effects, and tough measures and stricter punishments are necessary, but these can have both benefits and drawbacks.

The main advantage of stricter discipline is that it sends out a clear message that poor discipline will have appropriate consequences. If a pupil behaves badly in class, such as not doing the work assigned or swearing at a teacher, then they should be given a suitable punishment such as detention. In more extreme cases such as vandalism of school property or physical violence, then suspension or even expulsion from school should be considered.

If these rules are adhered to, any bad behaviour will be quickly dealt with and this will enable the other students to continue learning without major disruptions and ensure they make quicker progress.

On the other hand, there can also be disadvantages to having tougher measures and a less lenient approach as these can sometimes have a negative effect in that a restrictive, controlled atmosphere may limit some pupils' development. It is likely that some young people may have difficult family backgrounds and need more personalized support to help them achieve success.

There is no doubt that poor discipline in schools needs to be handled effectively but it is important to ensure that the balance between tough, stricter measures and a sensitive approach to dealing with bad behaviour should be considered carefully.

(264 words)

Comments

In the introduction the writer clarifies the question and signals that there are both advantages and disadvantages but uses different words (*benefits* and *drawbacks*). The opposing ideas are expressed in the two paragraphs in the main body with examples and supporting evidence, giving the answer balance. The writer includes a good range of topic-related vocabulary (*detention*, *vandalism*, *violence*, *suspension*, *expulsion*, *lenient*) and the conclusion sums up the main points.

Unit 5
Model answer for Task 1 on page 63

The pie chart and bar chart show the proportion of men and women doing full- and part-time work in the UK, comparing the amount earned by each of these groups in 2010.

Of a total workforce of nearly 25 million, just over half are men, the majority working in full-time employment. In contrast, women make up 49% of the workforce and are more likely than men to have a part-time job, 21% of the total compared to only 6% of the total for men.

The figures for average hourly pay are noticeably greater for full-time work than part-time work. Interestingly, men with full-time jobs earn slightly more than women, £13 an hour compared to almost £12 an hour. However, for part-time work the opposite is true, with women earning an average of £8 an hour, a little more than part-time men.

Overall, the information in the charts shows small but significant differences between the different groups in the workforce.

(158 words)

Comments

There is a clear introductory statement describing what the two charts show. The writer has chosen to organize the text by describing the pie chart in the second paragraph and the bar chart in the third. The most significant facts are highlighted and the different groups compared. Relevant structures and vocabulary are used (*just over half*, *the majority*, *noticeably greater*, *slightly more than*, *almost*, *a little more than*).

Unit 6
Model answer for Task 1 on page 75

This diagram shows the process of extracting sugar from sugar beets. First, the sugar beets arrive at the plant and are unloaded from the trucks. They are dirty because they have come straight from the farm, so they are shaken in order to remove the dirt and rocks, and then washed in a machine called a beet washer.

Next the beets are cut up into small pieces, which are called cossettes. After this, sugar is drawn from the beets using hot water, which makes a kind of sugar 'juice'.

As this juice may still be dirty, milk of lime is added in order to clean it. The mixture is then filtered so that the milk of lime can be removed.

Following this, the sugar juice is heated several times, which evaporates the water. This results in a purer sugar solution.

Finally, the sugar is boiled and spun in a centrifuge to create crystals. *(153 words)*

Comments

There is a clear introductory sentence describing what the diagram shows. Sequencers (*First*, *Next*, *Following this*), connectors indicating purpose (*in order to ...*) and reason clauses (*so that the milk of lime can be ...*) are used correctly. The passive voice is employed appropriately to show the process (*they are shaken*; *the sugar juice is heated*) and to keep the text impersonal and factual.

Unit 7
Model answer for Task 1 on page 84

This fire extinguisher is a strong metal container filled with water used to put out fires. Inside this is a cartridge containing gas. Near the lever of the extinguisher, there is a pull pin to prevent the handle being pressed accidentally.

In order to use the extinguisher, first the pin must be removed. Secondly, the lever is pressed. This pushes a rod into the valve of the cartridge and opens it. The gas is then released at high pressure from the cartridge into the main container, putting pressure on the water within it. This pressure causes the water to be forced up the siphon tube and out of the nozzle to extinguish the fire. If the lever is released, the rod will move upwards. This closes the valve on the cartridge of gas and removes the pressure on the water. Therefore the water will stop rising up the siphon and out of the nozzle.

The fire extinguisher is a useful device which can save lives. *(165 words)*

Comments

The opening sentence explains what the object is and what it does. Parts are identified (*a pull pin*) and the function (*to prevent the handle being pressed accidentally*), location (*inside this is a cartridge*) and what happens in the process are described using a range of structures (*If the lever is released, the rod will move upwards.*). The description is clear, simple and follows the sequence shown in the diagram. The final sentence sums up the device's usefulness.

Unit 8
Model answer for Task 2 on page 100

There is no doubt that finding possible cures and treatments for diseases is vital and a great deal of money is spent each year on funding such medical research. However, it is clear that money used for research should not be diverted from maintaining and improving the health services currently available.

There have been many medical advances, which have only been possible due to the work of scientists. It could be argued that without medical research, some common treatments which most people take for granted nowadays, like immunization and x-rays, would not have been possible. We now have a much better understanding of the causes of life-threatening diseases like cancer and how best to treat them and this has increased survival rates for many cancer sufferers.

However, all research is expensive and it can take years of work and a great deal of money before the work of a scientist achieves a successful result. Some research is also viewed by many to be less important and even dangerous or unethical, for example, research into infertility or cloning.

For this reason, it is important that sufficient money is also made available for the maintenance and development of hospitals, equipment and drugs, as well as the training of medical professionals. Obviously, without these, patients would not receive the high standards of care that they need to recover.

In conclusion, whilst it is clear that medical research is vital in providing new cures and treatments, the importance of maintaining a well-equipped system of healthcare with professionally trained staff should not be forgotten. Both are necessary to improve the lives and welfare of patients and money should be made available to fund them equally.   *(280 words)*

Comments

In the introduction the writer states that both of the points mentioned in the question are vital and the answer provides a well-balanced coverage of the topic. The second paragraph discusses the importance of scientific research in the medical field with specific examples (*x-rays, immunization*) demonstrating a good range of vocabulary. The third paragraph mentions some of the arguments against scientific research (*expensive, ... dangerous or unethical*). The fourth paragraph puts forward the main points in favour of maintaining good facilities and healthcare. The conclusion states that both areas are important and makes the suggestion that they are funded equally. In this answer the writer uses an impersonal style throughout.

Unit 9
Model answer for Writing Task 2 on page 111

There is no doubt that people are often judged in terms of their educational success. People need to pass exams to go to university and study for a degree and the majority of jobs and careers require these types of qualifications. However, this is surely not the only way to assess intelligence.

There are many people who leave school at the age of 16 yet go on to have successful careers in more practical jobs. This is often particularly true of those who have trades, such as plumbers and carpenters. Although they may not have passed many exams, they have successfully learned a skill which definitely requires intelligence.

Intelligence may also be demonstrated in creative or artistic ability. Musicians have the skills to perform complex pieces of music, while artists can create beautiful pieces of work through painting or sculpture. Such skills cannot necessarily be learned on a course or from a book, yet could be considered to be a more natural form of intelligence.

A final example of another aspect of intelligence is knowledge, which people often acquire through self-study or experience. They may not have done well at school or university, but have become 'educated' by learning about a subject independently or by dealing with a variety of real-life situations and problems. Indeed there are many highly qualified, successful

people who often lack 'common sense' and who would be less able to cope with such difficulties.

In conclusion, there is far more to the idea of intelligence than academic achievement. Skills and knowledge are important and give intelligence a broader meaning, proving that it cannot always be measured by educational success alone. *(274 words)*

Comments

This answer is a good example of the writer almost completely disagreeing with the statement. There are three main points made and each one is given a separate paragraph, with examples to back up the writer's opinion.

Model answer for Writing Task 2 on page 112

It is true to say that family background is an important factor in a child's learning and academic achievement, but whether parents have more influence than teachers on their children will depend on a number of factors.

Many people believe that we inherit intelligence from our parents and it is often the case that children of gifted parents go on to repeat their parent's success at school. However, this is not always the case. In fact, it is far more likely that children who have supportive and interested parents often have higher academic achievement than those who do not receive such support.

Early childhood is a key stage in a child's development and experiences at this time can have far-reaching consequences in the child's future. It is usually at this time when a parent's input is most influential. At this stage a parent often has sole charge of their child and therefore their influence is very significant.

Later in life, as the child starts school, teachers begin to have a greater influence. Often, one or more teachers can have considerable influence over a child's future, inspiring them in a particular subject or helping them to choose a career path. Teachers can have a particularly important role to play if a child lacks support from home due to emotional or financial difficulties which can have a negative effect on their learning. Therefore, it is definitely possible for a child to succeed academically, even without the help of a supportive family.

To conclude, it is clear that both parents and teachers can have a huge influence on a child's learning. However, in my view, positive support and help from the family may provide a more significant influence overall.   *(286 words)*

Comments

This is an example of a more balanced response to a 'to what extent do you agree' question. The writer gives arguments on both sides and concludes by giving a personal opinion. Notice that the writer frequently uses hedging to make her views more tentative (and thus balanced).

Unit 10

See model answer on page 124.

Unit 11

Model answer for Writing Task 2 on page 135

Perhaps the majority of people would agree that the young should not be encouraged to consume too many food products high in fat, salt and sugar. There is plenty of evidence that such foods are extremely bad for health, and growing numbers of obese children and teenagers. However, does this mean that there should be a total ban on the advertising of these products to under-16s?

Those who feel that such a ban is necessary argue that children and young people are particularly easily persuaded by advertisers. Many adverts are designed to appeal to the young by using cartoon characters or famous people, and their effect may be powerful as a result.

Others argue that it is the responsibility of parents to educate their children about the importance of a healthy diet, and to ensure that their children eat well, choosing unhealthy treats only occasionally. If parents buy plenty of fruit and vegetables rather than biscuits, chocolates and crisps, that will be what their children eat.

On balance I would say that there is certainly some truth in both arguments. Parents certainly do need to take some responsibility for their children's eating habits. However, young people will also spend a good part of their time at school or with friends, away from their parents, and may then choose to buy the foods that the advertisements have encouraged them to want. Overall, I think there can be no harm in banning these adverts from children's programmes, while there may be harm in letting them stay.   *(255 words)*

Comments

The essay is clearly structured. The introduction sets out the question, in different words, and the next two paragraphs lay out some of the arguments on each side. In the final paragraph the writer summarizes his reaction to both sides of the argument and gives his personal opinion.

Unit 12
Model answer for Writing Task 1 on page 142

The graph shows the number of medals won by four countries at six consecutive Olympic® Games over a 20-year period.

One of the most notable features is the enormous increase in medals won by China, whose medal total rose from only 28 in 1988 to 100 in 2008. The most significant increase came at the 2008 games when the medal total was almost 40 more than at the previous Olympics.

The United States won more medals than the Chinese team at the 2008 games but over the six games their overall increase was not as great, and in both 1996 and 2000 the total actually decreased slightly from earlier games.

There was also a decrease in the number of medals won by Great Britain in 1992 and 1996 but the amount won in 2008 was almost double that of 1988.

Japan's success at the six games was mixed with the total of medals fluctuating over these 20 years, the greatest success being 37 medals in 2004.

Overall, the four countries had different degrees of success over the six Olympic Games. *(180 words)*

Comments

The answer begins with a clear opening statement giving general information about the data. The most significant facts are highlighted (*One of the most notable features ...; The most significant increase ...*). More specific details are then considered with all four countries being mentioned. The writer uses different verbs and nouns to describe the changes (*increase, decrease, fluctuate*).

Model answer for Writing Task 2 on page 145

It is certainly true to say that for many people success is measured according to a person's wealth and possessions. Driving an expensive car, living in a nice house and enjoying a high standard of living would generally be considered as signs of success. This may indeed be true but there are many other ways, in my view, in which success can be achieved or measured.

Firstly, education and training are important ways to achieve, and therefore measure, success. Passing exams or completing a course are signs of successful activities. Similarly, gaining GCSEs, a diploma or a degree are also recognized as successful achievements, yet qualifications such as these do not always lead to riches.

Another type of success can be achieved in work situations simply by doing one's own particular job effectively. Furthermore, job satisfaction and career fulfilment are also indications of success, yet do not necessarily mean being in highly paid employment. For example, a voluntary worker for an aid agency in a developing country who has helped to construct buildings or to improve facilities has been part of a successful project.

Success can also be judged in other fields such as sport or music. For example, a person could gain individual success in a sport such as golf or tennis or play in a winning football or basketball team. I also believe that learning to play a musical instrument and being part of a group or orchestra is also a significant achievement.

There is no doubt that many people regard success purely in terms of wealth and materialistic values. However, in my opinion this does not account for the variety of other ways that success can be achieved.

(281 words)

Comments

The essay has been organized into five paragraphs with a clear introduction, main body and conclusion. In terms of opinions, the three central paragraphs on different types of success (education, work, sport/music) are introduced with a topic sentence (for example, *Success can also be judged in other fields such as sport or music ...*) followed by evidence and examples to support the main idea. The text is easy to follow as linkers and relevant phrases are used accurately (*Firstly, Another type of, I also believe*). The writer has also used a wide vocabulary range (*voluntary worker, materialistic*) and plenty of appropriate collocations (*achieve/gain success, significant achievement, passing exams*).

Audioscripts

1 Studying overseas

🔊 1.1

(**AO** = Admissions Officer; **LC** = Li Cha)

AO: Hello Li Cha, I'm Susie Shaw, the Admissions Officer.

LC: Hello, pleased to meet you.

AO: I'd just like to talk to you to find out a little more information to give your new tutor, Stephen Ennis.

LC: OK.

AO: How old are you, Li Cha?

LC: I'm eighteen.

AO: OK. Now your start date is next Monday, that's the 14th of February. And you're in class 2B.

LC: Sorry, 2D?

AO: No, 2B. B for Bravo. Do you know when you're finishing? October or November?

LC: I'd like to go home and see my family in November.

AO: Finishing at the end of October then, the 29th. We need a contact number here and one in China, Li Cha. Do you live with your parents?

LC: No, I live with my grandmother and brother, Shao, in Hong Kong. Their telephone number is 8731 4591. And my mobile number here is 0825 701 6924.

AO: Obviously you've studied English before. How long have you been studying?

LC: About three years.

AO: Is that all? You must work hard! I thought you'd been studying for at least five years. Do you have any other hobbies?

LC: Well, I like playing table tennis. I also spend a lot of time emailing friends. Oh, and I like reading. I read in English sometimes too.

AO: Great, that's probably why your English is so good. Now, you want to take IELTS, don't you? Why's that?

LC: Well, I want to go to the University of Sydney. I'd like to study IT and computing.

AO: Really? Would you like to get a job in IT in the future?

LC: Yes, I'd really like to work with computers, there are just so many possibilities.

🔊 1.2

Hello everyone. Thanks for coming this evening. I've been invited here tonight by the International Students' Society to talk a bit about culture shock. For many of you who have recently arrived from your home countries, life here in New Zealand must seem quite strange and different to you in many ways. Because of my work as an anthropologist, I've had the opportunity to work in quite a number of different countries with quite diverse cultures, so I've had my fair share of culture shock and know exactly how you might be feeling at this time.

Tonight, I want to talk a bit about my own experiences of culture shock and then go on to give you a few hints on how to minimize the effects.

I first left New Zealand when I was only 22 to do some research work on the island of Sumatra in Indonesia. I was interested in learning all about the country and the people, but I was particularly fascinated by the architecture.

In the part where I was working, the buildings have beautiful, curved rooves that I had never seen before and I loved them!

🔊 1.3

Life in Indonesia is very different from life in New Zealand, and at first I found it very difficult to adjust. The worst thing was looking different to everyone else. I'm about average height in New Zealand, but in Indonesia, I was much taller than most people, and it made me feel very uncomfortable. One of the best things, though, was the food. A change in diet can be one of the biggest problems of moving to a new country, but for me Indonesia was not difficult from that point of view. I'm very keen on spicy food, and there is an Indonesian chicken curry called 'Rendang' that is out of this world!

Climate can be another thing that people find it difficult to adjust to. I found working in Egypt very difficult because of the extreme heat. In contrast, living in Finland was hard because during the winter months the days are so short. Where I was, in the North, it was only light for about four or five hours a day in December. By the end I was pretty good at cross country skiing, though!

Language is often one of the biggest barriers when you're settling into a new country, but I'm quite good at learning them and this hasn't usually been a problem for me. However, Japan was quite different. I had learned some spoken Japanese before I went, but I hadn't tried to learn to write, so initially, I was a bit nervous about going to a country where I couldn't read anything. This did make life a lot more difficult for me. I couldn't read the destinations on buses, or menus in restaurants, or even road signs.

Sometimes it can be very small things that you're not used to that can make you feel the most homesick. For me, in China, it was connected with eating again. I really love Chinese food, but I found it very difficult to eat with chopsticks. I did learn eventually, but I still prefer a fork! One of the best things about my stay in China, though, was the Professor I was working with at the university. He was really enthusiastic about his work, and that made my job very satisfying.

OK, well enough about my experience. Having mentioned some of the problems I faced, I want to look a bit more generally at how you can adapt to culture shock ... (fade)

2 Earth today

🔊 1.4

⅓
3 million tonnes
59%
54 degrees Celsius
$450
¾
30 kilos
6,900 metres
27th December 2017

🔊 1.5

(**L** = Lecturer; **J** = James)

L: ... and today James is going to give us his presentation on household waste disposal. James, are you ready?

J: Yeah, thanks. Well, when I was deciding what to do for this presentation, this topic really attracted me, because it's such an important issue, and it's going to become even more important in the near future when new European law comes into effect. Um ... if you have any questions as I go along, please feel free to ask, and I'll do my best to clarify things.

OK. I think the facts and figures speak for themselves: on average we produce 30 million tonnes of solid household waste every year, or around half a tonne per person, which is a tremendous amount if you think about it, and obviously it's vital that waste is minimized and disposed of in a way that protects our environment and our health.

We're talking about waste food products, packaging, newspapers, glass, garden waste and so on. In fact some studies have shown that almost two thirds of our waste is biodegradable; food, paper, natural textiles for example and glass, which of course can be recycled, makes up about 10%.

L: Sorry, sorry to interrupt, but can I just ask you if those figures are for the UK only, or are the proportions the same in other countries?

J: No, that's fairly universal, at least in the developed world, but different countries do have very different levels of recycling. In Britain for example, we bury in the region of 25 million tonnes of biodegradable waste; this is known as landfill. I'm sure you can imagine that this is a limited option, particularly in a country with a small amount of land. As well as this, 2.5 million tonnes is burned to produce electricity, which is better, but still has environmental problems associated with it, and 2.5 million tonnes is recycled or composted.

L: This is the current situation in the UK?

J: Yes, it is. However, new European law requires us to reduce amounts of waste, and by 2020 we will only be able to send 10 million tonnes of this for landfill and the rest will have to be recycled, burned or treated in a different way. So clearly things are going to have to change, and everyone is involved in this issue in some way.

(**L** = Lecturer; **J** = James)

L: So what exactly is being done?

J: Well, the policy of the government and of environment agencies is firstly to reduce the amount of waste we create to begin with, and secondly, to reuse the waste that is created. Obviously some disposal is necessary but the aim is to limit this as much as possible. What we need to do is to conserve raw materials, like tin and aluminium, while still protecting the environment and public health.

L: Yes, but what does this mean in reality?

J: There are quite a few things that are being done, mostly by local councils. They're responsible for household 'dustbin' collections, or taking away all the rubbish you produce in the home. In recent years many more sites have been set up to collect waste separately for recycling. There are often containers in car parks or outside supermarkets for people to put bottles in; clear, green and brown bottles are separated. Also newspapers and magazines can be recycled, as well as tins made of aluminium. One of the problems with this, though, is that most people are not bothering to take their rubbish there. To overcome this, some local councils also provide special containers, often called 'recycling bins' for residents to collect glass and paper in. They put these outside their houses at the same time as their rubbish, and they are collected and recycled.

L: I see. So are you saying that recycling is more important than actually reducing waste?

J: No. Nowadays, many products are increasingly being designed with reuse or recycling in mind and I think, in general, people are far more aware about these issues. In some countries, like Switzerland for example, they have put a tax on black rubbish bags, so that people are encouraged not to just throw things straight in the bin, and to reduce their rubbish. Having said that, I think it's still absolutely crucial for the government to continue raising people's awareness of the importance of waste management and disposal. Overall, the situation has improved over the past 25 years, and this is mainly because of new laws with tighter controls and higher standards. Even so, individuals and businesses still need to work very hard to reduce and reuse waste as much as possible.

L: Thank you very much. That was a very nice presentation. Does anyone have any further questions?

1 I can't stand the fact that cars are still allowed in many city centres – they cause so much noise and pollution. At rush hour the traffic is always gridlocked. I much prefer city centres that are pedestrianized, where people can walk around with no worries about too much traffic.

2 I guess I'm quite lazy really as I don't bother recycling much except newspapers. I know we should try and reuse our resources if possible, but sometimes it's just not convenient. I do feel a bit guilty about adding to the amount of landfill, but

I'm convinced that more people would recycle stuff if there were better facilities, and it was generally easier.

3 Well, er, there are quite a lot of alternatives. There's solar power, wind power, even wave power. And, of course, nuclear power. Some people say that nuclear power is too dangerous. But if you ask me, it's our only real option. The others just don't produce enough power, do they?

3   All around the world

(**TEP** = Tele-enquiry person; **S** = Student)

TEP: Hello, National Train Enquiry Line. Can I help you?

S: Yes, please. I'd like to find out about times and prices of trains to Edinburgh.

TEP: Fine. And which station will you be travelling from?

S: Birmingham.

TEP: And when would you like to travel?

S: Umm. Friday March the 4th.

TEP: Will that be a Single or Return?

S: Return please.

TEP: Standard or First class?

S: Standard.

TEP: And what time of day would you like to travel?

S: In the morning, please, um, round about 8 o'clock.

TEP: Right, well, there's a train which leaves Birmingham New Street at 8.05 arriving in Edinburgh at 12.38.

S: OK, er, let me write that down ... leaving at five past eight and getting there at ... what time?

TEP: 12.38.

S: 12.38. Thanks. Do I have to change trains?

TEP: No, it's direct.

S: And what about the one after that?

TEP: The next one is at 9.15, arriving Edinburgh at 14.35, with a change at Stockport.

S: OK, leaving 9.50, arriving 2.35.

TEP: No, 9.15.

S: Oh. OK. And what about coming back?

TEP: What time would you like to leave?

S: Late afternoon, please.

TEP: Right. There's one at 16.45 which is direct and gets to Birmingham at 20.21, and the one after that leaves at 18.05 arriving at 21.57 including a change at Manchester.

S: Oh, would that be Manchester Oxford Road?

TEP: Erm, no it's Manchester Piccadilly.

S: Right. And how much is the cheapest ticket?

TEP: Well, it depends. If you can leave after 9am, it's cheaper. There's an Apex Super

Saver which you have to book at least 14 days before you want to travel. That costs £33.50.

S: Thirty three ... ?

TEP: Fifty.

S: OK. And what happens if I want to leave before 9am?

TEP: If you can book seven days in advance, then you can buy an Apex Peak Saver. That costs £41.30, but if you can't do that, the next cheapest ticket is the Standard Saver which costs £54 return.

S: So it's £41.30 if I book seven days in advance.

TEP: Yes.

S: And forty five if I don't.

TEP: No, it's £54 for the Standard Saver.

S: Oh, OK.

TEP: If you can travel on a different day of the week, then we have the Off Peak Saver at £38.

S: But I can't travel on a Friday for that fare?

TEP: That's right.

S: Fine. Thanks very much for your help.

TEP: You're welcome.

S: Bye.

TEP: Bye.

(**IDP** = Information desk person; **S** = Student)

IDP: Hello, can I help you?

S: Yes, I hope so. I've just arrived, and I'm trying to find my way around the train station. Can you tell me where the ticket office is?

IDP: Yes, of course. Look over there, to your right, the ticket office is to the right of the café as you look at it.

S: Oh yes. Thanks. And are those the platforms straight ahead of us?

IDP: Mmmm – which one do you need?

S: I think I need platform 15.

IDP: Yes – platform 15 is in the far corner.

S: Sorry, I can't see it ...

IDP: Just there, behind the flower shop.

S: Oh yes. Great – just one more thing – can you tell me where the toilets are?

IDP: Sure – they're over there, on the left, behind the newsagent's.

S: Thanks for all your help.

IDP: No problem.

Hello. Can I just have your attention for a minute? Thank you. My name is Mary Golding. Some of you may recognize me – I used to be a teacher here at the college, but I changed jobs last year, and I now work as the Student Officer. OK, well, I'm in today to tell you about a trip that we've got going to er … Paris. Well, this'll be a good chance for those of you who haven't been to France before to have a look at another country, and Paris is very beautiful. We'll be visiting many of the major tourist sites, sampling some French cuisine and you'll all be able to practise your language skills! This year there are 30 places available, a big increase on last year when only 20 were able to go. At least four members of staff will be travelling too. I think those of you who come will thoroughly enjoy it. The trip is going to be for five days. Originally we planned to leave on Friday the 30th of March but this has been changed and we will now depart on Saturday the 31st of March. We'll be leaving pretty early in the morning, seven o'clock from college, so you'll have to set your alarm clocks, and we'll be going through the Channel Tunnel on the train, so no ferries or coaches for those people who get seasick or travel sick! We aim to leave Paris on Wednesday at about 11 in the morning and should be back by 10pm that night.

🔊 **1.12**

So, what will we be doing when we get there? If you look at the diagram of Paris that I've given you, you can see that we're going to be staying in a small hotel near the centre of town. It's actually in the area called Montmartre. The accommodation will be shared, so you'll be in a room with one of your friends – you can obviously choose who you'd like to share with. On the first day we're in Paris, we'll be going on a boat trip, up the River Seine and up the Eiffel Tower, the famous monument in the middle of Paris. There should be a good view from up there. Both of these things are included in the cost of the trip, so you won't need to worry about spending extra money. On the second day, we'll be going to Notre Dame, which is a large cathedral with beautiful stained glass windows. There's no admission charge for this, but there are lots of souvenir shops around, so you might need some money for those! There will be lots of time for having a look around on your own, and doing some shopping – I know that some of you are very keen on that! On the third day, our last day in Paris, you'll be free to do whatever you like. You could go to an art gallery, for example the Louvre is a very famous one, where you can see the 'Mona Lisa'. You'll have to pay to get in there, but it's not expensive. The biggest problem is that the queue to get in is often very long. The cost of the whole trip is a hundred and twenty pounds, which includes all of the transport, the hotel, and breakfasts. You'll have to buy other food yourself, so you'll need more money for that. It's a really popular trip, we've had real success with it before, I'm sure those of you who come will really enjoy it.

If you'd like to go, can you sign up on this form on the student notice board by Friday. It'll be first come, first served, so do try and sign up as quickly as you can. Thank you very much, I hope to see some of you on the trip.

🔊 **1.13**

I'm going to talk about a place I have always wanted to visit which is Disneyland in Florida in the United States. It's famous all over the world as the place where you can meet all your favourite characters from Disney movies: Mickey Mouse, Snow White, Cinderella. There are many wonderful things to see there like fairytale castles and you can go on exciting rides from your favourite films. I know it's very popular and so I imagine it's crowded and busy all year round – I expect you have to wait a long time for some of the rides but I'm sure it would be worth it. I think there is a parade every day where you can see all the famous Disney characters walking and dancing down the streets with music and, and afterwards you can meet them and have your photo taken with them. The other thing I would like to do there is go shopping so I can buy lots of souvenirs to remember the trip and gifts for my friends and family. The reason I would like to visit Disneyland is it has been a dream of mine since I was very small. I have always loved Disney films and although I am much older now I still love them today. I think Disneyland is somewhere that the whole family can enjoy, whatever your age, and one day I hope to go with my own children.

4 Crime and punishment

🔊 **1.14**

It's very nice to see so many of you here tonight. I'm Constable Moore and I'm the Crime Prevention Officer for this area. I'm here tonight to talk about 'Neighbourhood Watch'. Can I ask how many of you have been involved with this before? Oh yes, a few of you – that's good. Well, for the rest of you, Neighbourhood Watch is a scheme set up between the police and local people and I'd like to tell you a bit about how it operates.

Basically, it's just common sense and community spirit. Fifty or a hundred years ago, people tended to live in the area that they grew up in and they didn't move around much, so most people would have known their neighbours. They probably knew each other's habits – what times they came home, who their friends were – that kind of thing, and so it was very obvious if something abnormal was happening. If a stranger was hanging around, or if someone was moving things out of a house, usually someone in the area would see what was happening and would call the police, or take some kind of action. In these days where people move around the country so much, you lose a lot of that community spirit. We don't tend to know our neighbours very well, and we feel a bit embarrassed to get involved.

Imagine this scene. One day, you see a large van outside your neighbour's house and some men carrying things out of the house into the van. Without any knowledge or information about your neighbour, most of us would feel too embarrassed to do anything. Meanwhile, your neighbour's house is being burgled and all of his possessions are being stolen in broad daylight!

Another example is vandalism – people might see someone smashing a telephone box or spraying paint on a wall, but usually they don't want to get involved or call the police.

🔊 **1.15**

These kinds of things happen every day. A Neighbourhood Watch scheme aims to bring back a bit of the 'nosy neighbour' in us all, so that we'll know if we see something suspicious, and feel as if we can contact the police.

How much you do is really flexible. It might be as simple as keeping an eye on a neighbour's home while they are away on holiday, or keeping a look out for suspicious things going on in your road. If you have time, you might want to take a more active role as a committee member, or volunteer to write, print or distribute newsletters. It's really up to you.

Another major benefit of being in a watch programme is that often insurance companies will lower your premium on your house insurance. Talk to your insurance company to check the details on this, sometimes you have to fit suitable locks on your windows and doors first – but this is a worthwhile thing to do, anyway.

Right – has anyone got any questions …

🔊 **1.16**

(P = Presenter; R = David Renshaw; L = Lorna Coates; J = Jennifer Simpson)

P: Today on 'Burning Issues' we are going to discuss the issue of school absenteeism or truancy. It's been in the news a lot recently because of the woman from Oxford who was jailed because she didn't make sure her two daughters were going to school regularly. First of all, let me introduce my guests, David Renshaw, a government spokesperson, Lorna Coates from The Crime Reduction Charity and Jennifer Simpson, a mother of three from Oxfordshire. Let me start with you, Mr Renshaw. What is the government doing about truancy?

R: Good morning. Well, obviously, children need to go to school. Truancy damages education, of course, but can also lead children to a life of crime.

P: But aren't the new laws about putting parents in prison rather tough?

R: Well, we have introduced imprisonment in some cases, and some people think this is too hard, but it does seem to work. Even the mother who was jailed said that it was a good thing for her children because they now realize how important it is to go to school. It's not the only measure we have, though. Something else we are thinking about is 'weekend' prison sentences. This means that the parent would only go to prison at the weekends, but could still keep their job in the week. We're also considering heavy fines.

P: OK. Thanks for that. Lorna, maybe you could tell us why you think children play truant.

L: Well I must say that I think the government isn't looking at the reasons why children play truant – they just want a quick answer, and I don't think it'll be successful. Children miss school for many reasons. For example, they might be unhappy at home, or they might have friends who play truant and encourage them to do the same. Peer pressure like this is very strong in teenagers, particularly. Bullying is another common reason. Children who are bullied at school will often avoid going. I strongly believe that more research needs to be conducted into this problem.

P: That's all very well but can you be more specific?

L: Well, for a start, I don't think punishing the parents will have long-term benefits. Everybody needs to work on this together –

parents, children, schools, the government and social services. It shouldn't be just the government sending parents to prison.

R: We are obviously trying to make that happen, but it's very difficult. For example, in the spring, there were over twelve thousand youngsters absent from school, and a lot of these were with their parents. Now, if children are missing school with their parent's consent, then the government needs to take tough measures.

L: Yes, but it's not always as simple as that, is it? What I'm saying is that we need to look at the reasons why this is happening.

🎧 1.17

P: Right. Let's look at it from a parent's point of view. Jennifer, you live in Oxford and have three teenage children?

J: That's right.

P: So how do you feel about this issue? Do you think that the parents are responsible for children playing truant?

J: Well, I think Lorna's right that it is a very complex issue and I tend to agree that you can't punish the parents for the child's behaviour. If a parent is sent to prison or fined heavily, this isn't going to help us to understand the main reasons why their child is missing school. If the child is unhappy or depressed about something at school, this isn't going to help, is it?

P: A good point Jennifer. So what would be better?

J: I think the emphasis should always be on the child. You need to find out why he or she is missing school. Then you can make decisions on that information about what to do.

L: Jennifer's right and can I just add that this is the approach that our charity would advocate too.

P: Counselling is another effective option. Wouldn't you agree, Lorna?

L: Well, it's certainly a possibility.

P: Do you have anything else to say, Mr Renshaw?

R: I can assure you that the government is considering all of these points and I should add that nothing is definite yet – we are still at the proposal stage.

P: OK. Thank you all very much for contributing to this discussion. And on tomorrow's programme … (fade)

🎧 1.18

Well, that's a good question … this has actually happened to me and some of my friends. Last year I left my mobile lying on a desk in a classroom and when I came back after break it was gone. I think what people should do is be very careful about personal security and always keep their valuables in a safe place. Personally I think it is a good idea not to show off expensive items like phones as this may tempt some people to steal them.

(pause)

Yes, I think that's very important that there are strict rules on the road to make sure that motorists drive more carefully. For example in my country the government introduced stricter speed limits about three ago which was very unpopular at the time. However, even though we have only had the law for a few years the number of accidents on the roads has decreased significantly. I'd say that stricter penalties have also made people think more carefully about the way they drive. Some people say that speed cameras are a good way to stop drivers going too fast but I'm not sure that they are effective.

(pause)

Possibly, but as far as I know the police in my country earn quite a lot compared with other jobs and although their job can be dangerous and difficult I believe that it would be better to put more money into education or healthcare.

5   A career or a job

🎧 1.19

(**S** = Sally; **J** = John)

S: Hi John, how're you doing?

J: Oh, Hi Sal, not too bad. Just beginning to realize that it won't be long before I have to start looking for a job.

S: But the Spring term's only just started!

J: I know, but think how fast the last two terms went – we'll be finished before we know it!

S: I guess you're right. It's a bit scary isn't it? What are you hoping to do?

J: With my degree in business I'd like to go into marketing but I'll probably end up in Sales as there may be more jobs there, so I'm not totally sure at the moment. Oh, that reminds me, there's a careers talk next week which we could go to if you fancy it. Anyway, what about you – any plans yet?

S: Well, I really want to get a job overseas. My sister and her two kids live in Australia. She's a doctor and I'd love to go out there, but before that I'm going to look for a job teaching English somewhere in Asia, possibly in China.

J: Really, that'd be great! I'll come and visit you!

S: Yeah, OK. Apparently there's a big demand for English teachers in China but I'm a bit worried as I'm not really sure how to go about finding a job or how to sell myself and to be honest I don't know how useful this type of experience will be for my long-term job prospects in this country.

J: It's difficult, isn't it? So what are you doing next Wednesday? Shall we go to this talk?

S: Who's the speaker then?

J: It's a guy called Adam Lorimer, one of the careers advisors – he once came in and talked to us about writing CVs. I thought he was quite good. He used to work in Human Resources apparently so he should know what he's talking about.

S: OK. Is that the 16th or the 17th of January? Let me just check. OK, it's the 17th.

J: So what do you think? Shall we go?

S: Maybe – what's he going to talk about?

J: Apparently the talk will cover looking for work and writing applications, including tips on how to impress your potential employers.

S: That sounds perfect, actually. What time does it start?

J: Umm, 7.30pm. Why don't we meet a bit earlier – say half past six and have a drink in the café?

S: And where did you say the talk is exactly?

J: Right. It's in the engineering block in … C something … I think … let me double-check … yes, C13 which is really easy to find as it's on the ground floor. I'll meet you there.

🎧 1.20

S: I've never been to Engineering. Is it the building opposite the Library?

J: No, that's the History faculty. It's opposite Modern Languages.

S: OK. Is there a small garden in front?

J: That's right, with a water fountain.

S: I know.

J: After you've walked in the main entrance you'll see a café directly in front of you. We could meet there and the room where the talk will take place is next to that.

S: Hold on, so C13, the venue for the talk, is straight ahead after I've entered the building?

J: Well, slightly to the left from where you are after you've gone into the foyer area. I think there's a laboratory immediately on your left when you go in. If you have any problems there's a reception area to your right next to a big lecture theatre.

S: Think I've got it. I'll give you a call if I'm running late. Better dash now as I'm meeting Tariq in 10 minutes. I'll see you in the café at 6.30 next Wednesday.

J: OK. See you then.

🎧 1.21

Hello everyone. It's good to see so many of you here. Starting your first full-time job is an important time in your lives and it's vital to make sure you find a job that is suitable for you and that you enjoy.

My talk tonight is going to be divided into two main parts: firstly, looking for a job and secondly, writing applications. Another important area is interviews, but they'll be discussed in a separate talk. There'll be time for questions afterwards so if you could wait until then to ask anything, I'd be grateful.

Right – looking for a job. I'm going to focus on four key ways to look for work. The first and probably the most traditional way is newspapers and magazines. These are still good places to find jobs although the internet is probably a more popular method nowadays. National papers are still an excellent source and often run adverts for different types of jobs on different days. Find out which day covers information about the line of work you are interested in for each paper. If you are less flexible about where you want to be, local papers are good sources if you are looking for work in specific areas. Another useful place to look is magazines, in particular specialist industry magazines relating to different sectors such as education or business for example. Of course, most newspapers and magazines will also have websites so let's briefly turn to online sources.

The majority of you will use this method and one of the main advantages is that you can search for information very quickly and complete applications online. At the end of the talk I'll give you a list of useful websites on a handout.

The third place to look for work I want to mention is through a job centre or agency. These are located in most towns and cities and this can be an efficient way to look for work as you're actually letting someone else do some of the job searching for you. Most agencies get a fee from your prospective employer so this service is usually free.

Finally, as many of you know, we organize regular Careers fairs here when representatives from major companies provide information about job opportunities. This is a great chance to have direct contact with a range of employers. Check the university website for news of future events.

🎧 **1.22**

So, you've found a job that you want to apply for. What next? The first step is usually to contact the company by phone or email and ask for an application form and a job description. Refer to the original job advert and make sure that you mention or include the job reference number. Next, read the job description – do your skills, qualifications and experience make you a suitable candidate? When you complete the application form, whether on paper or online, do it carefully and make sure the information you give is specific to the job and not just general. It's really important to say how your skills and experience match the job requirements and what personal qualities you have that would benefit the employer. Remember this may be your first contact with the employer and first impressions count so if the application form is untidy, incomplete or contains loads of spelling mistakes then it is likely to go straight in the bin! After you've completed the form, most applications will also ask you to include a covering letter. It is important to write a brief, formal letter or email about your interest in the job and your general suitability for this position – don't go into too much detail at this point as the vital information will be on the form. Finally, it's always a good idea to get someone you trust to check the form, maybe a close friend, a tutor or one of your parents. They might spot something that you haven't noticed. If it's all OK, send off the application form so that it reaches the company before the deadline. The main thing to remember is that the perfect job for you is out there – if you don't get the first one, just keep trying.

Does anyone have any questions?

6 Globalization
🎧 **1.23**

In the first part of today's lecture I would like to introduce you to the topic of globalization. I will start by considering what globalization is. Secondly, I will explain something of its history. Finally, I intend to look at who the main players

in globalization are, both for and against it, and briefly summarize their arguments.

So, let us begin with what may seem an obvious point. What exactly is globalization? A lot of people think it is mainly about economics, or increased global trade. However, it can also be seen as increased cultural and technological exchange between countries. Examples might be McDonald's in Calcutta and Japanese motor technology in Britain. Now let us look a little at the history of globalization. There is no agreed starting point, but it could have been about 100 years ago. Certainly, there was a big expansion in world trade and investment then. This was put back considerably as the capitalist world came up against the First World War and then the Great Depression in 1930.

However, the end of the Second World War set off another great expansion of capitalism in 1948 with the development of multinational companies. These were companies interested in producing and selling in the markets of countries all around the world. Finally, globalization really took off when the Soviet Union collapsed.

It's important not to forget the importance of air travel and the development of international communications. The telephone, the fax and now computers and email have all encouraged the progress of international business.

🎧 **1.24**

Turning now to the main players involved in globalization, we find that there is a clear division between those who are pro-globalization and those who are anti-.

The main organizations against globalization are the environmental organizations, such as Friends of the Earth and Greenpeace, who put forward the belief that globalization harms the environment.

In general, they blame global corporations for global warming and the depletion of natural resources. The most obvious is oil and gas, but there are others such as tropical rainforests, which are cut down for timber, and the resources of the sea, which may be affected by pollution.

Organizations which represent developing countries, including international aid agencies such as Oxfam, are also against globalization. They are concerned that the global organizations, such as the International Monetary Fund and the World Bank, are not doing enough to help the poor and, indeed, may be adding to their problems. Some are critical of the World Trade Organization. They argue that the WTO is making it difficult for poor countries to protect and build their own industries.

Many companies in rich countries also oppose globalization because they are worried that competition from imports will cost them money. A good example is companies that make clothing and shoes. These are among the few industries in which poor countries can provide effective competition with imports of cheap goods, because wages are so much lower than in America or Europe.

Lastly, some trade unions oppose globalization too. They say it leads to a lowering of wages and conditions of work in the developed and the developing world.

Having looked at some of the anti-globalization arguments, let's now consider those in favour. There are, of course, many organizations in favour of globalization. Perhaps the most important one is the World Trade Organization, or WTO. This was set up in 1995 and has 153 member countries. It administers the rules of international trade agreed to by its member countries. The WTO's rules make it difficult for a country to favour their own industry over imports from other countries.

The WTO argues that the growth of trade between countries increases the wealth of everyone. Trade allows those who can produce goods most cheaply to do so, thus giving everyone the best possible price.

Another pro-globalization organization is the International Monetary Fund or IMF. This was established after World War II in 1946. It aims to promote international cooperation on finance and provide temporary help for countries suffering financial problems. The IMF has 187 member countries.

Finally, the United Nations, which was established after the Second World War, has become a promoter of globalization. It has 193 member states and aims to promote a shared set of values in the areas of labour standards, human rights and environmental practices between the UN and the business community.

So, we've seen that there are powerful arguments and important players both for and against globalization. I'd now like to move on to look at some of the key issues for debate. Let us begin by considering the question of global inequality.

🎧 **2.1**

I'm going to talk about a company which is called Honda. It's a Japanese company and they sell a range of vehicles such as small family cars, estates and sports cars. They also produce motorbikes. It's a very good company and is well known all over the world. I'm sure Honda products are common in most countries but I've heard that they are especially popular in Asia and Europe.

There are many reasons why Honda is successful but I think one of the main ones is because it produces a new range of models every year. I expect the company has teams of skilled professionals who design and create cars using modern technology, which means new models have many of the latest features. Another reason for Honda's success is that the models are often more economical than some of their competitors – in both price and petrol consumption. Honda also makes expensive luxury cars too and some of these are designed to be very fast. This shows that Honda products appeal to a wide range of people. The company is also successful because parts for these cars are usually very cheap and easy to get in most countries.

As far as I know, Honda advertises new cars on TV quite a lot and these advertisements often look quite stylish. I've also seen their products advertised in newspapers and on large billboards by the side of the road.

In my country you see many Hondas on the road but these have been imported from overseas as we don't really have much of a car industry.

Well, there are clearly different ways of looking at it. Cheaper flights mean that more people can afford to travel. This has to be a good thing in that more people can experience different cultures and places. On the other hand, more flights cause more pollution and some tourist destinations have too many tourists and not enough clean water supplies, and so on. As far as I'm concerned though, the benefits outweigh the disadvantages.

7 Gadgets and gizmos
🔘 2.3

In today's lecture I want to give you a brief overview of the history of robotics, from ancient times up to the present day. We can then look at some of the key inventions in more detail over the next few weeks.

You may have wondered when I mentioned ancient times. Aren't robots a modern invention? Well, technically, yes, but ancient civilizations had very similar ideas, for example, there was the story of Talos, a man made from bronze, who guarded the island of Crete, in Greece. Then in Roman mythology the god Vulcan made two female robots out of gold to help him walk.

However, by 1774 myth had become fact, and two French brothers, Pierre and Henri Louis Jacquet-Droz were creating very complicated automatons, such as a boy robot, which could draw and write messages. They also created a robot woman, which could play a piano. Another example was a mechanical duck, which quacked, flapped its wings and pretended to eat and drink. This was invented at about the same time, by a man called Vaucanson. That's V–A–U–C–A–N–S–O–N.

In the next century robots started to be designed which were not so much toys, but had more practical, industrial uses. The industrial robots used in factories today have their origins in these early automated machines.

A good example is Joseph Jacquard's Textile Machine, invented in 1801, which was operated by punch cards.

Then, in 1834, Charles Babbage designed one of the first automatic computers, the Analytic Engine. This also used programs on punched cards to carry out mathematical operations. It had a memory capable of one thousand 50-digit numbers. The project was never finished, but it provided an excellent model for later developments.

🔘 2.4

The 20th century was a time which saw huge development in the science of robotics, particularly after the computer had been developed in the mid-forties. George Devol designed the Universal Automaton in 1954, which was the first programmable robot. The name was later shortened to Unimaton, which became the name of the first robot company.

Unimaton Inc sold designs to General Motors, who, in 1962, installed the first industrial robot on a production line. The 'Unimate' robot was used in a car factory to lift and stack hot pieces of metal.

In 1970, a computer-controlled robot called Shakey was developed. On one occasion

Shakey was asked to push a box off a platform. It couldn't reach the box, so it found a ramp, pushed the ramp against the platform, rolled up the ramp and pushed the box to the floor. Doesn't that seem like intelligence?

Since then hundreds of robots have been designed and developed for a variety of uses: assembling small parts in factories, providing the handicapped with artificial limbs, carrying out household chores and even carrying out surgical operations.

In 1967 Japan imported its first industrial robot from the United States, which was, at this time, about ten years ahead in robot technology. However, within a very short time, Japan started to catch up and then take over. Japan is now a world leader in robotics. Sony's Aibo robot dog was the first sophisticated robotic product to really sell well to the public. Now Honda have created Asimo, who has been made two-legged, in order to look more human. He is designed as 'a partner for people', or to work in the home. Asimo became the first non-human to open the New York Stock Exchange. Asimo will continue to be developed and, in the future, its power may come from hydrogen fuel cells, a technology whose only waste product is water. This may mean that Asimo will have to go to the toilet!

If these plans work out then society in the future could be very different. In fifty years' time, perhaps, no home or workplace will be without one.

8 Health and medicine
🔘 2.5
(**T** = Tutor; **B** = Barry; **A** = Alice)

T: Thank you Barry. As you said at the start of your presentation, human cloning is creating a genetically identical copy of another person and although this happens naturally, as you also mentioned, in the form of identical twins, the main topic we're discussing today is artificial human cloning. Alice, could you remind us of the two main types of cloning that Barry covered?

A: Yes, of course. Therapeutic cloning involves the creation of new cells or organs, embryos for example, for medical or research purposes. Reproductive cloning is actually growing a new human being.

T: And do you think that ethically there is really any difference between the two? Barry?

B: It's a good question, and I'm not really sure that I know the answer. Reproductive cloning is often the one that people fear. If you ask me, the idea of making a new person identical to someone living or who has lived, is a bit too close to science fiction.

T: Alice, what are your views on reproductive cloning?

A: Yes, it's true. People think of armies of clones, all the same, non-thinking machines, almost, who could be used in an attack by some mad dictator. There are so many books and films on this theme that people seem to imagine that it could really happen.

T: And couldn't it?

A: I don't think so. In my view, just because you have the same genes as someone, doesn't

mean you're going to act like a robot. What about identical twins? They don't do the same thing all the time but act as individuals so I think clones would be more like that.

B: Fair point. Twins have different personalities so it's unrealistic to think that clones would necessarily behave in the same way.

T: So Barry, is there a positive side to reproductive cloning? I mean would it be beneficial to anybody?

B: Childless couples. As far as I know, if reproductive cloning were legalized, those with fertility problems could have children.

T: That's a good point. So let's turn now to therapeutic cloning. What are your thoughts on that?

A: The possibilities are fascinating. If you could grow a new heart, kidney or lung for someone, you would address the problem of organ shortages. At the moment, people needing transplants usually have to wait for someone who wants to donate an organ and who has the same blood and tissue type.

B: Also, therapeutic cloning could be used to fight some degenerative diseases, you know, the type that get worse as you get older, such as Parkinson's.

T: So, going back to the question I asked at the beginning regarding the ethical issues …

B: I think that therapeutic cloning is easier for most people to accept as you're only talking about carrying out research on certain parts of a human, whereas reproductive cloning deals with making a complete human being, one that can think, feel and talk. Now, that's an entirely different matter.

🔘 2.6

T: So what do you think are the main barriers to progress or future developments in this area of medical science?

A: Well, as we touched on earlier, human cloning's always going to be a controversial topic particularly with certain religious and political groups who have serious ethical concerns. Many people have real issues about artificially creating human beings and the whole notion of 'playing God', as they feel it contradicts nature. 'If you cloned humans, we wouldn't be unique' is one of the key moral arguments against cloning.

B: That's true. Also, I think there are a number of significant issues relating to safety. If you remember, there were over 250 attempts to create Dolly the sheep, the first cloned mammal, and before a human being is successfully created it's highly likely there would be miscarriages, deformities or other side effects.

T: But isn't science all about challenging, experimenting and testing the limits of knowledge in the quest for progress?

B: Yes, you're right and there's no doubt there are benefits in terms of medical advances in this field but at the same time there's always going to be strong opposition.

A: Yet it's not stopping people carrying out research in this area. We know that human leg cells have already been cloned and human embryos have also been created from adult skin cells so developments in human cloning are happening now and will continue to happen whether we like it or not.

T: Ah yes, the inevitable march of progress. All interesting stuff. Right, let's move on to discuss … (fade)

9　All in the mind

🔘 2.7

(**A** = Announcer; **JG** = John Gregory)

A: As part of our series of study skills talks, John Gregory is going to talk to you today about the theory of multiple intelligences, a way of discovering more about how you, as an individual, may learn best.

JG: Hello. I'd like to start off today by giving you a little background information on the theory and then look at what these multiple intelligences are and how you can learn to make the most of your strengths in different areas.

The traditional view of intelligence, as measured by IQ tests, tends to focus on just two sorts of intelligence – Linguistic and Logical–Mathematical, or in other words being good with words or with numbers and logic. In his book *Frames of Mind*, Howard Gardner suggested that there were in fact other ways of being intelligent, that were not always recognized by the school system. He suggested seven different intelligences, which we will look at today, though he has since increased the number to eight, and thinks there may be more still.

So, what are the types of multiple intelligence? Firstly, those already mentioned: Linguistic and Logical–Mathematical. People with Linguistic or verbal intelligence are good at communicating with others through words. They will learn languages easily and enjoy writing and speaking. They tend to think in words rather than in pictures. They will be good at explaining and teaching and persuading others to their point of view. Not surprisingly, they will often become journalists, teachers, lawyers, politicians and writers.

Those who are strong in Logical–Mathematical intelligence are good at seeing patterns and making connections between pieces of information. They reason well, and can solve problems effectively. They're the kind of student that asks a lot of questions! They make good scientists, computer programmers, engineers, accountants or mathematicians.

Then there are the Personal intelligences – Interpersonal, meaning between people, and Intrapersonal, meaning within yourself. Those of you with good Interpersonal intelligence have the ability to see things from other people's points of view, understanding how others feel and think. You encourage people to co-operate and communicate well with others, both verbally and non-verbally. You'll make good counsellors, salespeople, politicians and managers.

Intrapersonal intelligence is more about being able to understand yourself, recognize your own strengths and weaknesses, and your inner feelings. If you're strong in this area you'll make good researchers, theorists and philosophers.

If you tend to think in pictures rather than words, you may be strong in Visual–Spatial intelligence. You enjoy drawing and designing as well as reading and writing. If you tend to doodle on your notes in class, that may be a sign of this intelligence. You'll have a good sense of direction and find graphs, charts and maps easy to understand. A good job for you might be a designer, an architect, a mechanic or engineer.

Bodily–Kinaesthetic intelligence is about the ability to control body movements and handle objects skilfully. Athletes, dancers, actors will be strong in this area. Sometimes physical skills are seen as something entirely separate from intelligence, something which Gardner strongly challenges by including this intelligence.

Finally, Musical intelligence. If you have a good deal of musical intelligence you'll often play an instrument, but not necessarily. If you often find yourself tapping out rhythms in class, this may be a sign that you're learning through your Musical intelligence. Not surprisingly you'll make a good musician or songwriter.

🔘 2.8

If you're aware of where your strengths lie, you can use this information to help you study more effectively. For example, if you have high Linguistic intelligence you'll learn well through group discussions, listening to lectures and reading, whereas if you're stronger in Logical Mathematical intelligence you may learn better through problem-solving activities. Those of you with strong Visual–Spatial intelligence will respond well to videos, diagrams and charts. You'll probably find it helpful to learn vocabulary through using word maps.

If you are Interpersonally intelligent, try working in groups or pairs or teaching someone else what you're trying to learn. Your good communication skills mean that you'll also learn well through listening to others. Or, if you're more Intrapersonally intelligent, it may be better for you to do some studying alone, setting yourself goals.

If you have high Bodily–Kinaesthetic intelligence you may find it easy to study while walking around – though perhaps you shouldn't try this in class! The Musically intelligent may learn well through songs, or with background music on while they study.

It is important to recognize that everyone is a combination of all the intelligences, just in different strengths. For many tasks and jobs you need to use a combination of strengths. So, what does the questionnaire you've completed tell you about how you learn? (fade)

🔘 2.9

I didn't learn to drive until I was about 25, which is pretty unusual in this country, I think. Most people learn as soon as they can, when they're 17. But I lived in London, where the public transport is pretty good, so I didn't really need a car.

When I got a job where I needed to drive, I wasn't really worried about learning, I thought I would pick it up pretty easily. I'm usually a quick learner so I decided to book myself an intensive driving course. A lesson every day for two weeks and then I'd take the test. Talk about throwing yourself in at the deep end!

Well, although I was so confident, it turned out I didn't really have an aptitude for driving. In fact, I was terrible. And I had to pass the test because my new job depended on it. It was certainly a steep learning curve! I didn't actually pass the first time. I think I was just too nervous, but I took the test again a week later, and this time I did pass!

🔘 2.10

(**DW** = Dr Williams; **S** = Sian)

DW: Hello there, Sian.

S: Hello Dr Williams – I'd like to talk to you about my assignment please.

DW: Fine. Come on in and have a seat. Have you started work on it yet?

S: Yes, I have. I've started doing some reading around and I've roughed out an outline of what I want to do, but I wanted to just check with you that I was going in the right direction.

DW: OK, good. So what have you decided to look at?

S: What really interests me is the idea of 'nature vs nurture' with regard to intelligence and looking at whether a child is just born clever, or whether their parents, teachers, friends – people like that influence them. Do you think that this is a suitable subject for me to focus on?

DW: Well, it's a big topic for a 2,000 word assignment. People have been debating that for years, and there's still no definitive answer.

S: Yes, I know. I've been researching in the library though and I've found several studies that have tried to compare the effects of genetic factors and environmental factors on children.

DW: Well, there's no shortage of literature on this subject, that's for sure!

S: Yes! And that's my main problem at the moment. For every study that shows that genetic potential is the most important factor, there's another to show the opposite!

DW: The best thing to do is to choose a selection of research that shows a similar pattern, and compare that in relation to one or two studies which don't follow the same trends. Then try to analyse why the results might differ.

S: OK. Another question I wanted to ask you was whether I should include my own opinion?

DW: It's fine to do that, but be careful not to make your writing sound too personal, that is make sure that you back up any statements with clear reasons or evidence and don't forget to make reference to where you found that information.

S: What do you mean, exactly?

DW: Well, for example, if you say that in Australia fewer children from lower income families go to university, even though that's a fairly well-known fact, you need to mention the source of that information.

S: You mean find a study that has shown that?

DW: Yes, and include the reference in your bibliography at the end of your assignment.

S: The bibliography – should that include all the books I've used for reference?

DW: No, only the ones that you've directly cited in the essay. Put them in alphabetical order according to author – not in the order that you use them in the essay. Remember, you were given a handout on this topic at the start of term.

S: Yes, that's right. Right – thanks for your time. I'll go and get on with it!

DW: OK – goodbye. If you have any further questions or points you want to discuss, then we can cover these in your next tutorial.

S: Great. Thank you for your help. Bye.

DW: Cheerio.

10 Leisure time

🔘 2.11

(**I** = Instructor; **J** = Julie)

I: Welcome to Fitness Fanatics Health Club. I'd just like to start by taking a few personal details, if I may. Your full name is …?

J: Julie Ann Edmonson.

I: Thank you, and you're 23, Julie, is that right?

J: Yes, oh actually, no, 24. It was my birthday last week.

I: And can I have a contact telephone number, please?

J: Yes, it's 0798 674 5689.

I: And what's the best time to contact you?

J: Oh, erm, after work would be better really. Any time between, say 6 and 9pm.

I: Fine. Now in a little while, we'll do some fitness tests and I'll ask you a bit more about your medical history, but first of all, I'd like to know a little more about why you've decided to join the gym. What kind of exercise do you do at the moment?

J: Well, I do quite a bit of walking. I bought myself a pedometer last year and I'm trying to do at least 10,000 steps a day. I don't always make it though!

I: That's great. Walking's a good start. And do you get much exercise at work?

J: No, not really. It's pretty much a desk job you see, there's a lot of sitting down. That's one of the reasons I felt I needed to join the gym.

(pause)

I: Yes, so what specific benefits are you looking for from joining the gym? For example, would you like to lose weight, or just get fitter?

J: I'm quite happy with my weight, but I'd like to keep it this way.

I: Uh huh, weight maintenance then. Anything else? Fitness goals?

J: Yes, although I'm doing the walking, it doesn't leave me out of breath, you know. I don't feel that I really get a lot of aerobic exercise – so I'd like to increase that.

I: Yes, that's fine. I think there are a number of ways we could help you achieve your targets. How many times a week were you thinking of coming, and for how long?

J: Er, well, I know I should come three times a week, but, if I'm honest it's only going to be twice a week, for about an hour or so.

I: Are you interested in doing any classes, or would you rather just use the gym?

J: I'm not sure, what classes do you have?

I: Oh, quite a range. We have a new class that's very popular, Zumba. That's all about getting a workout by dancing to Latin music. It's on a Wednesday night at 6.30.

J: That sounds interesting, but I'm not great at dancing, really, I prefer swimming. Do you have any aqua aerobics classes ?

I: Yes, we do. On a Thursday evening at 6.00pm. Shall I put you down for that?

J: Yes, I'll give it a try. And what about the gym? Will someone show me round?

I: Yes, we'll need to make an appointment with one of our fitness instructors. Could you come tomorrow evening?

J: Er, I could, but I'd rather come on Friday if that's possible? Any time after 7.00pm.

I: OK, then, you have an appointment at 7.00 with Mark.

J: Oh, I think I'd prefer to have a female trainer actually.

I: No problem, Siobhan is free at 7pm as well.

J: Could you spell that please?

I: S–I–O–B–H–A–N.

J: Thanks, that's great.

🔘 2.12

(**T** = Tutor; **R** = Rob; **J** = Julie)

T: So, Rob, you've been looking at the topic of internet addiction. How's your research going so far?

R: Well, I started off by looking at some research done by Cranfield University School of Management. They carried out a survey of 260 secondary school pupils and the results were quite interesting – a bit worrying, actually. They found that 26% of those surveyed spent more than six hours on the web a day.

J: That's incredible. Six hours?

R: More than six hours, actually. 63% of them felt that they were addicted to the internet and 53% felt that they couldn't live without their mobile phones. Interestingly, 62% of them were bought their first computer around the age of eight. So maybe it's down to their parents if they're addicted now. Most of them also had a mobile phone between the ages of eight and ten and started using a social networking site at the age of eleven. On average, they now spend 1–2 hours a day on social networking sites like Facebook.

T: But is it necessarily a bad thing to be online a lot?

R: Well, there are the physical issues for a start. If you spend that much time online, you tend to get less exercise and have a poor diet. You just eat junk food in front of the screen. And if you're staying up late, you're probably not getting enough sleep, which can affect your growth as a teenager. Teenagers need more sleep, not less.

You are probably consuming more caffeine as well, which can lead to poor concentration. You could also develop repetitive strain injury from typing on a keyboard, clicking a mouse or texting, and there was a recent case where someone had an accident on the motorway because she kept checking a social networking website page while she was driving along!

🔘 2.13

J: But surely these are all extreme cases. I mean most people wouldn't be so stupid as to be going online while trying to drive, would they?

R: No, I think that is pretty extreme. But I think being online for six or more hours a day is quite extreme too, and the research showed that this is pretty normal for those teenagers.

J: I think it depends what they are doing. If they're just playing games, then I guess that's a bit of a waste of time. But a lot of students use the internet to research stuff, don't they? There's a lot of useful information out there.

T: Yes, I think that's a good point. But I think they need to know how to navigate the web successfully. There's a lot of rubbish out there too and it's no good if students think that research just means going to a site like Wikipedia, where the information isn't always properly checked.

J: And I don't think there's anything wrong with social networking is there? It's just the same as chatting to friends on the phone or even face to face. Isn't it a good thing that we have more choices now? We can use email, or instant messaging or Twitter.

R: I don't think it is just the same thing, actually. A lot of people have 'friends' online that they've never met. How can that be a proper friendship? I think it's damaging people's ability to socialize actually, and it's definitely damaging people's ability to write properly, all these abbreviations that people use when they're texting. I read somewhere that students are starting to use them in essays now. How can that be a positive thing?

2.14

Well, probably my favourite thing to do in my free time is walking. I particularly like walking in the countryside or the mountains, you know, taking the whole day. But I do try to do some walking just about every day. Sometimes I go on my own, and sometimes with friends.

I don't need much equipment, really. Just a good pair of trainers or walking boots if I'm going a bit further, a map maybe, something to eat and drink. Oh, and if I'm on my own I take my mp3 player and listen to some music while I walk.

I find it really relaxing. Often when I start walking my mind is absolutely full of thoughts, but as I walk they just start to go away and I get more and more relaxed. And I have some of my best ideas when I'm walking too. And, of course, it's good for you, definitely good exercise.

2.15
(**E** = Examiner; **R** = Ravi)

E: Do you think that people have more or less time for leisure now than in the past?

R: Oh, I think people have less time, definitely. Everyone works so hard these days, don't they? Take email for example. Now everyone expects you to reply to emails even in the evenings or at weekends. That's got to affect how much time you have for leisure. For instance, I work 9 to 5 in the office, but I always spend another hour looking at emails when I get home.

11 The art of advertising
2.16
(**S** = Student; **T** = Tutor)

S: Can you explain what the problem was with my assignment on advertising standards?

T: Well, to begin with, it was much too long. We can accept up to 10% over the word limit, but you mustn't do more than that. We aren't allowed to accept an assignment of that length.

S: Oh, OK. I didn't realize that.

T: Then you really should have read the question more carefully. The question asked you to compare and contrast the rules applied by advertising standards agencies around the world and you only wrote about your own country.

S: So, I ought to have given more examples?

T: Yes, and you were also supposed to compare and contrast them, or say how they're different or similar.

S: Oh, I didn't understand that I had to do that. OK. Was that the only problem?

T: I'm afraid your handwriting wasn't very good either. You didn't need to word-process it, but it would have helped me to understand what

you wanted to say. Having said all that, you did have some very good ideas about … (fade)

2.17
(**K** = Kate; **T** = Tom; **I** = Isabelle)

K: So, I think we should try and make some decisions about the presentation we're doing next week. Do you think we should talk for a third of the time each, or divide it up some other way?

T: I think we should probably divide it up by topic, rather than time. Isabelle?

I: Yes, I think that makes more sense.

K: OK, agreed.

T: We have 20 minutes, but don't forget we need to leave five minutes for questions at the end, so it's only 15 minutes for the talk itself.

K: Good point. Well, the obvious way to divide it is to have four sections, for the four parts of the marketing mix. You know, um, product, price, place and promotion.

I: Sure. Shall we start with product? I'm happy to do that.

K: Yeah, that's fine.

T: Actually, would you mind if I did that section? That's the one I feel most confident about.

I: Oh, OK. No problem. Shall I look at promotion then?

K: That depends if you want to follow on from Tom. I think the next areas to look at would be price and place.

I: Yes, you're probably right. How about if I do those then and you finish up with promotion.

K: Fine.

T: OK, but we still need to look at the main points we're making, to make sure that what we're saying doesn't overlap.

2.18

I: OK, so what about if we go through each section and try and identify the main points?

T: Yes, good idea.

I: What are the main points we want to make about the product?

K: Well, it's important to say that a product can be either an actual item or a service.

T: Yes. Perhaps we could give some examples of different products at this point?

I: Good idea. That would help us with getting across the other key things to think about. For example the design of a product and what its key features are.

K: And the brand name.

T: Yes, that's important. And the packaging too, if it's a product rather than a service.

K: Well, you can package a service too, can't you?

T: Well, I guess so, in a way.

I: OK, shall we move onto price? This very much depends on the product, doesn't it?

K: Yes, and the target market of course. In fact, I think the target market is very important.

If it's aimed at people with money, they may well pay more regardless of whether the quality is really that high.

T: Mmm. Though quality is important, isn't it? It's important to be competitive in your pricing. If what you're selling is more expensive than the competition and not any better a product then you can't expect people not to notice, no matter how good your marketing is …

K: I think that brings us onto place, or how to get the product out to the consumers, or people who will buy it. Will it be sold only to wholesalers, who then sell it on, or sold directly to shops?

I: Or even directly to individuals, online for example.

T: Yes, that's happening more and more these days.

K: Yes, so then you really need to think about the design of your website.

I: Yes, that's important. That's connected with promotion, isn't it? The key points there are about communicating with people who might buy the product and encouraging them to buy it.

T: Persuade them to buy it!

K: Ideally, yes.

T: OK, I think we have the key points now.

12 Success and achievement
2.19
(**A** = Announcer; **AK** = Ali Khan)

A: Good afternoon. It's very nice to see so many of you here for our Open Day. I hope that you've enjoyed looking around the campus and have been able to get any questions you have about courses answered. We open this afternoon with a short talk from one of our success stories. Ali Khan is a former student of the university who we are very proud of. He is here this afternoon to tell us a little about his career and how his studies here have helped him. I hope that he will be an inspiration to you.

AK: Thank you very much and good afternoon. It's very nice to be back to visit the university. I have many happy memories of my time here – although I have to admit that the best of these are of social occasions rather than lectures!

I first came from Pakistan eleven years ago to study here. I think that the main reason was the reputation that England has. So many English universities have such a strong reputation for academic excellence and a great academic tradition. Also, to be frank, a good British degree is a passport to a higher position and a good job in Pakistan and it has certainly worked that way for me. I'm quite sure I wouldn't have done so well if I hadn't studied here.

I originally came to the UK wanting to study Economics and did so here for the first year, but then I found that actually I was much more interested in Politics. I never wanted to become a politician. In my country most people think that they are only a step away from criminals, but I was really fascinated by the way that government functions and the effects that this can have on ordinary people. I wish I had realized this earlier, as it cost me a year's study. When you're choosing your field of study, I think that it's very important to balance what you think will make you employable, with what you're interested in. In my case, as my parents were supporting me, the balance also included what they wanted me to do! Luckily, they were very sympathetic!

🔊 2.20

When I graduated in Politics, I went back to Pakistan and began looking for work in the public sector. As I said, I had no intention of becoming a politician, but I felt as if I wanted to do something positive to help my country to develop. I applied for work in the Ministry of Education. The competition for jobs like this is fierce but the fact that I had a good degree from a well-regarded British university made a huge difference. Partly this was because of the standard of education, but I think that there were other reasons why employers favour graduates who have studied overseas. Language, of course, is a major one. Even in Pakistan, where all educated people speak English and the standard is generally high, if an employer knows that you've studied in English to tertiary level, it gives them confidence in your abilities. It's not only language, though. To have had the experience of studying overseas gives you a lot of independence and flexibility. You definitely need to be flexible in order to cope with all of the cultural differences of a different country. Employers value that, I think.

So, I got the job I wanted and worked for six years in the Education sector, before coming back to England to get a Masters degree in Development Studies. I was actually sponsored to do this by the Ministry, and when I finished, last year, I went back to take up a new position of Director of a project to improve technical education in one region of the country. It's an important post and a very interesting one. I suppose that it would be too strong to say that I owe it all to this university, but the education I received here has certainly been a major factor in my success.

🔊 2.21

I'm going to talk about a competition which I entered quite a few years ago when I was 14 or 15. I was never good at sports or music and I couldn't dance or sing but I had a good imagination so I was very excited when my teacher told us about a national writing competition. I remember we had six weeks to write either a short story or a poem about any subject. I wanted to write a story but I had real difficulty thinking of a good idea and it was only on the day before we had to hand it in that I finally managed to come up with one. I was walking home from school and I was thinking about what present to get my mum for her birthday when I had the idea of writing a poem about my mum. Once I had the idea, it was easy to write and I handed it in on time. I didn't hear anything for weeks but finally I got a letter saying I was in the final 20. I was invited to a special prize giving ceremony at a hotel with all the other finalists who came from different schools all over the country. It was really exciting and although I didn't win first prize I did win a medal and certificate and I was able to meet one of my favourite writers, who was presenting the prizes. The whole experience made me realize that it is possible to achieve your goals and it gave me more confidence in myself. I still love writing today and I hope I'll be able to use my talent in my future career.

🔊 2.22

(**T** = Tutor; **E** = Eva; **P** = Pawel)

T: Well, guys, your IELTS test is next week. How are you feeling?

E: Um, to be honest, a bit nervous but quite excited too.

P: Yes, I really want to get on with it now but I have to say it's the listening I'm most worried about. Could you give us some general advice about this part?

T: Yes, of course. Well as you know, there are 4 parts and they get more difficult as the test goes on but before each section you do have a short time to look at the questions. My first piece of advice is quite simple: read the instructions carefully.

E: Yes, you need to know how many words you can use. I've lost marks on that before.

T: Also, after you've looked at the test paper it should help give you an idea about the kind of situation you're listening to – is it a conversation in a shop or restaurant or a monologue about a particular subject? Make sure you establish the context as this will help activate vocabulary relating to that topic.

E: Good point. And I remember you mentioned the importance of predicting answers to questions, for example are they looking for a person's name, a place, a date or a price?

T: That's right. It helps to be aware of the kind of information that is being asked for.

E: Didn't you say something about grammar too?

T: Yes. Try and predict what part of speech is coming up.

P: You mean like a noun or verb ... or adverb maybe.

T: Exactly. All these strategies should make the actual listening tasks easier.

P: The other thing I keep doing is missing an answer and then losing track of which point I'm at.

T: Right. While you're listening, it's vital to write down answers as quickly as you can but make sure you stay focused on the recording. Try and make a note of possible answers and guess later if you need to.

P: And how much time do we have at the end?

T: You'll get 10 minutes to transfer your answers. Don't forget to check your spelling because you'll lose marks if you make silly mistakes with this. So what's your biggest concern Eva?

🔊 2.23

T: How are you feeling at the moment?

E: To be honest I'm a bit anxious about all of it so any advice you could give at this stage would be useful but it's probably the reading that I find most difficult.

T: Well, I'd say the biggest problem most students have with this is poor time management. They spend too long on the first two passages then run out of time. I would suggest doing some more practice papers giving the same amount of time to each text and make sure you attempt all the answers in the hour.

P: Yes, me too, I find some of the passages really hard to understand and I think my main problem is that I don't understand the academic vocabulary

T: It's probably too late to start learning new words at this stage so it's all about working out the meaning from context. Make sure you don't stop or get 'blocked' when you meet an unknown word but try to guess what it means.

E: What about speaking? Is there anything I can do to improve these skills?

T: Yes definitely, many students find they don't have enough to say in Parts 2 and 3. Why don't you get together with a friend and practise the whole speaking test – ask and answer questions on familiar subjects for Part 1 and for the other sections that focus on common IELTS topics – you know, health, travel, education, leisure, that sort of thing.

P: OK. We could do that. And writing? Is it too late to do anything?

T: It's never too late. Apart from not knowing enough about the subject which I touched on before, the biggest difficulty students face and often get marked down for is grammatical accuracy.

P: Yeah, I'm usually ok with tenses but not so good at using articles correctly in my writing. I always miss them out – probably as we don't have them in my language.

T: What you could do is find some writing you've done recently and look at the type of errors you made and the teacher's corrections.

P: Good idea.

T: OK. So you've got plenty of things to work on before your test so you'd better get started! Hope it goes well for both of you.

E: Thanks for all the tips.

P: Yes, it's been useful advice.

Macmillan Education
Between Towns Road, Oxford OX4 3PP
A division of Macmillan Publishers Limited

Companies and representatives throughout the world

ISBN 978-0-230-42210-0

Text © Andrew Preshous, Joanna Preshous, Rachael Roberts and
Joanne Gakonga 2012
Design and illustration © Macmillan Publishers Limited 2012

First edition published 2004
This edition published 2012

Original design updated by greenbird design
Page make-up by Roger Sharpe at greenbird design
Illustrated by Oxford Designers and Illustrators Ltd pp8, 39, 55, 66,
85, 115;
Cover photograph: Glow Images/Ingrid Firmhofer/LOOK-foto
Picture research by Catherine Dunn

Authors' acknowledgements

The authors would like to thank their families for their support
and patience throughout this project, in particular those who have
provided childcare for Laura, Eleanor, Sam and Sophie.

Special thanks go to Helen Forrest for her valuable feedback, hard
work and guidance throughout the preparation for this second
edition.

Finally, thanks go to all those at Macmillan Education who have
helped with this project.

The publishers would like to thank Rose Aravanis, Christine
Dowling and Sam McCarter.

The authors and publishers would like to thank the following for
permission to reproduce their photographs:

Apple Inc p88(all); **Bananastock** p6; **BrandX** p39(tc); **Corbis**/
Dave Bartruff p60(tl), Corbis/Niall Benvie p102, Corbis/Kevin Burke
p24(r), Corbis/Ashley Cooper p18(tl), Corbis/Digital Art p86(tc),
Corbis/The Food Passionates p94(tl), Corbis/Stephanie Grewel
pp94(tr), 147(bl), Corbis/Dave and Les Jacobs p42(tl), Corbis/Lizzie
Hemmel p48(tl), Corbis/Hill Street Images/Blend Studios p138(tr),
Corbis/Imagemore.co ltd p18(tr), Corbis/Imagesource pp138(cl),
146(r), Corbis/Steven Kaslowski p24(tl), Corbis/Jutta Klee/Able
Images p124, Corbis/Thom Lang p90(bl), Corbis/James Leynse
p18(cr), Corbis/Jerry McCrea p78(tl), Corbis/William Manning
p48(tr), Corbis/Robert Michael p138(tl), Corbis/Buero Monaco/
Zefa p54, Corbis/Moodboard p103(br), Corbis/Ocean p114(bl),
Corbis/Louie Psihoyos p24(cl), Corbis/Radius Images pp78(tr),
90(tl), Corbis/Neil C. Robinson p78(tr), Corbis/Michael Rosenfield/
Science Faction p86(tr), Corbis/Sion Touhig/Sigma p39(tl); **Digital
Vision** p82; **Fairtrade.co.uk** p70; **Getty Images** pp18 (tc), 21(c),
30(tc), 147(r), Getty Images/Caterina Bernardi p30(tr), Getty
Images/Bloomberg p136, Getty Images/A. Chederros p114(tl), Getty
Images/Cultura/K. Magnusson pp42(tr), 147(tl), Getty Images/
Stuart Dee p21(tll), Getty Images/Echo p60(tr), Getty Images/Lane
Oatey p10, Getty Images/MCT p142, Getty images/Monty Rukusen
pp60(tc), 147(br), Getty Images/Tetra Images p78(tc), Getty Images/
Dilip Vishwanat/Stringer p86(tl); **Macmillan Australia** pp21(tr,c),
39(tr), 146(l0); **Medio Images** p30(tl); **Parentstock** p103(tr);
Photodisc p28(t).

Dictionary cover taken from the *Macmillan Collocations Dictionary*
© Macmillan Publishers Limited 2010

The publishers would like to thank the following for allowing us to
reproduce graphs based on their statistical data:

www.parliament.co.uk p12 fig 1; 2007 Open Door Report published
by Institute of International Education with support from US
Dept of States Bureau of Cultural Affairs p12 Fig 2: Reproduced by
permission of the Higher Education Statistic Agency. HESA cannot
accept responsibility for any conclusions or inferences derived
from the data by third parties pp12 (figs 3, 4); CBI.org.ukCBI for
material from Future fit: preparing graduates for the world of
work, copyright © CBI 2009, www.cbi.org.uk. The content may
not be copied, distributed, reported or dealt with in whole or in
part without prior consent of the CBI p56(all); Office for National
Statistics pp16(both), 37, 41, 62, 63(pie & Bar charts), 114(tr,br), 142;
Tourism research Australia p35(table).

The authors and publishers are grateful for permission to reprint
the following copyright material:

pp6–7: UK Council for International Student Affairs for extracts
from *Guidance Notes for Students 2001-2003 'International students
and culture shock'*, copyright © UK Council for International
Student Affairs; p24 Greenpeace International for an extract from
How to save the climate, pp2–3, www.greenpeace.org.uk/files/pdfs/
climate/howtosavetheclimatepers.pdf, copyright © Greenpeace
International; p29 Extract from 'Car use is dropping' by Geoffrey
Lean, copyright © Telegraph Group Limited 2011, first published
in *The Daily Telegraph* 02.03.11, reprinted by permission of the
publisher; p44 Extract from 'Crazy driving laws' by David Williams,
copyright © Telegraph Group Limited 2011, first published in *The
Daily Telegraph* 09.02.11, reprinted by permission of the publisher;
p55 CBI for material from *Future fit: preparing graduates for the
world of work*, copyright © CBI 2009, www.cbi.org.uk. The content
may not be copied, distributed, reported or dealt with in whole
or in part without prior consent of the CBI; p79 Extract from 'Top
10 'inventions' that changed the world' by Richard Gray, copyright
© Telegraph Group Limited 2009, first published in *The Daily
Telegraph* 13.03.09, reprinted by permission of the publisher;
p91 Material from 'What's the alternative?' by Sanjida O'Connell,
copyright © News International Syndication Ltd, first published in
The Times 16.07.02, reprinted by permission of the publisher; p105
Guardian News & Media Ltd for an extract from 'Family Matters'
by Tim Radford, first published in The Guardian 21.05.03, copyright
© Guardian News & Media Ltd 2003; p116 Westfield Stratford City
Centre Management for an extract from 'A New Retail Landmark'
http://uk.westfield.com, reproduced with permission; pp126–7
Hodder Education for an extract from *Marketing: An Analytical
and Evaluative Approach to Business Studies* by Ian Swift, Hodder
Arnold. Reproduced by permission of Hodder Education; p139
How To Books Ltd for an extract from *How to Pass Exams without
Anxiety, 5th edition* by David Acres, reproduced with permission.

Dictionary extracts taken from the *Macmillan Essential Dictionary
for Learners of English* © Macmillan Publishers Limited 2003

Printed and bound in Thailand
2016 2015 2014 2013 2012
10 9 8 7 6 5 4 3 2 1